1969

This book may be kept

FOURTEEN DAYS

Backgrounds of Romanticism

BACKGROUNDS
OF
ROMANTICISM

*English Philosophical Prose
of the Eighteenth Century*

Edited by Leonard M. Trawick

INDIANA UNIVERSITY PRESS

BLOOMINGTON & LONDON

Contents

v

Introduction

THIS BOOK assembles in convenient form selections from a number of eighteenth-century works which nowadays are hard to find, except in rare or expensive editions, but which helped shape the thinking of the English romantics—specifically, Blake, Coleridge, Wordsworth, Byron, Shelley, Keats, and Hazlitt. We know that they actually read most of these works; at any rate, each selection represents an influential attitude or strain of thought in the air at the time.

The eight works included here are not intended to give a balanced view of the romantics' whole intellectual background. Any book which did that would come close to being a standard anthology of eighteenth-century masterpieces; for, however much they railed at Pope, Addison, or Dr. Johnson—and their railing was less unanimous than is popularly supposed—the romantics inevitably shared many ideas and assumptions with the great writers of the preceding generations. Even among more obviously "pre-romantic" writings, this anthology omits verse and other imaginative literature, and most literary criticism, because these are available elsewhere. The Suggested Readings (pp. xxiii) should help to fill in the eighteenth-century backgrounds of romanticism.

The selections in this book are seminal treatments of questions at the heart of English romanticism—questions of politics, history, and metaphysics, and especially questions in that area of epistemology where theology, psychology, and aesthetics meet. In spite of their praise of spontaneity and their taste for lusher poetic modes than that of the *Essay on Man*, the romantics took a deep interest in current philosophy, and expended their finest poetic energies in attempts to define the relation of the individual consciousness to nature, God, and other men. The writings in this anthology were prime forces in shaping their definitions.

DIVERSE ATTITUDES IN EIGHTEENTH-CENTURY THOUGHT

The earlier eighteenth century is often called England's Augustan Age, a phrase which implies not only polished literature but a respect for good sense, moderation, authority, tradition, and order. Though such a label is inevitably crude, it does suggest some of the attitudes shared by figures as different as Dryden, Pope, Swift, Addison, Steele, Chesterfield, and Dr. Johnson.

Above all, they prized reason, which included sound common sense as well as analytical thought. The recent accomplishments in science epitomized by Newton's discoveries, though distrusted by some Augustans, led others to hope that, if reason were properly applied in all human activities, men might achieve a new golden age. This trust in reason, on the Continent as well as in England, characterized the "Enlightenment"—a term which, though it overlaps "Augustan," implies an un-Augustan distrust of tradition, authority, and received opinion, and a belief in progress and the validity of the individual mind.

In addition to Augustan good sense and Enlightenment rationalism a third spirit of the age was gradually emerging, which might be called a "counter-enlightenment": an acceptance—or even celebration—of man's irrational side. In religion there were always some who felt that God operated in ways more mysterious than Newton and Locke could explain. Some people, jaded with social and political complexities, looked back nostalgically to more primitive societies. Even "neoclassical" critics, if they were as sensible as Dryden, Pope, and Dr. Johnson, honored in poets like Shakespeare the "nameless graces which no methods teach." Some experienced, and tried to justify, a pleasure in feeling for its own sake, even fear, pity, and melancholy; to them we owe sentimentalism, Gothicism, and the "Graveyard School." There was sometimes an inexplicable yearning toward disorder: even Addison explains a taste for wild, sublime scenery by suggesting in *Spectator* 412 that "the mind of man naturally hates everything that looks like a restraint upon it." The imagination, which, unlike reason, usually works unconsciously and spontaneously, and which seemed to Augustans at best a harmless source of diversion and at worst a form of madness, slowly usurped the place of reason as the most powerful and respected of the faculties.

Fundamental Premises: How God Manifests Himself

Beneath this diversity of attitudes almost everyone shared a core of assumptions about the universe. They knew, with such certainty that it scarcely needed justification, that somehow the world was an orderly whole presided over by a benevolent God. This belief most often took the form of a Platonic "Great Chain of Being," with God—the ONE, pure spirit—at the top, inanimate matter or pure nonbeing at the bottom, and in between a hierarchy ascending from vegetable life to animals, man, and spirits.

But exactly how God managed this orderly, unified creation was not so certain. The predominant, rationalist tendency played down miracles, immediate revelations, and day-to-day divine interventions. God, the common reasoning went, originally created the world as a perfect machine, and after that had only to sit back and watch it run. God has given man the physical universe itself as an adequate record of its Creator, and He has given each man sufficient reason to learn of Him and achieve salvation through natural means. Thomas Paine's unequivocal assertions in *The Age of Reason* sum up the extreme form of such "natural religion" or Deism: "It is only by the exercise of reason that man can discover God," and "the word of God is the Creation we behold"; hence "my own mind is my own church."

At the opposite pole from Deism was the less respectable view that God is constantly at work in nature and human affairs. Writers influenced by the Neoplatonic tradition, such as the Cambridge Platonists of the later seventeenth century—Cudworth, Glanvil, More, and Burthogge—conceived of the divine spirit as a sort of world soul diffused through the material world, unifying and shaping it. The Earl of Shaftesbury, in his influential miscellany *Characteristics* (1711), calls this shaping spirit Nature, and describes her as an "impowered creatress," the agent by which the "universal ONE" unfolds itself in "the various map of . . . this fair visible world." Abraham Tucker, too, incorporates a world soul in the often mechanistic and empirical arguments of his *Light of Nature Pursued* (1768-78)—probably one reason for his popularity with the romantics. In France toward the end of the seventeenth century the occasionalists, notably Malebranche, denied physical causation and considered every event the result of the immediate will of God. Bishop Berkeley, a generation later, maintained a kind of psychological occasionalism in his theory that—to state it crudely—the material world has no objective existence, but is merely a systematic illusion maintained in men's minds by a benevolent deity. Less sophisticated forms of belief in God's intervention in daily life might be found in such sects as the Anabaptists, Quakers, and Ranters, which flourished in the latter half of the seventeenth century and continued through the eighteenth especially among the lower classes. Members of these sects believed that the divine spirit descended upon them with truth more immediate than that provided by reason and traditional wisdom; their moments of illumination were usually accompanied by great emotion. Such antinomianism, scorned by the more rational as "enthusiasm," eventually came to exert considerable influence, especially in the powerful evangelism of Whitefield and the

Wesleys, and in the fervent piety of William Law's writings. Law, an admirer of the early seventeenth-century German mystic Jacob Boehme, reflected his ideas and encouraged the publication of a monumental four-volume translation of his works (1764-81).

Great Chain—or Ladder?

A second variable within the unquestioned assumptions of the age was man's place in the cosmic hierarchy. One strong tradition made it man's duty to remain fixed at his natural level in creation, between the animals and the angels; to sink below the human (as Edmund does in *King Lear* when he declares, "Thou, Nature, art my Goddess") and to aspire to higher knowledge and power (like Marlowe's Faustus) are equally sinful and dangerous. Ulysses' speech on degree in *Troilus and Cressida*, and the passage in the *Essay on Man* in which Pope warns, "Know then thyself: presume not God to scan," are classic statements of the idea, which derives ultimately from the Platonic doctrine of plenitude. It was easy to extend what was basically a metaphysical idea to justify a static social hierarchy (as Ulysses does); for it would seem eminently reasonable that the body politic should mirror, in its hierarchy from peasant to king, the order of the macrocosm from the lowest creature to God.

There coexisted with this Platonic tradition of "everything in its place" the opposite belief, also of Platonic or Neoplatonic origin, that man should strive to rise in the chain of being and approach God as nearly as he can—in other words, that the order of creation is not a fixed chain but a ladder which a creature may climb. Such an idea goes back to the mystics and ascetics who, since the beginning of history, have sought to increase spiritual insight by mortifying the flesh and rising above the dross of physical existence. In the Renaissance, in Petrarch for example, or the fourth book of Castiglione's *The Courtier*, this desire to transcend the body takes the form of the "ladder of love": through the beauty of his mistress, the lover eventually turns to ideal beauty and says, "Leave me, oh love which reachest but to dust." In the eighteenth century it became a commonplace that natural scenery, especially of the wild and rugged sort, was a "language" by which God led men to turn their minds to more sublime thoughts and eventually to rise in the ladder of creation closer to pure spirit.

The tendency to regard such a rise as desirable received reinforcement from the optimism of the Enlightenment. The belief in human progress which Bacon and Descartes inspired carried over from natural science both to man's spiritual and to his political status, and these two kinds of perfectibility often went together. The libertarianism of the Enlightenment, immediate inspiration of the political theories of Paine, Priestley, and Godwin, appeared in less rationalistic writings such as Gray's *The Bard* and Coleridge's *France: An Ode* in conjunction with the spiritual elevation of sublime scenery. It is not surprising that all the romantic poets, at least at some time in their careers, were committed to the cause of liberty in the form of the American and French revolutions, connected as it was with more than one of the philosophical attitudes near their hearts.

THE NEW SUBJECTIVISM

Without any direct challenge to the basic assumption of an orderly hierarchical creation, the fundamental orientation of people's thinking gradually shifted during the eighteenth century: a writer was increasingly likely to begin an inquiry not with premises about God or the external order of things, but with the peculiarities and limitations of the individual mind's perceptions and reasonings. Much of the original impetus for this shift undoubtedly came, again, from Bacon and Descartes, whose insistence on experiment, and rejection of authority and a priori reasoning as a source of knowledge, forced arguments to begin much closer to the individual reasoner. Although few of Locke's ideas in the *Essay Concerning Human Understanding* are original, the book was extremely influential both because of the unprecedented rigor with which it scrutinized the operations of the mind and because of its conclusion that all knowledge must build up anew in each mind from personal experience. Locke, more than any other single writer, stimulated the new tendency to approach a problem of aesthetics, ethics, politics, or theology through a consideration of the individual mind. For example, Shaftesbury and Francis Hutcheson treat morality as a form of taste, rather than seeking objective standards of right and wrong; so subtle a theologian as Jonathan Edwards applies Lockean psychology to free will and grace; and, whereas at the beginning of the century an essay on poetry was most likely to concentrate on the form of the poem itself or on its effect on the audience, a century later such an essay would be much more likely to consider the nature of the poet's mind. For Coleridge and his contemporaries, "metaphysics" was almost synonymous with "epistemology."

THE LOCKEAN TRADITION

Locke's *Essay Concerning Human Understanding*, first published in 1690, modestly proposed "to take a survey of our own understandings, examine our own powers, and see to what things they were adapted." One of its underlying purposes was to discredit innate ideas and with them "enthusiasm" (even—when they contradict reason—revelation and faith). Following the principle of Aristotle and the Stoics that the mind begins as "white paper," a *tabula rasa*, Locke showed how even the most complex ideas can be built up from no other sources than sensation and reflection (i.e., the mind's observation of its own activity).

Much of the energy of eighteenth-century philosophy went to working out the implications of Locke's *Essay*. One school pursued along mechanical lines his analysis of the mind's growth through the accumulation and interaction of simple sensations.

In France, Condillac explained the development of the mind by repeating the process in a hypothetical animated statue which added mental powers one by one until it was capable of all the activities of the human mind with never a recourse to an innate idea or to divine illumination. And the title of La Mettrie's most famous work triumphantly announces its thesis: *L'Homme machine*. In England the most fruitful of the strict sensationalists followed the lead of Hobbes in making the association of ideas, mentioned only briefly in the fourth edition of Locke's *Essay*, the main or exclusive principle by which simple ideas grow into complex ones. Hume's *Treatise of Human Nature* (1739) and Akenside's popular *Pleasures of Imagination* (1744) developed the theory of association; but David Hartley achieved the most thorough and influential application of it in *Observations on Man* (1749). Hartley derives man's entire stock of ideas, which he says are caused by vibrations in the nervous system and brain, from their cumulative physical interaction with each other. One idea calls up another, and yet another and another, because of the similarity or temporal propinquity of their vibrations. Unlike the French mechanists, Hartley maintains the existence of both matter and spirit, and in fact devotes the second half of his book to a proof that the association of ideas is merely God's means of leading men by their senses up the ladder from a gross love of the world to an eventual virtuous "self-annihilation" and "theopathy." Among the most influential of Hartley's disciples was Joseph Priestley, discoverer of oxygen, Unitarian minister, prolific author, and dabbler in many disciplines.

In his *Essay* Locke had maintained that though we cannot know an object directly, we at least do know that "the thing as it is in itself" *resembles* certain primary qualities which we sense in it, namely "bulk, figure, number, situation, and motion." But there are secondary qualities, such as colors, sounds, smells, and tastes, that exist only in the perceiver's mind. Locke's admission of these secondary qualities is a step towards subjective idealism carried much further by George Berkeley in *A New*

Theory of Vision (1709), which proves that the so-called primary qualities of sight and touch have no more of an absolute existence than the secondary ones. In his *Principles of Human Knowledge*, published a year later, Berkeley maintains that the very existence of an object is nothing more than its being perceived: *esse est percipi.* Those mental images over which we have no control—that is, "external nature"—are merely a vast system of ideas put in our minds by God. Traditional descriptions of causation therefore are meaningless; the regularity of events which seem to us trains of causation is really only the systematic consistency of the ideas aroused by God. Hume a few years later assents to Berkeley's reasoning, but goes a step farther: why even posit God? In the final analysis, nothing is certain.

Such skepticism was intolerable to most philosophers and theologians of the eighteenth century, especially the more orthodox Christians. The usual avenue of escape was to backtrack a little from Locke and attribute greater innate powers to the mind. Locke himself had assumed certain "natural faculties," but had not examined their powers carefully. Kant, the most sophisticated investigator along these lines, said that the mind has certain innate categories—quantity, quality, relation, and modality—through which it organizes the phenomena of the senses.

Over fifty years before Kant's *Critique of Pure Reason*, about the same time that Berkeley was extending Locke's reasoning to his own striking conclusions, Shaftesbury in *Characteristics* was directly flouting Locke's epistemological caution by praising a certain kind of "enthusiasm," a love of nature, as the manifestation of a divine, shaping spirit, and by asserting a clear innate taste for virtue as the basis of morality. Shaftesbury's theory of an innate taste for the moral and the beautiful (for him the two were ultimately the same) was more systematically developed by Francis Hutcheson, particularly in his *Inquiry into the Original of Our Ideas of Beauty and Virtue* (1726), and, after Hume's alarming investigations, the orthodox began to succumb to the useful potentialities of innate ideas for patching up shaky doctrines. The Scottish common-sense school, which flourished in the latter half of the century and of which the most important exponents were Thomas Reid and James Beattie, depended heavily on rather substantive innate promptings of "common sense." The philosophical validity of the common-sense school is about the equal (but without the saving touch of self-satire) of Dr. Johnson's "Sir, we *know* the will is free, and there's an end on't."

NEW USE OF PSYCHOLOGICAL APPROACHES

A number of treatises, especially in aesthetics, began to appear after mid-century applying the theory of association or presenting some new analysis of the mental faculties. Edmund Burke's *Philosophical Enquiry into the Origin of Our Ideas of the Sublime and Beautiful* (1757) uncompromisingly attempts to explain aesthetic responses by the association of ideas. Hugh Blair, Lord Kames, and James Beattie also inject associational theory into their criticism, along with Scottish common sense and more traditional approaches. Archibald Alison in his *Essays on Taste* (1790) follows Burke and others in attributing the aesthetic qualities of any object exclusively to the beholding mind and not to the object itself, and he sounds very much like a romantic in his emphasis on the role of emotional energy in aesthetic response. Adam Smith's *Theory of Moral Sentiments* (1759) stresses the power and validity of the imagination, particularly as a basis of benevolence; and Abraham Tucker in his rambling pursuit of the light of nature also dwells on the imagination's extensive powers.

PRIMITIVISM, ORIGINAL GENIUS, AND LOVE OF THE PAST

The trends of thought discussed so far touch in several ways on a collateral development in taste—a growing primitivism, manifested as an interest in original or natural genius, an attraction toward societies still uncorrupted by civilization, and a fascination for past ages, not because they possessed more highly developed cultures to be emulated, but because they were exotic, mysterious, and melancholy in their ruin, or because they exhibited a vigor and truth derived directly from nature and not yet vitiated by the accumulated refinements of generations.

The common reasoning went like this: if physical nature is the "language" with which God speaks to man, and if God gives to each man sufficient reason to read the language, then obviously the first men, and still uncivilized men, have the advantage over us moderns, since they possess the same share of reason, undistorted by tradition and a narrowing education, and have access to an unspoiled nature for instruction. One should not be surprised, therefore, that Homer, one of the earliest poets, is also the greatest, and that a noble savage may be the moral superior of a modern Londoner. The English, scantily supplied with unspoiled wilderness and native savages, looked for spontaneous genius in the rural population, especially in the wilder western and northern sections. And they found some: Stephen Duck, "The Thresher Poet"; Ann Yearsley, the milkmaid; Robert Burns; Robert Bloomfield; and later John Claire and James Hogg, "The Ettrick Shepherd." Wordsworth's poetical rustics have numerous forebears. Two important books of the time reflect the concern with the workings of individual genius, *An Essay on Original Genius* (1767) by William Duff, and *An Essay on Genius* (1774) by Alexander Gerard, who also wrote an *Essay on Taste* (1759). Both Duff and Gerard use the new psychological approach, emphasizing the activities of the imagination.

Other works showed a more general interest in the past. A fake dark-age atmosphere was the main attraction of Macpherson's Ossian forgeries, and Chatterton's Rowley poems owe their popularity to their pleasantly archaic flavor. Bishop Thomas Percy assembled (and doctored up) an immensely influential collection of ballads in *Reliques of Ancient English Poetry* (1765). Scandinavian myths, which had the advantage of being quasi-Gothic, also received attention, notably from

Gray and in Paul Henri Mallet's *Northern Antiquities*, translated by Percy in 1770 and studied by Blake, Coleridge, and Southey. Robert Lowth's lectures on the sacred poetry of the Hebrews (*De Sacra Poesi Hebraeorum Praelectiones*, 1753) aroused interest partly because the subject was religious, more because it was exotic, and most of all because Lowth dwelt on the sublimity and passion of the biblical "bards." Jacob Bryant's *New System* had the attraction, no doubt for both author and readers, of delving into ancient and exotic matters; but it also satisfied the Enlightenment longing to see rational order established in a muddled subject—particularly since the system described turns out to be the one taught all along by orthodox Christianity.

ANTICIPATIONS OF ROMANTICISM

The introductions to the individual selections that follow will point out particular influences on the romantics. But perhaps a few words are in order connecting romantic ideas to the general trends outlined above.

Certain predispositions, such as a taste for wild natural scenery, a belief in the importance of emotion, and a love of the exotic, the primitive, and the archaic, the romantics seem to have inherited from previous generations with little change. Libertarianism and social meliorism are direct legacies of the Enlightenment. The most original development of the English romantic poets is their peculiar combination of the subjective orientation of British empirical psychology with basically Neoplatonic assumptions about the universe.

Diverse as they are in many ways, they all believe that the individual soul must rise in a hierarchy of being through an expansion of consciousness, and they pursue this goal by a poetic investigation of the mind's powers. The romantics wrote more poems about poetry and poets (including themselves) than any comparable group in English literature, for the good reason that they considered the poetic experience the highest activity of the human mind—not just a peculiar talent granted to a few composers of poems, but the fundamental means by which every man achieves his "godlike hours" of illumination. Their modes of thinking about the mind—though not necessarily their conclusions—inevitably grew out of the tradition of Locke, Berkeley, Hume, Hartley, and other investigators of the same problems in preceding generations. Coleridge named his first two sons, born while he was writing his best poetry, after Hartley and Berkeley; a good argument may be made that an intelligent reading not only of his conversation poems but also of *Kubla Khan*, *The Ancient Mariner*, *Christabel*, and *Dejection* depends on an understanding of the epistemological theories he developed from his wide reading. Wordsworth picked up some theories from Coleridge, but was independently influenced by Hartley and Godwin. In the fragmentary introduction to *The Recluse*—that unfinished cathedral of which *The Prelude* is the porch, *The Excursion* part of the nave, and the shorter poems small oratories—he announces that his whole "high argument" is to be an exposition of the relation of the individual mind to the external world. Shelley, a disciple of Godwin and avowed follower of the "academical" (that is, skeptical) philosophy of Hume, returns again and again to the nature of consciousness and inspiration in poems like *Alastor, Mont Blanc*, and *Adonais;* and his most splendid achievement, *Prometheus Unbound*, attempts to show that evil is merely an accidental, and curable, disease of the human mind. Keats admired Hazlitt's philosophically based criticism, and not only in his letters but in his most ambitious works, *Endymion* and the *Hyperion* fragments, he is concerned with the growth of the imagination and the relation of the subjective ideal to the external world. Blake was satirizing Locke's "Easy of Huming Understanding" as early as 1784, and the whole body of his poetry may be conceived as a counter-blast against Bacon, Newton, and Locke; yet at the end of *Jerusalem* this trio appears, finally assimilated in the healthy intellectual strife of Eden, riding in a triumphal heavenly chariot and rubbing elbows with Milton, Shakespeare, and Chaucer.

Coleridge, Shelley, and Blake, at least, read Plato and Neoplatonic writers in the original or in translations, notably those
of their contemporary Thomas Taylor. But, directly or indirectly, the Neoplatonic hierarchy of being pervades the poetry
of all the romantics. Coleridge, Wordsworth, and Shelley refer
to a world soul which "rolls through all things" and shapes the
physical world; but, slipping into the subjective orientation of
British empirical psychology, and perhaps also influenced by
eighteenth-century religious enthusiasm, they tend much more
than their predecessors to think of this spirit as operating "in the
mind of man." Sometimes when they speak of this shaping
spirit, "plastic and vast," it is hard to tell whether they mean
some divine force working in external nature, or a unifying and
glorifying power projected by the mind of the individual perceiver. But such a distinction becomes less important as the distinction between subject and object itself dissolves: the romantics regarded external reality as at least partly, if not wholly,
"created" by the individual imagination. The very act of cog-
nition, consciousness itself, is a function of a godlike power
which wells up from within; not only for Coleridge but for all
the romantics the imagination becomes "a repetition in the
finite mind of the eternal act of creation in the infinite I AM."
When Blake says, "All deities reside in the human breast," he is
not contracting the sphere of the gods, but expanding the sphere
of the human mind.

As the finite mind partakes increasingly of the infinite I AM
—which is another way of saying, as it develops wider consciousness, or achieves more intensely the poetic experience—it
soars above the world of bare physical perception,

> that inanimate cold world allowed
> To the poor loveless ever-anxious crowd,*

and rises in the spiritual hierarchy toward a "fellowship with
essence." But though "our destiny . . . is with infinitude," we

---

* Coleridge, "Dejection: An Ode."

can reach the ideal only through the ladder of the senses; hence the romantics approach an ultimate spiritual unity by way of particulars in the natural world, which their love and imaginative perception endow with an increasingly "finer tone."

The works represented in this book contain in suspension ideas which only at the end of the eighteenth century coagulated in the special outlook of the English romantics. Some influence —especially in the systematic formulation of the ideas—came from Germany, where parallel lines of thought were developing, partly from English sources. But the selections below provide ample evidence of the sizable contribution of native writers, many of them today forgotten, to the shaping of English romanticism.

Suggested Readings

I. Writers not represented in this anthology, who particularly influenced or anticipated the ideas of the English romantic poets. Modern editions are noted, but not eighteenth- and nineteenth-century ones.

Addison, Joseph. *The Spectator*, nos. 411–421, "The Pleasures of the Imagination," June 21–July 3, 1712. Available in many editions and anthologies.

Suggests a number of themes developed later in the century.

Alison, Archibald. *Essays on Taste*, 1790. Rev. 2nd ed., with a much more Wordsworthian conclusion, 1810.

Blair, Hugh. *Lectures on Rhetoric and Belles-Lettres*, 1783. Ed. Harold F. Harding, Carbondale: Southern Illinois Univ. Press, 1965.

Influential as lectures even before published.

Boehme, Jacob [also spelled Böhme and Behmen]. Works. First English translations by John Sparrow, 1647–62. An imposing four-volume edition based on this translation, sometimes incorrectly attributed to William Law, 1764–81. *The Aurora*, New York: Hillary House, 1960. *Dialogues on the Supersensual Life,* ed. Bernard Holland, New York: Frederick Ungar, 1958. *Signatura Rerum,* Everyman's Library, London: Dent, 1912. *Six Theosophic Points*, Ann Arbor: Univ. of Michigan Press, 1958.

Burke, Edmund. *A Philosophical Enquiry into the Origin of Our Ideas of the Sublime and Beautiful*, 1757. Ed. J. T. Boulton, New York: Columbia Univ. Press, 1958.

Burthogge, Richard. *An Essay upon Reason and the Nature of Spirits,* 1694. *Of the Soul of the World and of Particular Souls,* 1699. *The Philosophical Writings of Richard Burthogge,* ed. Margaret W. Landes, Chicago: Open Court, 1921.

Description of the world soul and anticipation of the familiar romantic image of the "correspondent breeze."

Butler, Joseph. *The Analogy of Religion, Natural and Revealed, to the Constitution and Course of Nature,* 1736. New York: Frederick Ungar, 1961.

Treats nature as "God's book," but with anything but facile optimism.

Cudworth, Ralph. *The True Intellectual System of the Universe: The First Part, Wherein All the Reason and Philosophy of Atheism Is Confuted, and Its Impossibility Demonstrated,* 1678. No second part.

Refutes such pagan philosophers as Democritus, Pythagoras, Zoroaster, the stoics, Platonists, and many others, but, as the learned joke had it, Cudworth states their cases so convincingly that it did the cause of Christianity more harm than good.

Darwin, Erasmus. *The Loves of the Plants,* 1789. *The Botanic Garden,* 1791, New York: Johnson Reprint, 1965.

The latest science decked out in heroic couplets and grotesque personification. Darwin, a learned and original if eccentric poet, was highly respected in his day and anticipated some ideas of his grandson Charles.

Gerard, Alexander. *An Essay on Taste,* 1759: Facsimile of 3rd ed. (1780), Gainesville, Fla.: Scholars' Facsimiles & Reprints, 1963. *An Essay on Genius,* 1774.

Hume, David. *A Treatise of Human Nature,* 1739. *Inquiry Concerning Human Understanding,* 1748. *Dialogues of Natural Religion,* 1779. Available in many modern editions and abridgments.

The *Inquiry* repeats much the same arguments as the *Treatise* but in a shorter and more graceful form.

Hurd, Richard. *Letters on Chivalry and Romance,* 1762. Ed. Hoyt Trowbridge, Berkeley: Univ. of California Press, 1963.

Hutcheson, Francis. *An Inquiry into the Original of Our Ideas of Beauty and Virtue,* 1726.

Kames, Lord (Henry Home). *Elements of Criticism,* 1762.

An influential and representative critical survey, generally, but not rigorously, along the lines of the empirical psychology of the day.

Locke, John. *An Essay Concerning Human Understanding*, 1690. 4th ed. 1700. Many modern editions and abridgments.

Lowth, Robert. *Lectures on the Sacred Poetry of the Hebrews*, 1787. Original Latin version, 1753.

Plotinus. *Enneads*. Trans. Stephen Mackenna and B. S. Page, New York: Pantheon, 1957. A useful abridgment in paperback by A. H. Armstrong, New York: Collier Books, 1962.

Plotinus is ultimately the source of most of the romantics' "Platonism." Coleridge read him in the original; he was also available through Thomas Taylor's translations and, at one or two removes, through the writings of Berkeley, Shaftesbury, the Cambridge Platonists, and Renaissance Platonists.

Price, Uvedale. *An Essay on the Picturesque, as Compared with the Sublime and the Beautiful*, 1794.

Burke's psychological approach applied to landscape gardening.

Priestley, Joseph. *Course of Lectures on Oratory and Criticism*, 1777. Ed. Vincent M. Bevilicqua and Richard Murphy, Carbondale: Southern Illinois Univ. Press, 1965. *Disquisitions Relating to Matter and Spirit*, 1777. *Selections*, ed. Ira V. Brown, University Park: Pennsylvania State Univ. Press, 1962. *Priestley's Writings on Philosophy, Science, and Politics*, ed. John A. Passmore, New York: Collier Books, 1965.

Reid, Thomas. *An Inquiry into the Human Mind on the Principles of Common Sense*, 1764. *Essays on the Intellectual Powers of Man*, 1785. Ed. and abridged by A. D. Woozley, London: Macmillan, 1941.

Dean of the Scottish common-sense school.

Shaftesbury, Third Earl of (Anthony Ashley Cooper). *Characteristics of Men, Manners, Opinions, Times*, 1711. Ed. John M. Robertson, Indianapolis: Bobbs-Merrill, 1964. Of special relevance is Treatise V, "The Moralists, a Philosophical Rhapsody," first published in 1709.

Spinoza, Benedict de. *Theologico-Political Treatise* and *Ethics* in *Chief Works*, trans. R. H. M. Elwes, New York: Dover, 1951.

A powerful influence on Coleridge, Wordsworth, and Shelley.

Young, Edward. *Conjectures on Original Composition*, 1759.

II. Anthologies containing selections from most of the above writers and
other writings useful in the study of the backgrounds of romanticism.

Chapman, Gerald Wester. *Literary Criticism in England, 1660–1800.* New
York: Knopf, 1966.

Elledge, Scott. *Eighteenth-Century Critical Essays.* 2 vols. Ithaca: Cornell
Univ. Press, 1961.

Quintana, Ricardo, and Alvin Whitley. *English Poetry of the Mid and
Late Eighteenth Century.* New York: Knopf, 1963.

Contains several poems anticipating romantic ideas about nature, imagination, and the poetic process—notably those of Gray, Akenside, Col-
lins, Joseph Warton, and James Beattie.

III. Modern scholarly works particularly valuable as introductions to this
field. To these works the preceding introduction is often indebted.

Abrams, Meyer H. *The Mirror and the Lamp: Romantic Theory and the
Critical Tradition.* London: Oxford Univ. Press, 1953. Paperback, New
York: Norton, 1958.

Bate, Walter Jackson. *From Classic to Romantic: Premises of Taste in
Eighteenth-Century England.* Cambridge, Mass.: Harvard Univ. Press,
1946. Paperback, New York: Harper, 1961.

Cassirer, Ernst. *The Philosophy of the Enlightenment,* trans. Fritz C. A.
Koellen and James P. Pettegrove. Princeton: Princeton Univ. Press,
1951. Paperback, Boston: Beacon Press, 1955.

Lovejoy, A. O. *The Great Chain of Being.* Cambridge, Mass.: Harvard
Univ. Press, 1936. Paperback, New York: Harper, 1960.

Nicolson, Marjorie Hope. *Mountain Gloom and Mountain Glory: The
Development of the Aesthetics of the Infinite.* Ithaca: Cornell Univ.
Press, 1959. Paperback, New York: Norton, 1963.

Stephen, Leslie. *History of English Thought in the Eighteenth Century.*
London: Smith, Elder, 1876. Paperback, New York: Harcourt, Brace &
World, 1962.

Tuveson, Ernest Lee. *The Imagination as a Means of Grace: Locke and
the Aesthetics of Romanticism.* Berkeley: Univ. of California Press,
1960.

Wellek, René. *A History of Modern Criticism: 1715–1950.* Vols. I and II. New Haven: Yale Univ. Press, 1955.

Willey, Basil. *The Eighteenth Century Background.* London: Chatto & Windus, 1940. Paperback, Boston: Beacon Press, 1961.

Backgrounds of Romanticism

WILLIAM LAW

(1686–1761)

Law, son of a grocer, became a Fellow at Emmanuel College, Cambridge, but his career in both the University and the Church came to an end because of his allegiance to the Stuart Pretender. He eventually became tutor of Edward Gibbon, father of the historian, and then remained with the family as "honoured friend and spiritual director." In 1740, after the Gibbon household had broken up, he retired to his native Kings Cliffe in Northamptonshire, where he had already established a school for girls. He was joined by a rich widow, Mrs. Hutcheson, and Miss Hester Gibbon, the historian's aunt, who undertook to live as anchoresses under Law's spiritual guidance. Here he spent the rest of his life in half-seclusion, watching over his two charges, directing his school, and distributing alms—much to the annoyance of the rest of the parish, who disapproved of all the beggars who were attracted.

In spite of his otherworldliness, Law was never loath to plunge into controversy in support of his opinions, which were Tory, high-church, and mystical. He attacked, at various times, Benjamin Hoadly, Bishop of Bangor and center of the "Bangorian Controversy"; the deist Matthew Tindal; Mandeville, author of *Fable of the Bees*; Bishop Warburton; and Dr. Trapp, who published a sermon against being "righteous overmuch." His condemnation of the theater, *The Absolute Unlawfulness of the Stage Entertainment Fully Demonstrated* (1726), is more vehement than the similar attack of Jeremy Collier. The Wesleys and Whitefield were early disciples of Law, but eventually parted from him because of his

3

mysticism. He was strongly attracted to the writings of Jacob
Boehme, whose influence is evident in the selection below.

ʟ . ; read Boehme in the edition sponsored by Law (1764–81),
and his religious attitudes are closely related to Law's kind of "enthusiasm." Newton P. Stallknecht in *Strange Seas of Thought*
(Bloomington: Indiana Univ. Press, 1958) links Law with Boehme
as an influence on Wordsworth. And Coleridge praises "Behmen's
commentator, the pious and fervid William Law" in Chapter IX of
Biographia Literaria.

Modern selections of Law include *Selected Mystical Writings*, ed.
Stephen Hobhouse (2nd ed., rev.; New York: Harper, 1948) and
Selections on the Interior Life, ed. Mary Morrison (Wallingford,
Pa.: Pendle Hill, 1962). His most popular work, *A Serious Call to a
Devout and Holy Life* (1729) is available in several modern editions.
For a good introduction, see Henri Talon, *William Law: A Study in
Literary Craftsmanship* (London: Rockliff, 1948).

The *Appeal to All That Doubt or Disbelieve* first appeared in
1740; the text used here is from the third edition (London, 1768),
which is part of Vol. VI of the nine-volume *Works of the Reverend
William Law* (London, 1762–85). Capitalization and italics are mod-
ernized.

An Appeal to All that Doubt or Disbelieve the Truths of the Gospel, Whether They Be Deists, Arians, Socinians, or Nominal Christians

CHAP. I

1. It has been an opinion commonly received, though without any foundation in the light of nature, or Scripture, that God created this whole visible world and all things in it out of nothing; nay, that the souls of men and the highest orders of beings were created in the same manner. The Scripture is very decisive against this origin of the souls of men. For Moses saith, God *breathed into man* (spiraculum vitarum) *the breath of lives, and man became a living soul.* Here the notion of a soul created out of nothing is in the plainest, strongest manner rejected by the first written word of God; and no Jew or Christian can have the least excuse for falling into such an error: here the highest and most divine original is not darkly, but openly, absolutely, and in the strongest form of expression ascribed to the soul; it came forth as a breath of life, or lives, out from the mouth of God, and therefore did not come out of the womb of nothing, but is what it is, and has what it has in itself, from and out of the first and highest of all beings.

For to say that God breathed forth into man the breath of lives, by which he became a living soul, is directly saying, that

5

that which was life, light, and spirit in the living God, was breathed forth from Him to become the life, light, and spirit of a creature. The soul therefore being declared to be an effluence from God, a breath of God, must have the nature and likeness of God in it, and is and can be nothing else, but something or so much of the divine nature, become creaturely existing, or breathed forth from God, to stand before Him in the form of a creature.

When the animals of this world were to be created, it was only said, Let the earth, the air, the water, bring forth creatures after their kinds; but when man was to be brought forth, it was said, *Let us make man in our own image and likeness.* Is not this directly saying, Let man have his beginning and being out of us, that he may be so related to us in his soul and spirit, as the animals of this world are related to the elements from which they are produced. Let him so come forth from us, be so breathed out of us, that our tri-une divine nature may be manifested in him, that he may stand before us as a creaturely image, likeness, and representative of that which we are in ourselves. . . .

3. Thinking and willing are eternal, they never began to be. Nothing can think, or will now, in which there was not will and thought from all eternity. For it is as possible for thought in general to begin to be, as for that which thinks in a particular creature to begin to be of a thinking nature: therefore the soul, which is a thinking willing being is come forth, or created out of that which hath willed and thought in God from all eternity. The created soul is a creature of time, and had its beginning on the sixth day of the creation; but the essences of the soul, which were then formed into a creature, and into a state of distinction from God, had been in God from all eternity, or they could not have been breathed forth from God into the form of a living creature.

And herein lies the true ground and depth of the uncontroulable freedom of our will and thoughts: they must have a self-motion, and self-direction, because they came out of the self existent God. They are eternal, divine powers, that never began to be, and therefore cannot begin to be in subjection to any thing, that which thinks and wills in the soul, is that very same unbeginning breath which thought and willed in God, before it was breathed into the form of an human soul; and therefore it is, that will and thought cannot be bounded or constrained. . . .

5. That the souls of men were not created out of nothing, but are born out of an eternal original, is plain from hence; from that delight in, and desire of eternal existence, which are so strong and natural to the soul of man. For nothing can delight in or desire eternity, or so much as form a notion of it, or think upon it, or any way reach after it, but that alone which is generated from it, and come out of it. For it is a self-evident truth, that nothing can look higher, or further back, than into its own original; and therefore, nothing can look or reach back into eternity, but that which came out of it. This is as certain, as that a line reaches and can reach no further back, than to that point from whence it arose.

Our bodily eyes are born out of the firmamental light of this world, and therefore they can look no further than the firmament: but our thoughts know no bounds, therefore they are come out of that which is boundless. The eyes of our minds can look as easily backwards into that eternity which always hath been, as into that which ever shall be; and therefore it is plain, that that which thinks and wills in us, which so easily, so delightfully, so naturally penetrates into all eternity, has always had an eternal existence, and is only a ray or spark of the divine nature, brought out into the form of a creature, or a limited, personal existence, by the creating power of God. . . .

8. . . . O, dear reader, stay a while in this important place, and learn to know thyself: all thy senses make thee know and feel, that thou standest in the vanity of time; but every motion, stirring, imagination, and thought of thy mind, whether in fansying, fearing, or loving everlasting life, is the same infallible proof, that thou standest in the midst of eternity, art an offspring and inhabitant of it, and must be for ever inseparable

from it. Ask when the first thought sprung up, find out the birth-
day of truth, and then thou wilt have found out when the
essences of thy soul first began to be. Were not the essences of
thy soul as old, as unbeginning, as unchangeable, as everlasting
as truth itself, truth would be at the same distance from thee, as
absolutely unfit for thee, as utterly unable to have any communion with thee, as to be the food of a worm.

The ox could not feed upon the grass, or receive any delight
or nourishment from it, unless grass and the ox had one and
the same earthly nature and origin: thy mind could receive no
truth, feel no delight and satisfaction in the certainty, beauty,
and harmony of it, unless truth and the mind stood both in the
same place, had one and the same unchangeable nature, unbeginning original. If there will come a time when thought itself
shall cease, when all the relations and connections of truth shall
be untied, then, but not till then, shall the knot or band of thy
soul's life be unloosed. It is a spark of the Deity, and therefore
has the unbeginning unending life of God in it. It knows nothing of youth or age, because it is born eternal. It is a life that
must burn for ever, either as a flame of light and love in the
glory of the divine majesty, or as a miserable fireband in that
God, which is a consuming fire.

9. It is impossible that this world, in the state and condition
it is now in, should have been an immediate and original creation
of God: this is as impossible, as that God should create evil,
either natural or moral. That this world hath evil in all its parts,
that its matter is in a corrupt, disordered state, full of grossness,
disease, impurity, wrath, death, and darkness, is as evident, as
that there is light, beauty, order, and harmony, every where to
be found in it. Therefore it is as impossible that this outward
state and condition of things should be a first and immediate
work of God, as that there should be good and evil in God
Himself. . . .

Dark, sour, hard, dead earth, can no more be a first, immediate
creation of God, than a wrathful devil, as such, can be created
by Him. For dark, sour, dead earth is as disordered in its kind,

as the devils are, and has as certainly lost its first heavenly condition and nature, as the devils have lost theirs. But now, as in
man, the little world, there is excellency and perfection enough
to prove, that human nature is the work of an all-perfect being,
yet so much impurity and disease of corrupt flesh and blood,
as undeniably shews that, sin has almost quite spoiled the work
of God; so, in the great world, the footsteps of an infinite wisdom in the order and harmony of the whole sufficiently appear,
yet the disorders, tumults, and evils of nature, plainly demon-
strate that the present condition of this world is only the remains or ruins, first, of a heaven spoiled by the fall of angels,
and then of a paradise lost by the sin of man. . . .

11. . . . All the qualities of all beings are eternal; no real quality or power can appear in any creature, but what has its eternal
root or generating cause in the Creator. . . . But now if no
quality can begin to be, if all the qualities and powers of creatures must be eternal and necessary existent in God before they
can have any existence in any creature, then it undeniably follows, that every created thing must have its whole nature from
and out of the divine nature.

All qualities are not only good but infinitely perfect as they
are in God; and it is absolutely impossible that they should have
any evil or defect in them, as they are in the One God, who is
the great and universal All. Because where all properties are
there must necessarily be an all possible perfection; and that
by an absolute necessity be always all perfect. But the same
qualities, thus infinitely good and perfect in God, may become
imperfect and evil in the creature; because in the creature, being
limited and finite, they may be divided and separated from one
another by the creature itself. Thus strength and fire in the
divine nature are nothing else but the strength and flame of love,
and never can be any thing else; but in the creature, strength
and fire may be separated from love, and then they are become
an evil; they are wrath, and darkness, and all mischief: and thus
that same strength and quality, which in creatures making a right
use of their own will, or self-motion, becomes their goodness

and perfection, does in creatures making a wrong use of their will become their evil and mischievous nature: and it is a truth that deserves well to be considered, that there is no goodness in any creature, from the highest to the lowest, but in its continuing to be such an union of qualities and powers, as God has brought together in its creation. . . .

12. If a delicious fragrant fruit had a power of separating itself from that rich spirit, fine taste, smell, and colour, which it receives from the virtue of the sun, and the spirit of the air; or if it could in the beginning of its growth turn away from the sun, and receive no virtue from it, then it would stand in its own first birth of wrath, sourness, bitterness, and astringency, just as the devils do, who have turned back into their own dark root, and rejected the light and spirit of God: so that the hellish nature of a devil is nothing else but its own first forms of life, withdrawn, or separated from the heavenly light and love; just as the sourness, astringency, and bitterness of a fruit, are nothing else but the first forms of its own vegetable life, before it has reached the virtue of the sun, and the spirit of the air.

And as a fruit, if it had a sensibility of itself, would be full of torment as soon as it was shut up in the first forms of its life, in its own astringency, sourness, and stinging bitterness, so the angels, when they had turned back into these very same first forms of their own life, and broke off from the heavenly light and love of God, became their own hell. No hell was made for them, no new qualities came into them, no vengeance or pains from the God of love fell upon them; they only stood in that state of division and separation from the Son, and Holy Spirit of God, which by their own motion they had made for themselves. They had nothing in them but what they had from God, the first forms of an heavenly life; nothing but what the most heavenly beings have, and must have, to all eternity; but they had them in a state of self-torment, because they had separated them from that birth of light and love, which alone could make them glorious sons, and blessed images of the Holy Trinity.

The same strong desire, fiery wrath, and stinging motion are in holy angels, that are in devils, just as the same sourness, astringency, and biting bitterness are in a full ripened fruit, which were there before it received the riches of the light and spirit of the air. In a ripened fruit, its first sourness, astringency, and bitterness are not lost, nor destroyed, but become the real cause of all its rich spirit, fine taste, fragrant smell, and beautiful colour; take away the working, contending nature of these first qualities, and you annihilate the spirit, taste, smell, and virtue of the fruit, and there would be nothing left for the sun and spirit of the air to enrich.

Just in the same manner, that which in a devil is an evil selfishness, a wrathful fire, a stinging motion, is in an holy angel the everlasting kindling of a divine life, the strong birth of an heavenly love, it is a real cause of an ever-springing, ever-triumphing joyfulness, an ever-increasing sensibility of bliss. . . .

28. . . . Now as there is but one God, so there is but one nature, as unalterable as that God from whom it arises, and whose manifestation it is; so also there is but one religion founded in nature, and but one salvation possible in nature. Revealed religion is nothing else but a revelation of the mysteries of nature, for God cannot reveal, or require any thing by a spoken or written word, but that which he reveals and requires by nature; for nature is his great book of revelation, and he that can only read its capital letters, will have found so many demonstrations of the truth of the written revelation of God.

But to shew that there is but one salvation possible in nature, and that possibility solely contained in the Christian method: look from the top to the bottom of all creatures, from the highest to the lowest beings, and you will find that death has but one nature in all worlds, and in all creatures: look at life in an angel, and life in a vegetable, and you will find that life has but one and the same form, one and the same ground in the whole scale of beings: no omnipotence of God can make that to be life which is not life, or that to be death which is not death, according to nature; and the reason is, because nature is nothing else but God's own outward manifestation of what he inwardly is, and can do; and therefore no revelation from God can teach, or require any thing but that which is taught and required by God in and through nature. The mysteries of religion therefore are no higher, nor deeper than the mysteries of nature, and all the rites, laws, ceremonies, types, institutions, and ordinances given by God from Adam to the apostles, are only typical of something that is to be done, or instrumental to the doing of that, which the unchangeable working of nature requires to be done. As sure therefore as there is but one and the same thing that is death, and one and the same thing that is life throughout all nature, whether temporal or eternal, so sure is it, that there is but one way to life or salvation for fallen man. And this way, let it be what it will, must and can be only that which has its reason and foundation in that one universal nature, which is the one unchangeable manifestation of the Deity. For if there is but one thing that is life, and one thing that is death throughout all nature, from the highest angel to the hardest flint upon earth, then it must be plain, that the life which is to be raised or restored by religion must and can only be restored according to nature: and therefore true religion can only be the religion of nature, and divine revelation can do nothing else, but reveal and manifest the demands and workings of nature.

29. Now the one great doctrine of the Christian religion, and which includes all the rest, is this, that Adam by his sin died to the kingdom of heaven, or that the divine life extinguished in him; that he cannot be redeemed, or restored to its first divine life, but by having it kindled or regenerated in him by the Son and Holy Spirit of God: now that which is here called death, his losing the light and spirit of the kingdom of heaven, and that which is here made necessary to make him alive again to the kingdom of heaven, are the very same which are called, and are death and life throughout all nature, both temporal and eternal: and therefore, the Christian religion, requiring this

method of raising man to a divine life, has its infallible proof
from all nature. Consider death, or the deadness that is in a hard
flint, and you will see what is the eternal death of a fallen angel:
the flint is dead, or in a state of death, because its fire is bound,
compacted, shut up, and imprisoned; this are its chains and
bands of death: a steel struck against a flint will shew you, that
every particle of the flint consists of this compacted fire.

Now a fallen angel is in no other state of death, knows no
other death than this: it is in its whole spiritual intelligent being,
nothing else but that very same which the flint is, in its insensible materiality, *viz.* an imprisoned compacted darkened fire-
spirit, shut up, and tyed in its own chains of darkness as the
fire of the flint; and you shall see by and by, that the flint is
changed from its first state into its present hardness of death,
in the same manner, and by the same means, as the heavenly
angel is become a fiery serpent in the state of eternal death.

Now, look at every death that can be found betwixt that of
a fallen angel, and that of a hard flint, and you will find that
death enters no where, into no kind of vegetable, plant, or
animal, but as it has entered into the angel, and the flint, and
stands in the same manner in every thing where-ever it is.

. . . . .

CHAP. II

2. Every thing that is in being is either God, or nature, or
creature; and every thing that is not God is only a manifestation
of God; for as there is nothing, neither nature, nor creature, but
what must have its being in and from God, so every thing is,
and must be, according to its nature more or less a manifestation
of God. Every thing therefore by its form and condition speaks
so much of God, and God in every thing speaks and manifests
so much of himself. Temporary nature is this beginning created
system of sun, stars, and element; it is temporary nature,

because it begins and has an end, and therefore is only a temporary manifestation of God, or God manifested according to transitory things.

3. Properly and strictly speaking, nothing can begin to be: the beginning of every thing is nothing more than its beginning to be in a new state. Thus time itself does not begin to be, but duration, which always was, began to be measured by the earth's turning round, or the rising and setting of the sun, and that is called the beginning of time, which is, properly speaking, only the beginning of the measure of duration: thus it is with all temporal nature, and all the qualities and powers of temporal beings that live in it: no quality or power of nature then began to be, but such qualities and powers as had been from all eternity, began then to be in a new state. Ask what time is; it is nothing else but something of eternal duration become finite, measurable, and transitory. Ask what fire, light, darkness, air, water, and earth are; they are, and can be nothing else, but some eternal things become gross, finite, measurable, divisible, and transitory. For if there could be a temporal fire that did not spring out of eternal fire, then there might be time that did not come out of eternity. . . .

10. Temporal nature, opened to us by the spirit of God, becomes a volume of holy instruction to us, and leads us into all the mysteries and secrets of eternity: for as every thing in temporal nature is descended out of that which is eternal, and stands as a palpable visible out-birth of it, so when we know how to separate the grossness, death, and darkness of time from it, we find what it is in its eternal state. Fire, and light, and air in this world, are not only a true resemblance of the Holy Trinity in unity, but are the Trinity itself in its most outward lowest kind of existence or manifestation; for there could be no fire, fire could not generate light, air could not proceed from both, these three could not be thus united, and thus divided, but because they have their root and original in the tri-unity of the Deity. Fire compacted, created, separated from light and air, is the elemental fire of this world: fire uncreated, uncompacted, un-

separated from light and air, is the heavenly fire of eternity: fire kindled in any material thing is only fire breaking out of its created compacted state; it is nothing else but the awakening the spiritual properties of that thing, which being thus stirred up, strive to get rid of that material creation under which they are imprisoned: thus every kindled fire, with all its rage and fierceness, tears and divides, scatters and consumes that materiality under which it is imprisoned; and were not these spiritual properties imprisoned in matter, no material thing could be made to burn. And this is another proof, that the materiality of this world is come out of a higher, and spiritual state, because every matter upon earth can be made to discover spiritual properties concealed in it, and is indeed a compaction of nothing else. Fire is not, cannot be a material thing, it only makes itself visible and sensible by the destruction of matter: matter is its death and imprisonment, and it comes to life but by being able to agitate, divide, shake off, and consume that matter which held it in death and bondage; so that every time you see a fire kindled, you see nature striving in a low degree to get rid of the grossness of this material creation, and to do that which can alone be done by the last fire, when all the inward spiritual properties hid in every thing, in rocks, and stones, and earth, in sun, and stars, and elements, shall by the last trumpet be awakened and called forth: and this is a certain truth, that fire could no where now be kindled in any material thing, but for this reason, because all material nature was created to be restored, and stands by divine appointment in a fitness and tendency to have its deliverance from this created state by fire; so that every time you see a piece of matter dissolved by fire, you have a full proof, that all the materiality of this world is appointed to a dissolution by fire; and that then (O glorious day!) sun and stars, and all the elements, will be delivered from vanity, will be again that one eternal, harmonious, glorious thing which they were, before they were compacted into material distinctions and separations.

11. The elements of this world stand in great strife and contrariety, and yet in great desire of mixing and uniting with each

other; and hence arise both the life and death of all temporal
things: and hereby we plainly know that the elements of this
world were once one undivided thing; for union can no where
be desired, but where there has first been a separation: as sure
therefore as the elements desire each other, so sure is it, that
they have been parted from each other, and are only parts of
some one thing that has been divided. When the elements come
to such a degree of union a life is produced; but because they
have still a contrariety to each other, they soon destroy again
that same life which they had built, and therefore every four-
elementary life is short and transitory. . . .

13. . . . In eternal nature or the kingdom of heaven, materiality
stands in life and light; it is the light's glorious body, or that
garment wherewith light is cloathed, and therefore has all the
properties of light in it, and only differs from light, as it is its
brightness and beauty, as the holder and displayer of all its
colours, powers, and virtues. But the same materiality in this
world, being created or compacted into a separation from fire
united with light, is become the body of death and darkness, and
is therefore gross, thick, dark, heavy, divisible, &c. for death is
nothing else but the shutting up, or shutting out the united
power of fire and light: this is the only death that ever did, or
can happen to any thing whether earthly or heavenly. Therefore every degree of hardness, and darkness, stiffness, &c. is a
degree of death; and herein consists the deadness of the materiality of this world. When it shall be raised to life, that is when
the united power of fire and light shall kindle itself through all
temporal nature, then hardness, darkness, divisibility, &c. will
be all extinguished together. . . .

17. All beings, that are purely of this world, have their existence in and dependence upon temporal nature. God is no maker,
creator, or governor of any being or creature of this world,
immediately, or by himself, but he creates, upholds, and governs
all things of this world, by, and through, and with temporal
nature: as temporary nature is nothing else but eternal nature
separated, divided, compacted, made visible, and changeable for

a time, so heaven is nothing else but the beatifick visibility, the majestick presence of the abyssal, unsearchable, tri-une God: it is that light with which the Scripture saith, God is decked as with a garment, and by which he is manifested and made visible to heavenly eyes and beings; for Father, Son, and Holy Ghost, as they are the tri-une God, deeper than the kingdom of heaven or eternal nature, are invisible to all created eyes; but that beatifick visibility and outward glory, which is called the kingdom of heaven, is the manifestation of the Father, Son, and Holy Ghost, in, and by, and through the glorious union of eternal fire, and light, and spirit.

GEORGE BERKELEY

(1685–1753)

Berkeley was born in Kilkenny, Ireland, and attended Trinity College, Dublin, where he was elected Fellow in 1707. He spent time in London, where he knew Swift, Pope, and Addison. In 1724 he was appointed Dean of Derry, and in 1734 Bishop of Cloyne. Between 1724 and 1731 he worked, unsuccessfully, to raise support for a college in the Bermudas; from 1728 to 1731, in the pursuit of this scheme, he lived in Newport, Rhode Island. His works include *Essay Towards a New Theory of Vision* (1709), a scrupulously reasoned proof that there is no real resemblance between the perceptions of vision and of touch; *A Treatise Concerning the Principles of Human Knowledge* (1710), in which he argues his most important principle, that *esse* is *percipi*; *Three Dialogues Between Hylas and Philonous* (1713), maintaining the same principle in the more popular form of a Socratic dialogue; *De Motu* (1721), application of this principle to questions of gravity, force, and motion; *Alciphron: or the Minute Philosopher* (1732), a dialogue attacking freethinkers of his day; *The Querist* (1735–37), treating social and political problems of Ireland; and *Siris* (1744), popular in its day mainly for its practical message of the curative powers of tar-water.

Though *Siris* speculates on the physical causes of tar-water's virtues, it does not abrogate Berkeley's basic principle that all reality exists only in the mind of God and, imperfectly, in the minds of men. As he explains in sections 231, 234, and 249–54, all such mechanistic explanations are only *descriptions* of the systematic order implicit in the great ideal reality created by God. Berkeley's system is not solipsism—quite the opposite: *The Principles of Human Action* and *Siris* both maintain that, external to the individual mind, the mind of God is constantly sustaining the entire "physical" universe by thinking of it. When a man perceives "external nature" he is sharing a small portion of the mind of God; hence sense impressions are the language through which God partially conveys His nature to men.

For young men of Coleridge's day it was tremendously exciting to speculate on these questions raised by Berkeley; and, though few in the end accepted Berkeley's principles unmodified, after reading him they could never again quite regard the material world as an unquestioned "given." Prospero's "We are such stuff as dreams are made on" took on a new significance. Berkeley is no doubt at least an indirect source of Blake's assertion in *A Vision of the Last Judgment*, "Mental things are alone real; what is called corporeal, nobody knows of its dwelling place," and of the statement in Shelley's fragment "On Life," "Nothing exists but as it is perceived." Coleridge, of course, read Berkeley early, praised him at times exorbitantly, and reflects his influence as early as "Religious Musings" and as late as the *Biographia Literaria*, where even the famous definitions of the primary and secondary imagination probably owe something to him.

Berkeley's collected works are edited, with excellent introductions and notes, by A. A. Luce and T. E. Jessop in the Bibliotheca Britannica Philosophica series, 9 vols. (London: Nelson & Sons, 1948–57); *Siris* is Volume V of this series. A. A. Luce has written *The Life of George Berkeley* (London: Nelson & Sons, 1949). There are several popular editions of *The Principles of Human Knowledge*, the *Three Dialogues*, and other works. The reader is also referred to Arthur D. Ritchie, *George Berkeley's Siris* (London: Oxford Univ. Press, 1954), and John Wild, *George Berkeley: A Study of His Life and Philosophy* (New York: Russell & Russell, 1961).

This text follows the "second edition, improved and corrected by the author" (Dublin, 1744). A few idiosyncrasies may be misleading, for example, such spellings as "humane" for "human," and "unite" for "unit"; and the failure to follow the modern convention of capitalizing words that refer to the Deity, such as "First Mover" or "the One."

Siris: *A Chain of Philosophical Reflexions and Inquiries Concerning the Virtues of Tar Water, and Divers Other Subjects Connected Together and Arising One from Another*

1. In certain parts of America, tar-water is made by putting a quart of cold water to a quart of tar, and stirring them well together in a vessel, which is left standing till the tar sinks to the bottom. A glass of clear water being poured off for a draught is replaced by the same quantity of fresh water, the vessel being shaken and left to stand as before. And this is repeated for every glass, so long as the tar continues to impregnate the water sufficiently, which will appear by the smell and taste. But as this method produceth tar-water of different degrees of strength, I chuse to make it in the following manner: Pour a gallon of cold water on a quart of tar, and stir and mix them thoroughly with a ladle or flat stick for the space of three or four minutes, after which the vessel must stand eight and forty hours that the tar may have time to subside, when the clear water is to be poured off and kept for use, no more being made from the same tar, which may still serve for common purposes.

2. This cold infusion of tar hath been used in some of our colonies, as a preservative or preparative against the small-pox, which foreign practice induced me to try it in my own neighbourhood, when the small-pox raged with great violence. And the trial fully answered my expectation: all those, within my

knowledge, who took the tar-water having either escaped that distemper, or had it very favourably. In one family there was a remarkable instance of seven children, who came all very well through the small-pox, except one young child which could not be brought to drink tar-water as the rest had done.

4. It seemed probable, that a medicine of such efficacy in a distemper attended with so many purulent ulcers, might be also useful in other foulnesses of the blood; accordingly I tried it on several persons infected with cutaneous eruptions and ulcers, who were soon relieved, and soon after cured. Encouraged by these successes I ventured to advise it in the foulest distempers, wherein it proved much more successful than salivations and wood-drinks had done.

5. Having tried it in a great variety of cases, I found it succeed beyond my hopes; in a tedious and painful ulceration of the bowels, in a consumptive cough and (as appeared by expectorated pus) an ulcer in the lungs; in a pleurisy and peripneumony. And when a person, who for some years had been subject to erysipelatous fevers, perceived the usual fore-running symptoms to come on, I advised her to drink tar-water which prevented the erysipelas.

42. The balsam or essential oil of vegetables contains a spirit, wherein consist the specific qualities, the smell and taste of the plant. Boerhaave holds the native presiding spirit to be neither oil, salt, earth, or water; but somewhat too fine and subtile to be caught alone and rendered visible to the eye. This when suffered to fly off, for instance, from the oil of rosemary, leaves it destitute of all flavour. This spark of life, this spirit or soul, if we may so say, of the vegetable departs without any sensible diminution of the oil or water wherein it was lodged.

43. It should seem that the forms, souls, or principles of vegetable life, subsist in the light or solar emanation, which in respect of the macrocosm is what the animal spirit is to the microcosm; the interior tegument, the subtile instrument and vehicle of power. No wonder then that the ens primum [primary being] or scintilla spirituosa [spiritual spark], as it is called, of

plants should be a thing so fine and fugacious as to escape our nicest search. It is evident that nature at the sun's approach vegetates; and languishes at his recess; this terrestrial globe seeming only a matrix disposed and prepared to receive life from his light. . . .

44. The luminous spirit which is the form or life of a plant, from whence it's differences and properties flow, is somewhat extremely volatile. It is not the oil, but a thing more subtile, whereof oil is the vehicle, which retains it from flying off, and is lodged in several parts of the plant, particularly in the cells of the bark and in the seeds. This oil purified and exalted by the organical powers of the plant, and agitated by warmth, becomes a proper receptacle of the spirit; part of which spirit exhales through the leaves and flowers, and part is arrested by this unctuous humour that detains it in the plant. It is to be noted this essential oil animated, as one may say, with the flavour of the plant, is very different from any spirit, that can be procured from the same plant by fermentation.

51. It is a great maxim for health, that the juices of the body be kept fluid in a due proportion. Therefore, the acid volatile spirit in tar-water, at once attenuating and cooling in a moderate degree, must greatly conduce to health, as a mild salutary deobstruent, quickening the circulation of the fluids without wounding the solids, thereby gently removing or preventing those obstructions, which are the great and general cause of most chronical diseases; in this manner answering to the antihysterics, assa foetida, galbanum, myrrh, amber, and, in general, to all the resins and gums of trees or shrubs useful in nervous cases.

151. . . . Air . . . is a mass of various particles, abraded and sublimated from wet and dry bodies of all sorts, cohering with particles of æther; the whole permeated by pure æther, or light, or fire: for these words are used promiscuously by ancient philosophers.

152. This æther or pure invisible fire, the most subtile and elastic of all bodies, seems to pervade and expand it self throughout the whole universe. If air be the immediate agent or instru-

ment in natural things, it is the pure invisible fire that is the first natural mover or spring, from whence the air derives it's power. This mighty agent is every where at hand, ready to break forth into action, if not restrained and governed with the greatest wisdom. Being always restless and in motion, it actuates and enlivens the whole visible mass, is equally fitted to produce and to destroy, distinguishes the various stages of nature, and keeps up the perpetual round of generations and corruptions, pregnant with forms which it constantly sends forth and re-sorbs. So quick in it's motions, so subtile and penetrating in it's nature, so extensive in it's effects, it seemeth no other than the vegetative soul or vital spirit of the world.

153. The animal spirit in man is the instrumental or physical cause both of sense and motion. To suppose sense in the world, would be gross and unwarranted. But loco-motive faculties are evident in all it's parts. The Pythagoræans, Platonists, and Stoics held the world to be an animal. Though some of them have chosen to consider it as a vegetable. However the phænomena and effects do plainly shew there is a spirit that moves, and a mind or providence that presides. This providence, Plutarch saith, was thought to be in regard to the world, what the soul is in regard to man.

154. The order and course of things, and the experiments we daily make, shew there is a mind that governs and actuates this mundane system, as the proper real agent and cause. And that the inferior instrumental cause is pure æther, fire, or the substance of light which is applied and determined by an infinite mind in the macrocosm or universe, with unlimited power, and according to stated rules; as it is in the microcosm, with limited power and skill by the human mind. We have no proof either from experiment or reason, of any other agent or efficient cause than mind or spirit. When therefore we speak of corporeal agents or corporeal causes, this is to be understood in a dif-ferent, subordinate, and improper sense.

155. The principles whereof a thing is compounded, the in-strument used in its production, and the end for which it was

intended, are all in vulgar use termed Causes, though none of them be strictly speaking agent or efficient. There is not any proof that an extended corporeal or mechanical cause doth really and properly act, even motion itself being in truth a passion. Therefore though we speak of this fiery substance as acting, yet it is to be understood only as a mean or instrument, which indeed is the case of all mechanical causes whatsoever. They are nevertheless sometimes termed agents and causes, although they are by no means active in a strict and proper signification. When, therefore, force, power, virtue, or action are mentioned as subsisting in an extended and corporeal or mechanical being, this is not to be taken in a true, genuine, and real, but only in a gross and popular sense, which sticks in appearances, and doth not analyse things to their first principles. In compliance with established language, and the use of the world, we must employ the popular current phrase. But then in regard to truth we ought to distinguish its meaning. It may suffice to have made this declaration once for all, in order to avoid mistakes.

156. The calidum innatum, the vital flame, or animal spirit in man is supposed the cause of all motions, in the several parts of his body, whether voluntary or natural. That is, it is the instrument, by means whereof the mind exerts and manifests herself in the motions of the body. In the same sense may not fire be said to have force, to operate, and agitate the whole system of the world, which is held together and informed by one presiding mind, and animated throughout by one and the same fiery substance, as an instrumental and mechanical agent, not as a primary real efficient?

161. In the human body the mind orders and moves the limbs: but the animal spirit is supposed the immediate physical cause of their motion. So likewise in the mundane system, a mind presides, but the immediate, mechanical, or instrumental cause, that moves or animates all it's parts, is the pure elementary fire or spirit of the world. The more fine and subtile part or spirit is supposed to receive the impressions of the first mover,

and communicate them to the grosser sensible parts of this world. Motion, though in metaphysical rigor and truth, a passion or mere effect, yet, in physics, passeth for an action. And by this action all effects are supposed to be produced. Hence the various communications, determinations, accelerations of motion constitute the laws of nature.

164. The element of æthereal fire or light seems to comprehend, in a mixed state, the seeds, the natural causes and forms of all sublunary things. The grosser bodies separate, attract, and repel the several constituent particles of that heterogeneous element; which, being parted from the common mass, make distinct essences, producing and combining together such qualities and properties, as are peculiar to the several subjects, and thence often extracted in essential oils or odoriferous waters, from whence they exhale into the open air, and return into their original element.

175. This same heat is also what Hippocrates calls nature, the author of life and death, good and evil. It is farther to be noted of this heat, that he maketh it the object of no sense. It is that occult, universal nature, and inward invisible force, which actuates and animates the whole world, and was worshipped by the ancients under the name of Saturn; which Vossius judges, not improbably, to be derived from the Hebrew word Satar, to lye hidden or concealed. And what hath been delivered by Hippocrates agrees with the notions of other philosophers: Heraclitus, for instance, who held fire to be the principle and cause of the generation of all things, did not mean thereby an inanimate element, but, as he termed it, $\pi\hat{v}\rho\ \dot{\alpha}\epsilon\dot{\iota}\zeta\omega o\nu$, an everliving fire.

178. As the Platonists held intellect to be lodged in soul, and soul in æther; so it passeth for a doctrine of Trismegistus in the Pimander, that mind is cloathed by soul, and soul by spirit. Therefore as the animal spirit of man, being subtil and luminous, is the immediate tegument of the human soul, or that wherein and whereby she acts; even so the spirit of the world, that active fiery æthereal substance of light, that permeates and animates

the whole system, is supposed to cloath the soul, which cloaths the mind of the universe.

210. Plotinus supposeth, that from the sun's light which is corporeal, there springs forth another equivocal light which is incorporeal, and as it were the brightness of the former. Marsilius Ficinus also, observing it to be a doctrine in the Timæus of Plato, that there is an occult fire or spirit diffused throughout the universe, intimates that this same occult invisible fire or light is, as it were, the sight of the mundane soul. And Plotinus, in his fourth Ennead, sheweth it to be his opinion, that the world seeth it self and all it's parts. The Platonic philosophers do wonderfully refine upon light, and soar very high: from coal to flame; from flame to light; from this visible light to the occult light of the celestial or mundane soul, which they supposed to pervade and agitate the substance of the universe by it's vigorous and expansive motion.

214. The principles of motion and vegetation in living bodies seem to be delibations from the invisible fire or spirit of the universe. Which, though present to all things, is not nevertheless one way received by all; but variously imbibed, attracted, and secreted by the fine capillaries, and exquisite strainers in the bodies of plants and animals, whereby it becomes mixed and detained in their juices.

218. Tar-water serving as a vehicle to this spirit is both diuretic and diaphoretic, but seems to work it's principal effect by assisting the vis vitæ [life force], as an alterative and cordial, enabling nature by an accession of congenial spirit, to assimilate that which could not be assimulated by her proper force, and so to subdue the fomes morbi [source of disease]. And this should seem in most cases the best and safest course. Great evacuations weaken nature as well as the disease. And it is to be feared that they who use salivations and copious bleedings may, though they should recover of the distemper, in their whole life be never able to recover of the remedies.

220. Force or power, strickly speaking, is [in] the agent alone who imparts an equivocal force to the invisible elementary fire,

or animal spirit of the world, and this to the ignited body or visible flame, which produceth the sense of light and heat. In this chain the first and last links are allowed to be incorporeal: the two intermediate are corporeal, being capable of motion, rarefaction, gravity, and other qualities of bodies. It is fit to distinguish these things, in order to avoid ambiguity concerning the nature of fire.

231. The laws of attraction and repulsion are to be regarded as laws of motion, and these only as rules or methods observed in the productions of natural effects, the efficient and final causes whereof are not of mechanical consideration. Certainly, if the explaining a phænomenon be to assign its proper efficient and final cause, it should seem the mechanical philosophers never explained any thing, their province being only to discover the laws of nature, that is the general rules and methods of motion, and to account for particular phænomena by reducing them under, or shewing their conformity to such general rules.

234. Mechanical laws of nature or motion direct us how to act, and teach us what to expect. Where intellect presides, there will be method and order, and therefore rules, which if not stated and constant would cease to be rules. There is therefore a constancy in things, which is styled the course of nature. All the phænomena in nature are produced by motion. There appears an uniform working in things great and small, by attracting and repelling forces. But the particular laws of attraction and repulsion are various. Nor are we concerned at all about the forces, neither can we know or measure them otherwise than by their effects, that is to say, the motions, which motions only, and not the forces, are indeed in the bodies. Bodies are moved to or from each other, and this is performed according to different laws. The natural or mechanic philosopher endeavours to discover those laws by experiment and reasoning. But what is said of forces residing in bodies whether attracting or repelling, is to be regarded only as a mathematical hypothesis, and not as any thing really existing in nature.

249. The mechanical philosopher, as hath been already ob-

served, inquires properly concerning the rules and modes of operation alone, and not concerning the cause, forasmuch as nothing mechanical is or really can be a cause. And although a mechanical or mathematical philosopher may speak of absolute space, absolute motion, and of force as existing in bodies, causing such motion and proportional thereto; yet what these forces are, which are supposed to be lodged in bodies, to be impressed on bodies, to be multiplied, divided, and communicated from one body to another, and which seem to animate bodies like abstract spirits or souls, hath been found very difficult, not to say impossible, for thinking men to conceive and explain, as may be seen by consulting Borellus De vi percussionis, and Torricelli in his Lezioni academiche, among other authors.

250. Nor, if we consider the proclivity of mankind to realize their notions, will it seem strange that mechanic philosophers and geometricians should, like other men, be misled by prejudice, and take mathematical hypotheses for real beings existing in bodies, so far as even to make it the very aim and end of their science to compute or measure those phantoms; whereas it is very certain that nothing in truth can be measured or computed, beside the very effects or motions themselves. Sir Isaac Newton asks, have not the minute particles of bodies certain forces or powers by which they act on one another, as well as on the particles of light, for producing most of the phænomena in nature? But in reality, those minute particles are only agitated according to certain laws of nature, by some other agent, wherein the force exists and not in them, which have only the motion; which motion in the body moved, the Peripatetics rightly judge to be a mere passion, but in the mover to be ἐνέργεια or act.

251. It passeth with many, I know not how, that mechanical principles give a clear solution of the phænomena. The Democritic hypothesis, saith doctor Cudworth, doth much more handsomely and intelligibly solve the phænomena, than that of Aristotle and Plato. But things rightly considered, perhaps it will be found not to solve any phænomenon at all. For all phænomena are, to speak truly, appearances in the soul or mind;

and it hath never been explained, nor can it be explained, how external bodies, figures and motions should produce an appearance in the mind. Those principles, therefore, do not solve, if by solving is meant assigning the real, either efficient or final cause of appearances, but only reduce them to general rules.

252. There is a certain analogy, constancy, and uniformity in the phænomena or appearances of nature, which are a foundation for general rules: and these are a grammar for the understanding of nature, or that series of effects in the visible world, whereby we are enabled to foresee what will come to pass, in the natural course of things. Plotinus observes, in his third Ennead, that the art of presaging is in some sort the reading of natural letters denoting order, and that so far forth as analogy obtains in the universe, there may be vaticination. And in reality, he that foretells the motions of the planets, or the effects of medicines, or the result of chemical or mechanical experiments, may be said to do it by natural vaticination.

254. As the natural connexion of signs with the things signified is regular and constant, it forms a sort of rational discourse, and is therefore the immediate effect of an intelligent cause. This is agreeable to the philosophy of Plato and other ancients. Plotinus indeed saith, that which acts naturally is not intellection, but a certain power of moving matter, which doth not know, but only do. And it must be owned, that, as faculties are multiplied by philosophers according to their operations, the will may be distinguished from the intellect. But it will not therefore follow, that the will, which operates in the course of nature, is not conducted and applied by intellect, although it be granted that neither will understands, nor intellect wills. Therefore, the phænomena of nature, which strike on the senses and are understood by the mind, form not only a magnificent spectacle, but also a most coherent, entertaining, and instructive discourse; and to effect this, they are conducted, adjusted, and ranged by the greatest wisdom. This language or discourse is studied with different attention, and interpreted with different degrees of skill. But so far as men have studied and remarked it's

rules, and can interpret right, so far they may be said to be knowing in nature. A beast is like a man who hears a strange tongue, but understands nothing.

255. Nature, saith the learned Doctor Cudworth, is not master of art or wisdom: Nature is ratio mersa & confusa, reason immersed and plunged into matter, and as it were fuddled in it and confounded with it. But the formation of plants and animals, the motions of natural bodies, their various properties, appearances and vicissitudes, in a word, the whole series of things in this visible world, which we call the course of nature, is so wisely managed and carried on, that the most improved human reason cannot thoroughly comprehend even the least particle thereof; so far is it from seeming to be produced by fuddled or confounded reason.

256. Natural productions, it is true, are not all equally perfect. But neither doth it suit with the order of things, the structure of the universe, or the ends of providence that they should be so. General rules, we have seen, are necessary to make the world intelligible: and from the constant observation of such rules, natural evils will sometimes unavoidably ensue: things will be produced in a slow length of time, and arrive at different degrees of perfection.

257. It must be owned, we are not conscious of the systole and diastole of the heart, or the motion of the diaphragm. It may not nevertheless be thence inferred, that unknowing nature can act regularly, as well as ourselves. The true inference is, that the self-thinking individual, or humane person, is not the real author of those natural motions. And in fact no man blames himself if they are wrong, or values himself if they are right. The same may be said of the fingers of a musician, which some object to be moved by habit which understands not; it being evident, that what is done by rule must proceed from something that understands the rule; therefore, if not from the musician himself, from some other active intelligence, the same perhaps which governs bees and spiders, and moves the limbs of those who walk in their sleep.

258. Instruments, occasions, and signs occur in, or rather make up, the whole visible course of nature. These, being no agents themselves, are under the direction of one agent concerting all for one end, the supreme good. All those motions, whether in animal bodies or in other parts of the system of nature, which are not effects of particular wills, seem to spring from the same general cause with the vegetation of plants, an ætherial spirit actuated by a mind.

259. The first poets and theologers of Greece and the east considered the generation of things, as ascribed rather to a divine cause, but the Physici to natural causes subordinate to, and directed still by a divine; except some corporealists and mechanics, who vainly pretended to make a world without a God. The hidden force that unites, adjusts, and causeth all things to hang together, and move in harmony, which Orpheus and Empedocles styled love; this principle of union is no blind principle, but acts with intellect. This divine love and intellect are not themselves obvious to our view, or otherwise discerned than in their effects. Intellect enlightens, Love connects, and the sovereign Good attracts all things.

262. Plotinus supposeth that the soul of the universe is not the original cause or author of the species, but receives them from intellect, the true principle of order and distinction, the source and giver of forms. Others consider the vegetative soul only as some lower faculty of a higher soul, which animates the fiery ætherial spirit. As for the blots and defects which appear in the course of this world, which some have thought to proceed from a fatality or necessity in nature, and others from an evil principle, that same philosopher observes, that it may be the governing reason produceth and ordaineth all those things; and, not intending that all parts should be equally good, maketh some worse than others by design, as all parts in an animal are not eyes: And in a city, comedy, or picture, all ranks, characters, and colours are not equal or like; even so excesses, defects, and contrary qualities, conspire to the beauty and harmony of the world.

263. It cannot be denied, that with respect to the universe of things, we in this mortal state are like men educated in Plato's cave, looking on shadows with our backs turned to the light. But though our light be dim, and our situation bad, yet if the best use be made of both, perhaps something may be seen. Proclus, in his commentary on the theology of Plato, observes there are two sorts of philosophers. The one placed body first in the order of beings, and made the faculty of thinking depend thereupon, supposing that the principles of all things are corporeal: that body most really or principally exists, and all other things in a secondary sense, and by virtue of that. Others, making all corporeal things to be dependent upon soul or mind, think this to exist in the first place and primary sense, and the being of bodies to be altogether derived from, and presuppose that of the mind.

264. Sense and experience acquaint us, with the course and analogy of appearances or natural effects. Thought, reason, intellect, introduce us into the knowledge of their causes. Sensible appearances, though of a flowing, unstable, and uncertain nature, yet having first occupied the mind, they do by an early prevention, render the after task of thought more difficult: and as they amuse the eyes and ears, and are more suited to vulgar uses and the mechanic arts of life, they easily obtain a preference, in the opinion of most men, to those superior principles, which are the later growth of the humane mind arrived to maturity and perfection, but, not affecting the corporeal sense, are thought to be so far deficient in point of solidity and reality, sensible and real to common apprehensions being the same thing. Although it be certain, that the principles of science are neither objects of sense nor imagination; and that intellect and reason are alone the sure guides to truth.

265. The successful curiosity of the present age, in arts and experiments and new systems, is apt to elate men, and make them overlook the ancients. But notwithstanding that the encouragement and purse of princes, and the united endeavours of great societies in these later ages, have extended experi-

mental and mechanical knowledge very far, yet it must be owned, that the ancients too were not ignorant of many things, as well in physics as metaphysics, which perhaps are more generally, though not first known in these modern times.

266. The Pythagoreans and Platonists had a notion of the true system of the world. They allowed of mechanical principles, but actuated by soul or mind: they distinguished the primary qualities in bodies from the secondary, making the former to be physical causes, and they understood physical causes in a right sense: they saw that a mind infinite in power, unextended, invisible, immortal, governed, connected and contained all things: they saw there was no such thing as real absolute space: that mind, soul or spirit, truly and really exists: that bodies exist only in a secondary and dependent sense: that the soul is the place of forms: that the sensible qualities are to be regarded as acts only in the cause, and as passions in us: they accurately considered the differences of intellect, rational soul, and sensitive soul, with their distinct acts of intellection, reasoning, and sensation, points wherein the Cartesians and their followers, who consider sensation as a mode of thinking, seem to have failed. They knew there was a subtil æther pervading the whole mass of corporeal beings, and which was itself actually moved and directed by a mind: and that physical causes were only instruments, or rather marks and signs.

267. Those ancient philosophers understood the generation of animals to consist, in the unfolding and distending of the minute imperceptible parts of pre-existing animalcules, which passeth for a modern discovery: this they took for the work of nature, but nature animate and intelligent: they understood that all things were alive and in motion: they supposed a concord and discord, union and disunion in particles, some attracting, others repelling each other: and that those attractions and repulsions, so various, regular, and useful, could not be accounted for, but by an intelligence presiding and directing all particular motions, for the conservation and benefit of the whole.

268. The Ægyptians, who impersonated nature, had made her a distinct principle, and even deified her under the name of Isis. But Osiris was understood to be mind or reason, chief and sovereign of all. Osiris, if we may believe Plutarch, was the first, pure, unmixed and holy principle, not discernible by the lower faculties; a glympse whereof like lightening darting forth, irradiates the understanding; with regard to which Plutarch adds, that Plato and Aristotle termed one part of philosophy ἐποπτικόν; to wit, when having soared above common mixed objects, and got beyond the precincts of sense and opinion, they arrive to contemplate the first and most simple being, free from all matter and composition. This is that οὐσία ὄντως οὖσα [really existing essence] of Plato, which employeth mind alone; which alone governs the world, and the soul is that which immediately informs and animates nature.

274. Jamblichus declares the world to be one animal, in which the parts however distant each from other, are nevertheless related and connected by one common nature. And he teacheth, what is also a received notion of the Pythagoreans and Platonics that there is no chasm in nature, but a chain or scale of beings rising by gentle uninterrupted gradations from the lowest to the highest, each nature being informed and perfected by the participation of a higher. As air becomes igneous, so the purest fire becomes animal, and the animal soul becomes intellectual, which is to be understood not of the change of one nature into another, but of the connection of different natures, each lower nature being, according to those philosophers, as it were a receptable or subject for the next above it to reside and act in.

275. It is also the doctrine of Platonic philosophers, that intellect is the very life of living things, the first principle and exemplar of all, from whence by different degrees are derived the inferior classes of life; first the rational, then the sensitive, after that the vegetal; but so as in the rational animal there is still somewhat intellectual, again in the sensitive there is somewhat rational, and in the vegetal somewhat sensitive, and lastly

in mixt bodies, as metals and mineral, somewhat of vegetation: By which means the whole is thought to be more perfectly connected. Which doctrine implies that all the faculties, instincts, and motions of inferior beings, in their several respective subordinations, are derived from, and depend upon mind and intellect.

276. Both Stoics and Platonics held the world to be alive, though sometimes it be mentioned as a sentient animal, sometimes as a plant or vegetable. But in this, notwithstanding what hath been surmised by some learned men, there seems to be no atheism. For so long as the world is supposed to be quickened by elementary fire or spirit, which is it self animated by soul, and directed by understanding, it follows that all parts thereof originally depend upon, and may be reduced unto, the same indivisible stem or principle, to wit, a supreme mind; which is the concurrent doctrine of Pythagoræans, Platonics, and Stoics.

277. There is according to those philosophers a life infused throughout all things: the πῦρ νοερόν, πῦρ τεχνικόν, an intellectual and artificial fire, an inward principle, animal spirit, or natural life producing and forming within as art doth without, regulating, moderating and reconciling the various motions, qualities and parts of this mundane system. By virtue of this life the great masses are held together in their orderly courses, as well as the minutest particles governed in their natural motions, according to the several laws of attraction, gravity, electricity, magnetism, and the rest. It is this gives instincts, teaches the spider her web, and the bee her honey. This it is that directs the roots of plants to draw forth juices from the earth, and the leaves and cortical vessels to separate and attract such particles of air, and elementary fire, as suit their respective natures.

278. Nature seems to be not otherwise distinguished from the anima mundi, than as life is from soul, and, upon the principles of the oldest philosophers, may not improperly or incongruously be styled the life of the world. Some Platonics indeed, regard life as the act of nature, in like manner as intellection is of the mind or intellect. As the first intellect acts by understanding, so

nature according to them acts or generates by living. But life is the act of the soul, and seems to be very nature it self, which is not the principle, but the result of another, and higher principle, being a life resulting from soul, as cogitation from intellect.

279. If nature be the life of the world, animated by one soul, compacted into one frame, and directed or governed in all parts by one mind: This system cannot be accused of atheism; tho' perhaps it may of mistake or impropriety. And yet, as one presiding mind gives unity to the infinite aggregate of things, by a mutual communion of actions and passions, and an adjustment of parts, causing all to concur in one view to one and the same end, the ultimate and supreme good of the whole, it should seem reasonable to say, with Ocellus Lucanus the Pythagorean, that as life holds together the bodies of animals, the cause whereof is the soul; and as a city is held together by concord, the cause whereof is law; even so the world is held together by harmony, the cause whereof is God. And in this sense, the world or universe may be considered either as one animal or one city.

286. Aristotle hath observed there were indeed some who thought so grosly, as to suppose the universe to be one only corporeal and extended nature: but in the first book of his Metaphysics he justly remarks they were guilty of a great mistake; forasmuch as they took into their account the elements of corporeal beings alone; whereas there are incorporeal beings also in the universe; and while they attempted to assign the causes of generation and corruption, and account for the nature of all things, they did at the same time destroy the very cause of motion.

290. Body is opposite to spirit or mind. We have a notion of spirit from thought and action. We have a notion of body from resistance. So far forth as there is real power, there is spirit. So far forth as there is resistance, there is inability or want of power. That is, there is a negation of spirit. We are embodied, that is, we are clogged by weight, and hindered by resistance. But in respect of a perfect spirit, there is nothing hard or impenetrable: there is no resistance to the Deity: Nor hath he any body: nor

is the supreme being united to the world, as the soul of an animal is to it's body, which necessarily implieth defect, both as an instrument, and as a constant weight and impediment.

291. Thus much it consists with piety to say, that a divine agent doth by his virtue permeate and govern the elementary fire or light, which serves as an animal spirit to enliven and actuate the whole mass, and all the members of this visible world. Nor is this doctrine less philosophical than pious. We see all nature alive or in motion. We see water turned into air, and air rarified and made elastic by the attraction of another medium, more pure indeed, more subtil, and more volatile than air. But still, as this is a moveable extended, and, consequently, a corporeal being, it cannot be itself the principle of motion, but leads us naturally and necessarily to an incorporeal spirit or agent. We are conscious that a spirit can begin, alter, or determine motion, but nothing of this appears in body. Nay the contrary is evident, both to experiment and reflection.

292. Natural phænomena are only natural appearances. They are, therefore, such as we see and perceive them. Their real and objective natures are, therefore, the same; passive without any thing active, fluent and changing without any thing permanent in them. However, as these make the first impressions, and the mind takes her first flight and spring, as it were, by resting her foot on these objects, they are not only first considered by all men, but most considered by most men. They and the phantomes that result from those appearances, the children of imagination grafted upon sense, such for example as pure space are thought by many the very first in existence and stability, and to embrace and comprehend all other beings.

294. It is with our faculties as with our affections: what first seises, holds fast. It is a vulgar theme, that man is a compound of contrarieties, which breed a restless struggle in his nature, between flesh and spirit, the beast and the angel, earth and heaven, ever weighed down and ever bearing up. During which conflict the character fluctuates: when either side prevails, it is then fixed for vice or virtue. And life from different principles

takes a different issue. It is the same in regard to our faculties. Sense at first besets and overbears the mind. The sensible appearances are all in all, our reasonings are employed about them; our desires terminate in them: we look no farther for realities or causes; till intellect begins to dawn, and cast a ray on this shadowy scene. We then perceive the true principle of unity, identity, and existence. Those things that before seemed to constitute the whole of being, upon taking an intellectual view of things, prove to be but fleeting phantomes.

295. From the outward form of gross masses which occupy the vulgar, a curious inquirer proceeds to examine the inward structure and minute parts, and from observing the motions in nature, to discover the laws of those motions. By the way he frames his hypothesis and suits his language to this natural philosophy. And these fit the occasion and answer the end of a maker of experiments or mechanic, who means only to apply the powers of nature, and reduce the phænomena to rules. But, if proceeding still in his analysis and inquiry, he ascends from the sensible into the intellectual world, and beholds things in a new light and a new order, he will then change his system and perceive, that what he took for substances and causes are but fleeting shadows; that the mind contains all, and acts all, and is to all created beings the source of unity and identity, harmony and order, existence and stability.

301. The humane mind is so much clogged, and born downward, by the strong and early impressions of sense, that it is wonderful, how the ancients should have made even such a progress, and seen so far into intellectual matters, without some glimmering of a divine tradition. Whoever considers a parcel of rude savages left to themselves, how they are sunk and swallowed up in sense and prejudice, and how unqualified by their natural force to emerge from this state, will be apt to think that the first spark of philosophy was derived from heaven. . . .

313. . . . It was the Platonic doctrine, that humane souls or minds descended from above, and were sowed in generation, that they were stunned, stupified, and intoxicated by this descent and

immersion into animal nature. And that the soul, in this ὀνείρωξις or slumber, forgets her original notions, which are smothered and oppressed by many false tenets and prejudices of sense. Insomuch that Proclus compares the soul, in her descent invested with growing prejudices, to Glaucus diving to the bottom of the sea, and there contracting divers coats of sea-weed, coral, and shells, which stick close to him and conceal his true shape.

314. Hence, according to this philosophy, the mind of man is so restless to shake off that slumber, to disengage and emancipate herself from those prejudices and false opinions, that so straitly beset and cling to her, to rub off those covers, that disguise her original form, and to regain her primæval state and first notions: Hence, that perpetual struggle to recover the lost region of light, that ardent thirst and endeavour after truth and intellectual ideas, which she would neither seek to attain, nor rejoice in, nor know when attained, except she had some præ-notion or anticipation of them, and they had lain innate and dormant like habits and sciences in the mind, or things laid up, which are called out and roused by recollection or reminiscence. So that learning seemeth in effect reminiscence.

317. Neither Plato nor Aristotle by matter, ὕλη, understood corporeal substance, whatever the moderns may understand by that word. To them certainly it signified no positive actual being. Aristotle describes it as made up of negatives, having neither quantity nor quality nor essence. . . .

319. If any one should think to infer the reality or actual being of matter from the modern tenet, that gravity is always proportionable to the quantity of matter, let him but narrowly scan the modern demonstration of that tenet, and he will find it to be a vain circle, concluding in truth no more than this, that gravity is proportionable to weight, that is to it self. Since matter is conceived only as defect and mere possibility; and since God is absolute perfection and act; it follows there is the greatest distance and opposition imaginable between God and matter. Insomuch that a material God would be altogether inconsistent.

320. The force that produces, the intellect that orders, the

goodness that perfects all things, is the supreme being. Evil, defect, negation, is not the object of God's creative power. From motion the Peripatetics trace out a first immoveable mover. The Platonics make God author of all good, author of no evil, and unchangeable. According to Anaxagoras there was a confused mass of all things in one chaos, but mind supervening, ἐπελθών, distinguished and divided them. Anaxagoras, it seems, ascribed the motive faculty to mind, which mind some subsequent philosophers have accurately discriminated from soul and life, ascribing to it the sole faculty of intellection.

323. . . . [Plutarch] concludes, that in the sense of those philosophers God is a mind, χωριστὸν εἶδος [separable form] not an abstract idea compounded of inconsistencies and prescinded from all real things, as some moderns understand abstraction; but a really existing spirit, distinct or separate from all sensible and corporeal beings. . . .

326. Now whether the νοῦς [mind] be abstracted from the sensible world, and considered by it self, as distinct from, and presiding over the created system, or whether the whole universe, including mind together with the mundane body, is conceived to be God, and the creatures to be partial manifestations of the divine essence, there is no atheism in either case, whatever misconceptions there may be; so long as mind or intellect is understood to preside over, govern, and conduct the whole frame of things. And this was the general prevailing opinion among the philosophers.

330. These disquisitions will probably seem dry and useless, to such readers as are accustomed to consider only sensible objects. The employment of the mind on things purely intellectual is to most men irksome: whereas the sensitive powers, by constant use acquire strength. Hence, the objects of sense more forcibly affect us, and are too often counted the chief good. For these things men fight, cheat and scramble. Therefore, in order to tame mankind and introduce a sense of virtue, the best humane means is to exercise their understanding, to give them a glympse of another world, superior to the sensible, and while

they take pains to cherish and maintain the animal life, to teach them not to neglect the intellectual.

331. Prevailing studies are of no small consequence to a state, the religion, manners and civil government of a country ever taking some bias from it's philosophy, which affects not only the minds of its professors and students, but also the opinions of all the better sort and the practice of the whole people, remotely and consequentially, indeed, though not inconsiderably. Have not the polemic and scholastic philosophy been observed to produce controversies in law and religion? And have not Fatalism and Sadducism gained ground, during the general passion for the corpuscularian and mechanical philosophy, which hath prevailed for about a century? This indeed might usefully enough have employed some share of the leisure and curiosity of inquisitive persons. But when it entered the seminaries of learning as a necessary accomplishment, and most important part of education, by engrossing men's thoughts, and fixing their minds so much on corporeal objects, and the laws of motion, it hath, however undesignedly, indirectly, and by accident, yet not a little indisposed them for spiritual, moral, and intellectual matters. Certainly had the philosophy of Socrates and Pythagoras prevailed in this age, among those who think themselves too wise to receive the dictates of the gospel, we should not have seen interest take so general and fast hold on the minds of men, nor public spirit reputed to be γενναῖαν εὐήθειαν, a generous folly, among those who are reckoned to be the most knowing as well as the most getting part of mankind.

332. It might very well be thought serious trifling to tell my readers that the greatest men had ever an high esteem for Plato; whose writings are the touchstone of a hasty and shallow mind; whose philosophy has been the admiration of ages; which supplied patriots, magistrates, and lawgivers to the most flourishing states, as well as fathers to the church, and doctors to the schools. Albeit in these days, the depths of that old learning are rarely fathomed, and yet it were happy for these lands, if our young nobility and gentry instead of modern maxims would imbibe

the notions of the great men of antiquity. But in these free thinking times many an empty head is shook at Aristotle and Plato,
as well as at the holy scriptures. And the writings of those celebrated ancients are by most men treated on a foot, with the dry
and barbarous lucubrations of the schoolmen. It may be modestly presumed, there are not many among us, even of those who
are called the better sort, who have more sense, virtue, and love of
their country than Cicero, who in a letter to Atticus could not
forbear exclaiming, O Socrates et Socratici viri! numquam vobis
gratiam referam. [O Socrates and followers of Socrates! I shall
never be able to thank you enough!] Would to God many of
our countrymen had the same obligations to those Socratic
writers. . . .

333. Proclus, in the first book of his commentary on the
theology of Plato observes that, as in the mysteries, those who
are initiated, at first meet with manifold and multiform Gods,
but being entered and thoroughly initiated they receive the divine illumination and participate the very deity; in like manner,
if the soul look abroad she beholds the shadows and images of
things; but returning into herself she unravels and beholds her
own essence: At first she seemeth only to behold her self:
But having penetrated farther she discovers the mind. And again,
still farther advancing into the innermost sanctuary of the soul
she contemplates the θεῶν γένος. And this, he saith, is the most
excellent of all human acts, in the silence and repose of the
faculties of the soul to tend upwards to the very divinity; to
approach and be closely joined with that which is ineffable and
superior to all beings. When come so high as the first principle
she ends her journey and rests. Such is the doctrine of Proclus.

337. The most refined humane intellect exerted to its utmost
reach can only seize some imperfect glympses of the divine
ideas, abstracted from all things corporeal, sensible, and imaginable. Therefore Pythagoras and Plato treated them in a mysterious manner, concealing rather than exposing them to vulgar
eyes; so far were they from thinking, that those abstract things,
altho' the most real, were the fittest to influence common minds,

or become principles of knowledge, not to say duty and virtue, to the generality of mankind.

339. In the Timæus of Plato mention is made of ancient persons, authors of traditions, and the offspring of the gods. It is very remarkable, that in the account of the creation contained in the same piece, it is said that God was pleased with his work, and that the night is placed before the day. The more we think, the more difficult shall we find it to conceive, how mere man, grown up in the vulgar habits of life, and weighed down by sensuality, should ever be able to arrive at science, without some tradition or teaching, which might either sow the seeds of knowledge, or call forth and excite those latent seeds that were originally sown in the soul.

340. Humane souls in this low situation, bordering on mere animal life, bear the weight and see through the dusk of a gross atmosphere, gathered from wrong judgments daily passed, false opinions daily learned, and early habits of an older date than either judgment or opinion. Through such a medium the sharpest eye cannot see clearly. And if by some extraordinary effort the mind should surmount this dusky region, and snatch a glympse of pure light, she is soon drawn backward and depressed by the heaviness of the animal nature, to which she is chained. And if again she chanceth, amidst the agitation of wild fancies and strong affections, to spring upwards, a second relapse speedily succeeds into this region of darkness and dreams.

341. Nevertheless, as the mind gathers strength by repeated acts, we should not despond, but continue to exert the prime and flower of our faculties, still recovering, and reaching on, and struggling into the upper region, whereby our natural weakness and blindness may be in some degree remedied, and a taste attained of truth and intellectual life. Beside the constant prevailing opinion of the greatest men of antiquity, that there is both an universal spirit author of life and motion, and an universal mind enlightening and ordering all things, it was a received tenet among them, that there is also τὸ ἓν [the one] or

τἀγαθόν [the good], which they looked on as the fons deitatis, the first hypostasis in the divinity.

342. The one or τὸ ἕν, being immutable and indivisible, always the same and entire, was therefore thought to exist truly and originally, and other things only so far as they are one and the same, by participation of the τὸ ἕν. This gives unity, stability, reality to things. Plato describes God, as Moses, from his being. According to both, God is he who truly is, ὁ ὄντως ὄν. Change and division were esteemed defects or bad. Evil scatters, divides, destroys: Good, on the contrary, produceth concord and union, assembles, combines, perfects, and preserves entire. The several beings which compose the universe are parts of the same system, they combine to carry on one end, and perfect one whole. And this aptness and concurrence thereunto furnishes the partial particular idea of good in the distinct creatures. Hence it might have come to pass, that τἀγαθὸν and τὸ ἕν were regarded as one and the same.

343. Light and sight (saith Plato in the sixth book of his Republic) are not the sun; even so truth and knowledge are not the good itself, altho' they approach thereunto. And again, what the sun is in a visible place with respect to sight and things seen, that same is τἀγαθὸν or good in an intelligible place, with respect to understanding and things understood. Therefore the good or one is not the light that enlightens, but the source of that light.

345. It is the opinion of Plato and his followers, that in the soul of man, prior and superior to intellect, there is somewhat of an higher nature, by virtue of which we are one; and that by means of our one or unit, we are most closely joined to the deity. And, as by our intellect we touch the divine intellect, even so by our τὸ ἕν or unit the very flower of our essence, as Proclus expresseth it, we touch the first one.

346. According to the Platonic philosophy, ens and unum are the same. And consequently our minds participate so far of existence as they do of unity. But it should seem that personality is the indivisible center of the soul or mind, which is a monad so

far forth as she is a person. Therefore person is really that which exists, inasmuch as it participates of the divine unity. In man the monad or indivisible is the αὐτὸ τὸ αὐτό the self same self or very self, a thing, in the opinion of Socrates, much and narrowly to be inquired into and discussed, to the end that, knowing ourselves, we may know what belongs to us and our happiness.

347. Upon mature reflexion the mind of all created beings seemeth alone indivisible, and to partake most of unity. But sensible things are rather considered as one than truly so, they being in a perpetual flux or succession, ever differing and various. Nevertheless, all things together may be considered as one universe, one by the connection, relation and order of it's parts, which is the work of mind whose unit is by Plato, supposed a participation of the first τὸ ἕν.

350. The displeasure of some readers may perhaps be incurred, by surprising them into certain reflexions and inquiries for which they have no curiosity. But perhaps some others may be pleased, to find a dry subject varied by digressions, traced through remote inferences, and carried into ancient times, whose hoary maxims scattered in this essay are not proposed as principles, but barely as hints to awaken and exercise the inquisitive reader, on points not beneath the attention of the ablest men. Those great men, Pythagoras, Plato, and Aristotle, the most consummate in politics, who founded states, or instructed princes, or wrote most accurately on publick government, were at the same time most acute at all abstracted and sublime speculations; the clearest light being ever necessary to guide the most important actions. And whatever the world thinks, he who hath not much meditated upon God, the humane mind, and the Summum bonum, may possibly make a thriving earthworm, but will most indubitably make a sorry patriot and a sorry statesman.

355. Plato teacheth, that the doctrine concerning the one or unite is a means to lead and raise the mind to the knowledge of him who truly is. And it is a tenet both of Aristotle and Plato, that identity is a certain unity. The Pythagoreans also, as well as

the Platonic philosophers, held unum and ens to be the same. Consistently with which that only can be said to exist, which is one and the same. In things sensible and imaginable, as such, there seems to be no unity, nothing that can be called one prior to all act of the mind; since they being in themselves aggregates, consisting of parts or compounded of elements, are in effect many. Accordingly it is remarked by Themistius, the learned interpreter of Aristotle, that to collect many notions into one, and to consider them as one, is the work of intellect, and not of sense or fancy.

356. Aristotle himself, in his third book of the Soul, saith it is the mind that maketh each thing to be one. . . . How this is done, Themistius is more particular, observing, that as being conferreth essence, the mind by virtue of her simplicity conferreth simplicity upon compounded beings. And, indeed, it seemeth that the mind, so far forth as person, is individual therein resembling the divine one by participation, and imparting to other things what itself participates from above. This is agreeable to the doctrine of the ancients, however the contrary opinion of supposing number to be an original primary quality in things, independent of the mind, may obtain among the moderns.

357. The Peripatetics taught, that in all divisible things there was somewhat indivisible, and in all compounded things somewhat simple. This they derived from an act of the mind. And neither this simple indivisible unite, nor any sum of repeated unites, consequently no number, can be separated from the things themselves, and from the operation of the mind. Themistius goeth so far as to affirm, that it cannot be separated from the words or signs; and, as it cannot be uttered without them, so saith he, neither can it be conceived without them. Thus much upon the whole may be concluded, that, distinct from the mind and her operations, there is in created beings neither unite nor number.

358. Of inferior beings the human mind, self, or person is the most simple and undivided essence. And the supreme father is the most perfect one. Therefore the flight of the mind towards

God is called by the Platonics φυγὴ μόνου πρὸς μόνον [the flight of the one to the one]. The supreme being, saith Plotinus, as he excludes all diversity, is ever alike present. And we are then present to him, when, recollected and abstracted from the world and sensible objects, we are most free and disengaged from all variety. He adds, that in the intuition of the supreme deity the soul finds her wished for end and repose; which that philosopher calls awaking out of his body into himself.

359. In the tenth book of the arcane, or divine wisdom of the Ægyptians, we are taught that the supreme being is not the cause of any created thing; but that he produced or made the word; and that all created beings were made by the word, which is accordingly styled the cause of all causes; and that this was also the doctrine of the Chaldæans. Plato, likewise, in his letter to Hermias, Erastus, and Coriscus, speaks of God the ruler and cause of all things, as having a father: And in his Epinomis, he expresly teacheth that the word or λόγος made the world. Accordingly saint Augustine in his commentary on the beginning of saint John's Gospel, having declared that Christ is the wisdom of God by which all things were made, observes that this doctrine was also found in the writings of philosophers, who taught that God had an only begotten Son by whom are all things.

360. Now, though Plato had joined with an imagination the most splendid and magnificent, an intellect not less deep and clear; yet it is not to be supposed, that either he or any other philosophers of Greece or the east, had by the light of nature attained an adequate notion of the Holy Trinity, nor even that their imperfect notion, so far as it went, was exactly just; nor perhaps that those sublime hints, which dart forth like flashes of light in the midst of a profound darkness, were originally struck from the hard rock of human reason; but rather derived, at least in part, by a divine tradition from the author of all things. It seems a remarkable confirmation of this, what Plotinus observes in his fifth Ennead, that this doctrine of a Trinity,

father, mind, and soul, was no late invention, but an ancient tenet.

361. Certain it is, that the notion of a Trinity is to be found in the writings of many old heathen philosophers, that is to say, a notion of three divine hypostases. Authority, light, and life did, to the eye of reason, plainly appear to support, pervade, and animate the mundane system or macrocosm. The same appeared in the microcosm, preserving soul and body, enlightening the mind, and moving the affections. And these were conceived to be necessary, universal principles, co-existing and co-operating in such sort, as never to exist asunder, but on the contrary to constitute one Sovereign of all things. And, indeed, how could power or authority avail or subsist without knowledge? or either without life and action?

362. In the administration of all things there is authority to establish, law to direct, and justice to execute. There is first the source of all perfection, or *fons deitatis*, secondly the supreme Reason, order, or λόγος, and lastly the Spirit which quickens and inspires. We are sprung from the father, irradiated or enlightened by the son, and moved by the spirit. Certainly, that there is father, son, and spirit; that these bear analogy to the sun, light, and heat; and are otherwise expressed by the terms, principle, mind, and soul; by one or τὸ ἕν, intellect, and life; by good, word, and love; and that generation was not attributed to the second hypostasis, the νοῦς or λόγος, in respect of time, but only in respect of origine and order, as an eternal necessary emanation; these are the express tenets of Platonists, Pythagoreans, Ægyptians, and Chaldæans.

365. But Plato himself consider'd that doctrine as a venerable mystery, not to be lightly treated of or rashly divulged. . . . Plato enjoins Dionysius over and over, with great earnestness not to suffer, what he communicates concerning the mystery of the divine nature, to fall into illiterate or vulgar hands, giving it withal as a reason for this caution, that nothing would seem more ridiculous or absurd to the common run of mankind. . . .

366. And, indeed, what this philosopher in his Phædrus speaketh of the super-celestial region, and the divinity resident therein, is of a strain not to be relished or comprehended by vulgar minds; to wit, essence realy existent, object of intellect alone, without colour, without figure, without any tangible quality. He might very justly conceive that such a description must seem ridiculous to sensual men.

367. As for the perfect intuition of divine things, that he supposeth to be the lot of pure souls, beholding by a pure light, initiated, happy, free and unstained from those bodies, wherein we are now imprisoned like oysters. But in this mortal state, we must be satisfy'd to make the best of those glympses within our reach. It is Plato's remark in his Theætetus, that while we sit still we are never the wiser, but going into the river and moving up and down, is the way to discover its depths and shallows. If we exercise and bestir ourselves, we may even here discover something.

368. The eye by long use comes to see even in the darkest cavern: and there is no subject so obscure, but we may discern some glympse of truth by long poring on it. Truth is the cry of all, but the game of a few. Certainly where it is the chief passion, it doth not give way to vulgar cares and views; nor is it contented with a little ardour in the early time of life, active perhaps to pursue, but not so fit to weigh and revise. He that would make a real progress in knowledge, must dedicate his age as well as youth, the later growth as well as first fruits, at the altar of truth.

Cujusvis est errare, nullius nisi insipientis in errore perseverare. [Anyone can make a mistake, but only a fool persists in his error.]

CICERO

DAVID HARTLEY

(1705–57)

"The excellent and pious Hartley," as Coleridge calls
him in *Biographia Literaria,* received an M.A. at Cambridge and
was destined for the ministry; but he felt reservations about
certain of the thirty-nine articles and so became a physician instead.
He published *Observations on Man,* the great work of his life, in
1749, after, as he says in his preface, at least eighteen years of thought
and work on it. Regarded by many as the last word in psychology,
it was especially popular because it seemed to place orthodox
Christianity on a scientific footing scarcely less firm than physics or
algebra.

Joseph Priestley published in 1775 an abridgment of the *Observations* which left out the physiological doctrine of vibrations and also
the moral and religious matter. In 1791 appeared a new edition with
a biographical introduction by Hartley's son David, and notes
"translated from the German of the Rev. Herman Andrew Pistorius,
Rector of Poseritz in the Island of Rugen." The author's portrait in
the front of this edition was, incidentally, engraved by Blake.

James Mill admired the *Observations,* and John Stuart Mill's
autobiography describes his own study of Hartley's psychology.
Between about 1794 and 1798 Coleridge was an avid disciple of
Hartley, whose influence is particularly clear in "Religious
Musings," where Coleridge even cites him in a footnote. Words-
worth too reflects Hartley's ideas in the 1800 Preface to *Lyrical
Ballads* and in "Tintern Abbey," *The Prelude,* and other poems;
Arthur Beatty describes Wordsworth's indebtedness in *William*

Wordsworth: His Doctrine and Art in Their Historical Relations,
University of Wisconsin Studies in Language and Literature, No.
24 (Madison: Univ. of Wisconsin Press, 1927). Shelley ordered
"Hartley on Man" in July 1812 and presumably read it. A good
case is even made for the book's influence on Keats, by James
Ralston Caldwell in *John Keats' Fancy: The Effect on Keats of the
Psychology of His Day* (Ithaca: Cornell Univ. Press, 1945).

Hartley also became important as a whipping boy for those who
wished to reject the mechanical psychology and necessitarianism
which his work so eminently embodies. Coleridge devotes three
chapters of the *Biographia Literaria* to discrediting the associational psychology, and Hazlitt's first book is a direct attempt at
refutation *(An Essay on the Principles of Human Action . . . to
Which Are Added, Some Remarks on the Systems of Hartley and
Helvetius,* 1805).

Hartley develops his argument in an ostensibly logical series of
propositions, first stated briefly in italics and then expounded in
sections ranging from one to a couple of dozen pages. A number of
the proposition headings are given below without their detailed development, so that the reader can follow at least the skeleton of
Hartley's argument. But several extensive sections of his reasoning,
in both the physiological and the theological parts, are included as
samples of his method. The reader will probably not be able to
follow all of the details of such an abridgment, much less find them
convincing; but even in the driest and most far-fetched sections
one is surprised by the frequent appearance of topics important to
the romantics: synesthesia, the closeness of pleasure to pain, the
ability of the imagination to equal the vividness of reality, the
spiritual ladder leading from sensation to unity with God.

The 1749 edition of *Observations on Man* has been reprinted in
facsimile with an introduction by Theodore L. Huguelet (Gainesville, Fla.: Scholars' Facsimiles & Reprints, 1966). This selection follows the 1749 edition, with capitalization and italics modified.

Observations on Man, His Frame, His Duty, and His Expectations

Part I

Introduction

Man consists of two parts, body and mind.

The first is subjected to our senses and inquiries, in the same manner as the other parts of the external material world.

The last is that substance, agent, principle, &c. to which we refer the sensations, ideas, pleasures, pains, and voluntary motions.

Sensations are those internal feelings of the mind, which arise from the impressions made by external objects upon the several parts of our bodies.

All our other internal feelings may be called *ideas*. Some of these appear to spring up in the mind of themselves, some are suggested by words, others arise in other ways. Many writers comprehend *sensations* under *ideas*; but I every-where use these words in the senses here ascribed to them.

The ideas which resemble sensations, are called *ideas of sensation*: all the rest may therefore be called *intellectual ideas*.

It will appear in the course of these Observations, that the

53

ideas of sensation are the elements of which all the rest are compounded. Hence *ideas of sensation* may be termed *simple, intellectual* ones *complex.*

The *pleasures* and *pains* are comprehended under the sensations and ideas, as these are explained above. For all our pleasures and pains are internal feelings, and, conversely, all our internal feelings seem to be attended with some degree either of *pleasure* or *pain.* However, I shall, for the most part, give the names of *pleasure* and *pain* only to such degrees as are considerable; referring all low, evanescent ones to the head of *mere sensations* and *ideas.*

The pleasures and pains may be ranged under seven general classes; *viz.*

1. sensation;
2. imagination;
3. ambition;
4. self-interest;
5. sympathy;
6. theopathy; and,
7. the moral sense; according as they arise from,
1. the impressions made on the external senses;
2. natural or artificial beauty or deformity;
3. the opinions of others concerning us;
4. our possession or want of the means of happiness, and security from, or subjection to, the hazards of misery;
5. the pleasures and pains of our fellow-creatures;
6. the affections excited in us by the contemplation of the Deity; or,
7. moral beauty and deformity.

The human mind may also be considered as indued with the faculties of *memory, imagination* or *fancy, understanding, affection,* and *will.*

Memory is that faculty, by which traces of sensations and ideas recur, or are recalled, in the same order and proportion, accurately or nearly, as they were once actually presented.

When ideas, and trains of ideas, occur, or are called up, in a vivid manner, and without regard to the order of former actual impressions and perceptions, this is said to be done by the power of *imagination* or *fancy*.

The *understanding* is that faculty, by which we contemplate mere sensations and ideas, pursue truth, and assent to, or dissent from, propositions.

The *affections* have the pleasures and pains for their objects; as the *understanding* has the mere sensations and ideas. By the affections we are excited to pursue happiness, and all its means, fly from misery, and all its apparent causes.

The *will* is that state of mind, which is immediately previous to, and causes, those express acts of memory, fancy, and bodily motion, which are termed *voluntary*.

The *motions* of the body are of two kinds, *automatic* and *voluntary*. The *automatic* motions are those which arise from the mechanism of the body in an evident manner. They are called *automatic*, from their resemblance to the motions of *automata*, or machines, whose principle of motion is within themselves. Of this kind are the motion of the heart, and peristaltic motion of the bowels. The *voluntary motions* are those which arise from ideas and affections, and which therefore are referred to the mind; the immediately preceding state of the mind, or of the ideas and affections, being termed *will*, as noted in the last article. Such are the actions of walking, handling, speaking, &c. when attended to, and performed with an express design.

This may serve as a short account of the chief subjects considered in the First Part of these *Observations*. These subjects are so much involved in each other, that it is difficult, or even impossible, to begin any-where upon clear ground, or so as to proceed intirely from the *data* to the *quaesita*, from things known to such as are unknown. I will endeavour it as much as I can, and for that purpose shall observe the following order.

First, I shall lay down the general laws, according to which the sensations and motions are performed, and our ideas generated.

Secondly, I shall consider each of the sensations and motions in particular, and inquire how far the phaenomena of each illustrate, and are illustrated by, the foregoing general laws.

Thirdly, I shall proceed in like manner to the particular phaenomena of ideas, or of understanding, affection, memory, and imagination; applying to them what has been before delivered.

Lastly, I shall endeavour to give a particular history and analysis of the six classes of intellectual pleasures and pains; *viz.* those of imagination, ambition, self-interest, sympathy, theopathy, and the moral sense.

•   •   •   •   •

PROP. I

The white medullary substance of the brain, spinal marrow, and the nerves proceeding from them, is the immediate instrument of sensation and motion.

•   •   •   •   •

PROP. 2

The white medullary substance of the brain is also the immediate instrument, by which ideas are presented to the mind: or, in other words, whatever changes are made in this substance, corresponding changes are made in our ideas; and vice versa.

•   •   •   •   •

PROP. 3

The sensations remain in the mind for a short time after the sensible objects are removed.

•   •   •   •   •

PROP. 4

*External objects impressed upon the senses occasion, first in the
nerves on which they are impressed, and then in the brain,
vibrations of the finall, and, as one may say, infinitesimal,
medullary particles.*

.   .   .   .   .

PROP. 5

*The vibrations mentioned in the last Proposition are excited,
propagated, and kept up, partly by the æther,* i.e. *by a very
subtle and elastic fluid, and partly by the uniformity, continuity, softness, and active powers of the medullary substance of the brain, spinal marrow, and nerves.*

.   .   .   .   .

PROP. 6

*The phænomena of sensible pleasure and pain appear to be very
suitable to the doctrine of vibrations.*

The most vigorous of our sensations are termed sensible
pleasures and pains, as noted above, in the Introduction. And
the vivid nature of these engages us to be very attentive to their
several properties, relations, and oppositions. It is requisite
therefore, in our inquiry into the doctrine of vibrations, to
examine, how far the phænomena of sensible pleasure and pain
can be deduced from, or explained by it.

First then, the doctrine of vibrations seems to require, that
each pain should differ from the corresponding and opposite

pleasure, not in kind, but in degree only; *i.e.* that pain should be nothing more than pleasure itself, carried beyond a due limit. For of the four differences of vibrations mentioned in the First Corollary of the foregoing Proposition, three are given, *viz.* those of kind, place, and line of direction, in the pleasures and pains which correspond, as opposites to each other: there is therefore nothing left, from whence the difference of such pleasures and pains can arise, except the difference of degree. But the phænomena appear to be sufficiently suitable to this reasoning, inasmuch as all pleasure appears to pass into pain, by increasing its cause, impression, duration, sensibility of the organ upon which it is impressed, &c. Thus an agreeable warmth may be made to pass into a troublesome, or burning heat, by increase, or continuance; and the same thing holds, in respect of friction, light, and sounds. . . .

It agrees well with the doctrine of vibrations, that all evident solutions [i.e., breaks] of continuity in the living parts occasion pain, inasmuch as a solution of continuity cannot happen without a violent impression of some sensible object, nor, by consequence, without violent mutual actions between the object, nerves, and æther. The solution of continuity does therefore presuppose that degree of violence in the vibrations, which exceeds the limit of pleasure, and is proper to pain, according to the foregoing paragraph. . . .

We may, in like manner, give a reason, from the doctrine of vibrations, both why a moderate degree of distention in the parts is necessary to their growth, and pleasurable state; and also why all great distentions are attended with pain for a considerable time, before they are raised to such a pitch as to cause a visible solution of continuity. For a great distention is equivalent to a vigorous impression of a sensible object, being often caused by such; and as the situation of the small particles is changed in great distentions, their mutual actions will be changed also, and so may give rise to more vigorous vibrations; and these increased vibrations may either fall within the limits of pleasure, or go beyond them, according to their degree. We are also to consider, that, in all considerable distentions there is an increase of friction between the vessels and circulating fluids, and consequently of heat, *i.e.* of vibrations.

But besides this, it seems not improbable, that in preternatural and painful distentions, the small particles are perpetually separating themselves from their former cohesions, and running into new ones; so that a minute and invisible solution of continuity is carried on during the whole distention, till such time as this degree of distention becomes familiar to the parts, and the situation and mutual actions of the small particles be accommodated to it. Thus the cause of the pain in distentions will arise from the solution of continuity, and may be referred to the foregoing head. And conversely it appears, that in manifest solutions of continuity, occasioned by wounds, burns, &c. there always arises in the neighbouring parts, which are inflamed, a preternatural distention of the small fibres and vessels; by which means the pain is renewed and continued. Every manifest solution of continuity does therefore, according to the explanation of distention just laid down, include within itself an infinite number of minute invisible solutions.

Hence we may ask, whether this minute invisible solution of continuity in the infinitesimal medullary particles of the brain, is not that common limit, and middle point, which separates pleasure from pain, and of which the visible solutions of continuity, which are caused by external injuries, are a type, and also a means, *viz.* by propagating violent vibrations up to the brain. . . .

All the mere sensations, which enter the mind by the five external senses, admit of a general analysis, upon the same principles as the pleasures and pains do. For all the mere sensations were, in their original state, either pleasures or pains, and vary now from their original state only by the diminution of the degree. Let therefore all the differences of kind, place, and line of direction, be combined in all their varieties, the degree being supposed every-where evanescent; and we shall have all the particular vibrations from whence each mere sensation arises. This is the general account. But it is a most difficult problem to explain, by what differences of kind the particular sensations, either of the same, or of different senses, are distinguished from each other.

It seems probable to me, that the limits of the seven primary colours, *viz.* the extreme red, the limit of the red and orange, of the orange and yellow, yellow and green, green and blue, blue and indigo, indigo and violet, and the extreme violet, excite vibrations in the optic nerve, whose times are proportional to the times of vibration of a string which sounds the notes in order, according to the key mentioned by Sir Isaac Newton in his *Optics; i.e.* the notes D, E, F, G, A, B, C, D. This hypothesis affords at least a probable reason for the several very particular breadths of the primary colours, in the prismatic oblong image of the sun, as I shall endeavour to shew in its place, Prop. 56.

If the frequency of the vibrations excited by the several sapid and odorous bodies in the nerves of the tongue and membrana schneideriana, could be discovered, it is not improbable but this would be a clue to lead us into the inner constitution of natural bodies, since one may reasonably suppose, that each sapid and odorous body excites vibrations of the same frequency as those which take place in it before it is tasted or smelt to.

·   ·   ·   ·   ·

PROP. 7

The phænomena of sleep appear to be very suitable to the doctrine of vibrations.

·   ·   ·   ·   ·

PROP. 8

Sensations, by being often repeated, leave certain vestiges, types, or images, of themselves, which may be called, simple ideas of sensation.

·   ·   ·   ·   ·

PROP. 9

Sensory vibrations, by being often repeated, beget, in the medullary substance of the brain, a disposition to diminutive vibrations, which may also be called vibratiuncles and miniatures, corresponding to themselves respectively.

·   ·   ·   ·   ·

PROP. 10

Any sensations A, B, C, *&c. by being associated with one another a sufficient number of times, get such a power over the corresponding ideas* a, b, c, *&c. that any one of the sensations* A, *when impressed alone, shall be able to excite in the mind* b, c, *&c. the ideas of the rest.*

Sensations may be said to be associated together, when their impressions are either made precisely at the same instant of time, or in the contiguous successive instants. We may therefore distinguish association into two sorts, the synchronous, and the successive.

The influence of association over our ideas, opinions, and affections, is so great and obvious, as scarce to have escaped the notice of any writer who has treated of these, though the word *association*, in the particular sense here affixed to it, was

first brought into use by Mr. Locke. But all that has been delivered by the antients and moderns, concerning the power of
habit, custom, example, education, authority, party-prejudice,
the manner of learning the manual and liberal arts, &c. goes
upon this doctrine as its foundation, and may be considered as
the detail of it, in various circumstances. I here begin with the
simplest case, and shall proceed to more and more complex
ones continually, till I have exhausted what has occurred to me
upon this subject.

·   ·   ·   ·   ·

PROP. I I

*Any vibrations, A, B, C, &c. by being associated together a
sufficient number of times, get such a power over a, b, c,
&c. the corresponding miniature vibrations, that any of the
vibrations A, when impressed alone, shall be able to excite
b, c, &c. the miniatures of the rest.*

This Proposition may be deduced from the foregoing, in the
same manner as the Ninth has been from the Eighth.

But it seems also deducible from the nature of vibrations, and
of an animal body. Let *A* and *B* be two vibrations, associated
synchronically. Now, it is evident, that the vibration *A* (for I
will, in this Proposition, speak of *A* and *B* in the singular number, for the sake of greater clearness) will, by endeavouring to
diffuse itself into those parts of the medullary substance which
are affected primarily by the vibration *B*, in some measure
modify and change *B*, so as to make *B* a little different from
what it would be, if impressed alone. For the same reasons the
vibration *A* will be a little affected, even in its primary seat,
by the endeavour of *B* to diffuse itself all over the medullary
substance. Suppose now the vibrations *A* and *B* to be impressed
at the same instant, for a thousand times; it follows, from the
Ninth Proposition, that they will first overcome the disposition

to the natural vibrations *N*, and then leave a tendency to themselves, which will now occupy the place of the original natural tendency to vibrations. When therefore the vibration *A* is impressed alone, it cannot be intirely such as the object would excite of itself, but must lean, even in its primary seat, to the modifications and changes induced by *B*, during their thousand joint impressions; and therefore much more, in receding from this primary seat, will it lean that way; and when it comes to the seat of *B*, it will excite *B*'s miniature a little modified and changed by itself.

. . . . .

Simple ideas will run into complex ones, by means of association.

In order to explain and prove this Proposition, it will be requisite to give some previous account of the manner in which simple ideas of sensation may be associated together.

Case 1. Let the sensation *A* be often associated with each of the sensations *B*, *C*, *D*, &c. *i.e.* at certain times with *B*, at certain other times with *C*, &c. it is evident, from the Tenth Proposition, that *A*, impressed alone, will, at last, raise *b*, *c*, *d*, &c. all together, *i.e.* associate them with one another, provided they belong to different regions of the medullary substance; for if any two, or more, belong to the same region, since they cannot exist together in their distinct forms, *A* will raise something intermediate between them.

Case 2. If the sensations *A*, *B*, *C*, *D*, &c. be associated together, according to various combinations of twos, or even threes, fours, &c. then will *A* raise *b*, *c*, *d*, &c. also *B* raise *a*, *c*, *d*, &c. as in Case the First.

It may happen, indeed, in both cases, that *A* may raise a particular miniature, as *b*, preferably to any of the rest, from its being more associated with *B*, from the novelty of the impression of B, from a tendency in the medullary substance to favour b, &c. and, in like manner, that b may raise c or d preferably to the rest. However, all this will be over-ruled, at last, by the recurrency of the associations; so that any one of the sensations will excite the ideas of the rest, at the same instant, *i.e.* associate them together.

Case 3. Let A, B, C, D, &c. represent successive impressions, it follows from the Tenth and Eleventh Propositions, that A will raise b, c, d, &c. B raise c, d, &c. And though the ideas do not, in this case, rise precisely at the same instant, yet they come nearer together than the sensations themselves did in their original impression; so that these ideas are associated almost synchronically at last, and successively from the first. The ideas come nearer to one another than the sensations, on account of their diminutive nature, by which all that appertains to them is contracted. And this seems to be as agreeable to observation as to theory.

Case 4. All compound impressions $A + B + C + D$, &c. after sufficient repetition leave compound miniatures $a + b + c + d$, &c. which recur every now and then from slight causes, as well such as depend on association, as some which are different from it. Now, in these recurrencies of compound miniatures, the parts are farther associated, and approach perpetually nearer to each other, agreeably to what was just now observed; *i.e.* the association becomes perpetually more close and intimate.

Case 5. When the ideas a, b, c, d, & c. have been sufficiently associated in any one or more of the foregoing ways, if we suppose any single idea of these, a for instance, to be raised by the tendency of the medullary substance that way, by the association of A with a foreign sensation or idea X or x, &c. this idea a, thus raised, will frequently bring in all the rest, b, c, d, &c. and so associate all of them together still farther.

And, upon the whole, it may appear to the reader, that the simple ideas of sensation must run into clusters and combinations, by association; and that each of these will, at last, coalesce into one complex idea, by the approach and commixture of the several compounding parts.

It appears also from observation, that many of our intellectual ideas, such as those that belong to the heads of beauty, honour, moral qualities, &c. are, in fact, thus composed of parts, which, by degrees, coalesce into one complex idea. . . .

Cor. 1. If the number of simple ideas which compose the complex one be very great, it may happen, that the complex idea shall not appear to bear any relation to these its compounding parts, nor to the external senses upon which the original sensations, which gave birth to the compounding ideas, were impressed. The reason of this is, that each single idea is overpowered by the sum of all the rest, as soon as they are all intimately united together. Thus, in very compound medicines, the several tastes and flavours of the separate ingredients are lost and overpowered by the complex one of the whole mass: so that this has a taste and flavour of its own, which appears to be simple and original, and like that of a natural body. Thus also, white is vulgarly thought to be the simplest and most uncompounded of all colours, while yet it really arises from a certain proportion of the seven primary colours, with their several shades, or degrees. . . .

Cor. 2. One may hope, therefore, that, by pursuing and perfecting the doctrine of association, we may some time or other be enabled to analyse all that vast variety of complex ideas, which pass under the name of ideas of reflection, and intellectual ideas, into their simple compounding parts, *i.e.* into the simple ideas of sensation, of which they consist. This would be greatly analogous to the arts of writing, and resolving the colours of the sun's light, or natural bodies, into their primary constituent ones. The complex ideas which I here speak of, are generally excited by words, or visible objects; but they are also connected with other external impressions, and depend upon them, as upon symbols. . . .

Cor. 7. When a variety of ideas are associated together, the visible idea, being more glaring and distinct than the rest, performs the office of a symbol to all the rest, suggests them, and connects them together. In this it somewhat resembles the first letter of a word, or first word of a sentence, which are often made use of to bring all the rest to mind. . . .

Cor. 9. When the pleasure or pain attending any sensations, and ideas, is great, all the associations belonging to them are much accelerated and strengthened. For the violent vibrations excited in such cases, soon over-rule the natural vibrations, and leave in the brain a strong tendency to themselves, from a few impressions. The associations will therefore be cemented sooner and stronger than in common cases; which is found agreeable to the fact.

．　．　．　．　．

PROP. 13

When simple ideas run into a complex one, according to the foregoing Proposition, we are to suppose, that the simple miniature vibrations corresponding to those simple ideas run, in like manner, into a complex miniature vibration, corresponding to the resulting complex idea.

．　．　．　．　．

PROP. 14

It is reasonable to think, that some of the complex vibrations attending upon complex ideas, according to the last Proposition, may be as vivid as any of the sensory vibrations excited by the direct action of objects.

For these complex vibrations may consist of so many parts co-existent and successive, and these parts may so alter and exalt one another, as that the resulting agitations in the medullary substance may no longer be miniature vibrations, but vivid ones, equal to those excited by objects impressed on the senses. This process may be farther favoured by a mixture of vivid real impressions among the ideas, by the irritability of the medullary substance, by a previous disposition to the vibrations to be excited, &c.

Cor. 1. When the complex miniature vibrations are thus exalted in degree, we are to conceive, that the corresponding complex ideas are proportionally exalted, and so pass into intellectual affections and passions. We are therefore to deduce the origin of the intellectual pleasures and pains, which are the objects of these affections and passions, from the source here laid open.

Cor. 2. Since the present Proposition unfolds the nature of the affections and will, in the same manner, and from the same principles, as the Twelfth does that of ideas, intellect, memory, and fancy, it follows, that all these are of the same original and consideration, and differ only in degree, or some accidental circumstances. They are all deducible from the external impressions made upon the senses, the vestiges or ideas of these, and their mutual connexions by means of association, taken together, and operating on one another.

Cor. 3. It follows also from this Proposition, that the intellectual pleasures and pains may be greater, equal, or less, than the sensible ones, according as each person unites more or fewer, more vivid or more languid miniature vibrations, in the formation of his intellectual pleasures and pains, &c.

Cor. 4. It is evident, that all the vibrations which belong to ideas, and intellectual affections, must reside in the brain, or even in the most internal parts of it, not in the spinal marrow, or nerves. The brain is therefore the seat of the rational soul, *i.e.* of the soul, as far as it is influenced by reasons and moral motives, even tho' we should admit, that the spinal marrow and nerves are, in part, the sensorium, or the seat of the sensitive soul; which is some argument, that this ought not to be admitted, but that the sensorium, in men at least, ought to be placed in the internal parts of the brain.

Cor. 5. It is of the utmost consequence to morality and religion, that the affections and passions should be analysed into their simple compounding parts, by reversing the steps of the associations which concur to form them. For thus we may learn how to cherish and improve good ones, check and root out such as are mischievous and immoral, and how to suit our manner of life, in some tolerable measure, to our intellectual and religious wants. And as this holds, in respect of persons of all ages, so it is particularly true, and worthy of consideration, in respect of children and youth. The world is, indeed, sufficiently stocked with general precepts for this purpose, grounded on experience; and whosoever will follow these faithfully, may expect good general success. However, the doctrine of association, when traced up to the first rudiments of understanding and affection, unfolds such a scene as cannot fail both to instruct and alarm all such as have any degree of interested concern for themselves, or of a benevolent one for others. It ought to be added here, that the doctrine of association explains also the rise and progress of those voluntary and semivoluntary powers, which we exert over our ideas, affections, and bodily motions (as I shall shew hereafter, Prop. 21.); and, by doing this, teaches us how to regulate and improve these powers.

Cor. 6. If beings of the same nature, but whose affections and passions are, at present, in different proportions to each other, be exposed for an indefinite time to the same impressions and associations, all their particular differences will, at last, be overruled, and they will become perfectly similar, or even equal. They may also be made perfectly similar, in a finite time, by a proper adjustment of the impressions and associations.

Cor. 7. Our original bodily make, and the impressions and associations which affect us in passing through life, are so much alike, and yet not the same, that there must be both a great general resemblance amongst mankind, in respect of their intellectual affections, and also many particular differences. Cor. 8. Some degree of spirituality is the necessary consequence of passing through life. The sensible pleasures and pains must be transferred by association more and more every day, upon things that afford neither sensible pleasure nor sensible pain in themselves, and so beget the intellectual pleasures and pains.

Cor. 9. Let the letters *a*, *b*, *c*, *d*, *e*, &c. represent the sensible pleasures; *x*, *y*, and *z*, the sensible pains, supposed to be only three in number; and let us suppose all these, both pleasures and pains, to be equal to one another: if now the ideas of these sensible pleasures and pains be associated together, according to all the possible varieties, in order to form intellectual pleasures and pains, it is plain, that pleasure must prevail in all the combinations of seven or more letters; and also, that when the several parts of these complex pleasures are sufficiently united by association, the pains which enter their composition will no longer be distinguished separately, but the resulting mixed and complex pleasures appear to be pure and simple ones, equal in quantity to the excess of pleasure above pain, in each combination. Thus association would convert a state, in which pleasure and pain were both perceived by turns, into one in which pure pleasure alone would be perceived; at least, would cause the beings who were under its influence to an indefinite degree, to approach to this last state nearer than by any definite difference. Or, in other words, association, under the supposition of this corollary, has a tendency to reduce the state of those who have eaten of the Tree of the Knowledge of Good and Evil, back again to a paradisiacal one. Now, though the circumstances of mankind are not the same with those supposed in this corollary, yet they bear a remarkable resemblance thereto, during that part of our existence which is exposed to our observation. For our sensible pleasures are far more numerous than our sensible pains; and tho' the pains be, in general, greater than the pleasures, yet the sum total of these seems to be greater than that of those; whence the remainder, after the destruction of the pains by the opposite and equal pleasures, will be pure pleasure.

Cor. 10. The intellectual pleasures and pains are as real as the sensible ones, being, as we have seen, nothing but the sensible ones variously mixed and compounded together. The intellectual pleasures and pains are also all equally of a factitious and acquired nature. We must therefore estimate all our pleasures equally, by their magnitude, permanency, and tendency to procure others; and our pains in like manner.

Cor. 11. The sensible pleasures and pains have a greater tendency to destroy the body, than the intellectual ones; for they are of a particular local nature, and so bear hard upon the organs which convey them. But the destruction of any one considerable part of the body is the destruction of the whole, from the sympathy of the parts; whereas the intellectual pleasures and pains, being collected from all quarters, do not much injure any organ particularly, but rather bring on an equable gradual decay of the whole medullary substance, and all the parts thereon depending.

Cor. 12. This Proposition, and its corollaries, afford some pleasing presumptions; such are, that we have a power of suiting our frame of mind to our circumstances, of correcting what is amiss, and improving what is right: that our ultimate happiness appears to be of a spiritual, not corporeal nature; and therefore that death, or the shaking off the gross body, may not stop our progress, but rather render us more expedite in the pursuit of our true end: that association tends to make us all ultimately similar; so that if one be happy, all must: and, lastly, that the same association may also be shewn to contribute to introduce pure ultimate spiritual happiness, in all, by a direct argument, as well as by the just mentioned indirect one.

[Propositions 15–22 and 73–77 treat automatic and voluntary muscular motions in the light of the doctrines of vibration and association; 23–72, the senses of touch, taste, smell, sight, and hearing; 79–88, language and the nature of assent.]

PROP. 89

To explain the origin and nature of the passions in general.

Here we may observe,

First, that our passions or affections can be no more than aggregates of simple ideas united by association. For they are excited by objects, and by the incidents of life. But these, if we except the impressed sensations, can have no power of affecting us, but what they derive from association; just as was observed above of words and sentences.

Secondly, since therefore the passions are states of considerable pleasure or pain, they must be aggregates of the ideas, or traces of the sensible pleasures and pains, which ideas make up by their number, and mutual influence upon one another, for the faintness and transitory nature of each singly taken. This may be called a proof *a priori*. The proof *a posteriori* will be given, when I come to analyse the six classes of intellectual affections; *viz.* imagination, ambition, self-interest, sympathy, theopathy, and the moral sense.

Thirdly, as sensation is the common foundation of all these, so each in its turn, when sufficiently generated, contributes to generate and model all the rest. . . .

Fourthly, as all the passions arise thus from pleasure and pain, their first and most general distribution may be into the two classes of love and hatred; *i.e.* we may term all those affections of the pleasurable kind, which objects and incidents raise in us, love; all those of the painful kind, hatred. Thus we are said to love not only intelligent agents of morally good dispositions, but also sensual pleasures, riches, and honours; and to hate poverty, disgrace, and pain, bodily and mental.

Fifthly, when our love and hatred are excited to a certain degree, they put us upon a variety of actions, and may be termed desire and aversion; by which last word I understand an active hatred. Now the actions which flow from desire and aversion, are intirely the result of associated powers and circumstances, agreeably to the 20th, 21st, and 22d Propositions, with their corollaries. . . .

Sixthly, the will appears to be nothing but a desire or aversion sufficiently strong to produce an action that is not automatic primarily or secondarily. At least it appears to me, that the substitution of these words for the word *will* may be justified by the common usage of language. The will is therefore that desire or aversion, which is strongest for the then present time. For if any other desire was stronger, the muscular motion connected with it by association would take place, and not that which proceeds from the will, or the voluntary one, which is contrary to the supposition. Since therefore all love and hatred, all desire and aversion, are factitious, and generated by association; *i.e.* mechanically; it follows that the will is mechanical also.

Seventhly, since the things which we pursue do, when obtained, generally afford pleasure, and those which we fly from affect us with pain, if they overtake us, it follows that the gratification of the will is generally attended or associated with pleasure, the disappointment of it with pain. Hence a mere associated pleasure is transferred upon the gratification of the will; a mere associated pain upon the disappointment of it. . . .

Eighthly, we often desire and pursue things which give pain rather than pleasure. Here it is to be supposed, that at first they afforded pleasure, and that they now give pain on account of a change in our nature and circumstances. Now, as the continuance to desire and pursue such objects, notwithstanding the pain arising from them, is the effect of the power of association, so the same power will at last reverse its own steps, and free us from such hurtful desires and pursuits. . . .

[Propositions 90–93 treat memory, dreams, madness, and the faculties of brutes.]

*To examine how far the just-mentioned pleasures and pains of
imagination are agreeable to the doctrine of association.*

Of the Pleasures Arising from the Beauty of the Natural World.

The pleasures arising from the contemplation of the beauties
of the natural world seem to admit of the following analysis.

The pleasant tastes, and smells, and the fine colours of fruits
and flowers, the melody of birds, and the grateful warmth or
coolness of the air, in the proper seasons, transfer miniatures of
these pleasures upon rural scenes, which start up instantaneously
so mixed with each other, and with such as will be immediately
enumerated, as to be separately indiscernible.

If there be a precipice, a cataract, a mountain of snow, &c.
in one part of the scene, the nascent ideas of fear and horror
magnify and enliven all the other ideas, and by degrees pass
into pleasures, by suggesting the security from pain.

In like manner the grandeur of some scenes, and the novelty
of others, by exciting surprize and wonder, *i.e.* by making a
great difference in the preceding and subsequent states of mind,
so as to border upon, or even enter the limits of pain, may
greatly enhance the pleasure.

Uniformity and variety in conjunction are also principal
sources of the pleasures of beauty, being made so partly by their
association with the beauties of nature; partly by that with the
works of art; and with the many conveniences which we receive
from the uniformity and variety of the works of nature and art.
They must therefore transfer part of the lustre borrowed from
the works of art, and from the head of convenience, upon the
works of nature.

Poetry and painting are much employed in setting forth the
beauties of the natural world, at the same time that they afford

us a high degree of pleasure from many other sources. Hence the beauties of nature delight poets and painters, and such as are addicted to the study of their works, more than others. Part of this effect is indeed owing to the greater attention of such persons to the other sources; but this comes to the same thing, as far as the general theory of the factitious, associated nature of these pleasures is concerned.

The many sports and pastimes, which are peculiar to the country, and whose ideas and pleasures are revived by the view of rural scenes, in an evanescent state, and so mixed together as to be separately indiscernible, do farther augment the pleasures suggested by the beauties of nature.

To these we may add, the opposition between the offensiveness, dangers, and corruption of populous cities, and the health, tranquillity, and innocence, which the actual view, or the mental contemplation, of rural scenes introduces; also the pleasures of sociality and mirth, which are often found in the greatest perfection in country retirements, the amorous pleasures, which have many connexions with rural scenes, and those which the opinions and encomiums of others beget in us, in this, as in other cases, by means of the contagiousness observable in mental dispositions, as well as bodily ones.

Those persons who have already formed high ideas of the power, knowledge, and goodness, of the Author of Nature, with suitable affections, generally feel the exalted pleasures of devotion upon every view and contemplation of his works, either in an explicit and distinct manner, or in a more secret and implicit one. Hence, part of the general indeterminate pleasures, here considered, is deducible from the pleasures of theopathy.

We must not omit in this place to remind the reader of a remark made above; *viz.* that green, which is the middle colour of the seven primary ones, and consequently the most agreeable to the organ of sight, is also the general colour of the vegetable kingdom, *i.e.* of external nature.

These may be considered as some of the principal sources of

the beauties of nature to mankind in general. Inquisitive and philosophical persons have some others, arising from their peculiar knowlege and study of natural history, astronomy, and philosophy, in general. For the profusion of beauties, uses, fitnesses, elegance in minute things, and magnificence in great ones, exceed all bounds of conception, surprize, and astonishment; new scenes, and those of unbounded extent, separately considered, ever presenting themselves to view, the more any one studies and contemplates the works of God.

And, upon the whole, the reader may see, that there are sufficient sources for all those pleasures of imagination, which the beauties of nature excite in different persons; and that the differences which are found in different persons in this respect, are sufficiently analogous to the differences of their situations in life, and of the consequent associations formed in them.

An attentive person may also, in viewing or contemplating the beauties of nature, lay hold, as it were, of the remainders and miniatures of many of the particular pleasures here enumerated, while they recur in a separate state, and before they coalesce with the general indeterminate aggregate, and thus verify the history now proposed.

It is a confirmation of this history, that an attentive person may also observe great differences in the kind and degree of the relish which he has for the beauties of nature in different periods of his life; especially as the kind and degree may be found to agree in the main with this history.

To the same purpose we may remark, that these pleasures do not cloy very soon, but are of a lasting nature, if compared with the sensible ones; since this follows naturally from the great variety of their sources, and the evanescent nature of their constituent parts.

When a beautiful scene is first presented, there is generally great pleasure from surprize, from being struck with objects and circumstances which we did not expect. This presently declines; but is abundantly compensated afterwards by the gradual alternate exaltation of the several constituent parts of the complex pleasures, which also do probably enhance one another. And thus we may take several reviews of the same scene, before the pleasure, which it affords, comes to its maximum. After this the pleasure must decline, if we review it often: but if at considerable intervals, so as that many foreign states of mind intervene, also so as that new sources of the pleasures of this kind be broken up, the pleasure may recur for many successions of nearly the same magnitude.

The same observations hold in respect of the pleasures from the beauties of nature in general, and indeed from all the other sources, works of art, liberal arts, sciences, &c. These all strike and surprise the young mind at first, but require a considerable time before they come to their maximum; after which some or other will always be at its maximum for a considerable time. However, the pleasures of imagination in general, as well as each particular set and individual, must decline at last from the nature of our frame. In what manner they ought to decline, so as to be consistent with our *summum bonum*, by yielding, in due time, to more exalted and pure pleasures, whose composition they enter, I will endeavour to shew hereafter.

These pleasures are a principal source of those which are annexed to the view of uniformity with variety, as above noted, *i.e.* of analogies of various orders; and consequently are a principal incitement to our tracing out real analogies, and forming artificial ones.

The novel, the grand, and the marvellous, are also most conspicuous in the works of nature; and the last strikes us particularly in many of the phænomena of nature, by seeming to exceed all bounds of credibility, at the same time that we are certified by irrefragable evidences of the truth of the facts. The satiety which every pleasure begets in us, after some continuance, makes us thirst perpetually after the grand and novel; and, as it were, grasp at infinity in number and extent; there being a kind of tacit expectation, that the pleasure will be in proportion to the magnitude and variety of the causes, in the same manner as we observe, in other cases, the effects to be in some degree proportional to their causes. . . .

Of Music.

Now, in respect of music, it is to be observed, that the simple sounds of all uniform sonorous bodies, and particularly the single notes of the several musical instruments, also all the concords, or notes, whose vibrations bear to each other the simple ratio's of 1 to 2, 2 to 3, 3 to 4, &c. sounded together, or near to each other, may, be considered as originally pleasant to the ear. Discords are originally unpleasant, and therefore, as in other like cases, may be made use of to heighten our pleasures, by being properly and sparingly introduced, so as to make a strong contrast. To which if we add the uniformity and variety observable in all good music, we shall have the chief pleasures affecting children, and young persons, upon their being first accustomed to hear music.

By degrees the discords become less and less harsh to the ear, and at last even pleasant, at least by their associations with the concords, that go before, or follow them; so that more, and also more harsh discords, are perpetually required to give a relish, and keep the sweetness of the concords from cloying. Particular kinds of air and harmony are associated with particular words, affections, and passions, and so are made to express these; besides which there is often a natural aptitude in the music to represent the affection, as in quick music, and concords, to represent mirth. Music in general is connected with gaiety, public rejoicings, the amorous pleasures, riches, high-rank, &c. or with battles, sorrow, death, and religious contemplations. There is an ambition to excel in taste, in performance, and in composition, and a difficulty which enhances the pleasure, &c. &c.; till, by these and such-like ways, the judgments and tastes of different persons, in respect of music, become as different, as we find them to be in fact.

Of Painting.

Our pleasures from pictures are very nearly related to those of imitation, which, as was observed above, take up a considerable part of our childhood; and the several playthings representing men, houses, horses, &c. with which children are so much delighted, are to be considered, both as augmenting and gratifying this taste in them.

To this it is to be added, that as the ideas of sight are the most vivid of all our ideas, and those which are chiefly laid up in the memory as keys and repositories to the rest, pictures, which are something intermediate between the real object and the idea, and therefore in cases of sufficient likeness more vivid than the idea, cannot but please us by thus gratifying our desire of raising up a complete idea of an absent object. This an attentive person may observe in himself in viewing pictures.

The surprize and contrast which arise in children, upon their seeing persons and objects present in their pictures, which yet they know to be absent, by striking the mind with the impossible conception of the same thing in two places, are probably the sources of considerable pleasure to them.

To these causes let us add the gay colours, and fine ornaments, which generally go along with pictures; and we shall have the chief sources of the pleasures which painting affords to young persons, and to those who have not yet been much affected with the various incidents of life, and their representations, or acquired a taste and skill in these things. . . .

Painting has a great advantage over verbal description, in respect of the vividness and number of ideas to be at once excited in the fancy; but its compass is, upon the whole, much narrower; and it is also confined to one point of time.

The representations of battles, storms, wild beasts, and other objects of horror, in pictures, please us peculiarly, partly from the near alliance which the ideas suggested bear to pain, partly from the secret consciousness of our own security, and partly because they awaken and agitate the mind sufficiently to be strongly affected with the other pleasures, which may then be offered to it.

Of Poetry.

The beauties and excellencies of good poetry are deducible from three sources. First, the harmony, regularity, and variety of the numbers or metre, and of the rhyme. Secondly, the fitness and strength of the words and phrases. Thirdly, the subject-matter of the poem, and the invention and judgment exerted by the poet, in regard to his subject. And the beauties arising from each of these are much transferred upon the other two by association.

That the versification has of itself a considerable influence, may be seen by putting good poetical passages into the order of prose. And it may be accounted for from what has been already observed of uniformity and variety, from the smoothness and facility with which verses run over the tongue, from the frequent coincidence of the end of the sentence, and that of the verse, at the same time that this rule is violated at proper intervals in all varieties, lest the ear should be tired with too much sameness, from the assistance which versification affords to the memory, from some faint resemblance which it bears to music, and its frequent associations with it, &c. &c.

The beauties of the diction arise chiefly from the figures; and therefore it will be necessary here to inquire into the sources of their beauties.

Now figurative words seem to strike and please us chiefly from that impropriety which appears at first sight, upon their application to the things denoted by them, and from the conse-quent heightening of the propriety, as soon as it is duly per-ceived. For when figurative words have recurred so often as to excite the secondary idea instantaneously, and without any pre-vious harshness to the imagination, they lose their peculiar beauty and force; and, in order to recover this, and make our-selves sensible of it, we are obliged to recal the literal sense, and to place the literal and figurative senses close together, that so we may first be sensible of the inconsistency, and then be more affected with the union and coalescence. . . .

As the pleasures of imagination are very prevalent, and much cultivated, during youth; so, if we consider mankind as one great individual, advancing in age perpetually, it seems natural to expect, that in the infancy of knowlege, in the early ages of the world, the taste of mankind would turn much upon the pleasures of this class. And agreeably to this it may be observed, that music, painting, and poetry, were much admired in antient times; and the two last brought to great perfection. . . .

Of the Beauty of the Person.

The word *beauty* is applied to the person, particularly in the female sex, in an eminent manner; and the desires and pleasures arising from beauty, in this sense, may be considered as an intermediate step between the gross sensual ones, and those of pure esteem and benevolence; for they are, in part, deduced from both these extremes; they moderate, spiritualize, and improve the first, and, in the virtuous, are ultimately converted into the last. . . .

Of Wit and Humour.

I come now to examine the pleasures of mirth, wit, and humour.

But, first, it will be necessary to consider the causes of laughter, and particularly the mental ones.

Now it may be observed, that young children do not laugh aloud for some months. The first occasion of doing this seems to be a surprize, which brings on a momentary fear first, and then a momentary joy in consequence of the removal of that fear, agreeably to what may be observed of the pleasures that follow the removal of pain. This may appear probable, inasmuch as laughter is a nascent cry, stopped of a sudden; also because if the same surprize, which makes young children laugh, be a very little increased, they will cry. It is usual, by way of diverting young children, and exciting them to laughter, to repeat the surprize, as by clapping the hands frequently, reiterating a sudden motion, &c.

This is the original of laughter in children, in general; but the progress in each particular is much accelerated, and the occasions multiplied, by imitation. They learn to laugh, as they learn to talk and walk; and are most apt to laugh profusely, when they see others laugh; the common cause contributing also in a great degree to produce this effect. The same thing is evident even in adults; and shews us one of the sources of the sympathetic affections.

To these things it is to be added, that the alternate motions of the chest follow the same degrees of mental emotion with more and more facility perpetually, so that at last children (who are likewise more exquisitely sensible and irritable than adults) laugh upon every trifling occasion.

By degrees they learn the power of suspending the actions both of laughing and crying, and associate this power with a variety of ideas, such as those of decency, respect, fear, and shame: the incidents and objects, which before occasioned emotion sufficient to produce laughter, now occasion little or none, from the transmutation of their associations: their new-associated pleasures and pains are of a more sedate kind, and do not affect them so much by surprize; and, which is a principal cause in respect of individuals, their equals laugh less, and, by forming them to the same model with themselves, make the disposition to laughter decrease still faster. For whatever can be shewn to take place at all in human nature, must take place in a much higher degree, than according to the original causes, from our great disposition to imitate one another, which has been already explained.

It confirms this account of laughter, that it follows tickling, as noted above; *i.e.* a momentary pain and apprehension of pain, with an immediately-succeeding removal of these, and their alternate recurrency; also that the softer sex, and all nervous persons, are much disposed both to laugh and cry profusely, and to pass quickly from one state to the other. And it may deserve to be inquired, how far the profuse, continued laughter and mirth on one hand, sorrow, hanging the lip, and crying, on the other, which occur in madness, agree with it.

As children learn the use of language, they learn also to laugh at sentences or stories, by which sudden alarming emotions and expectations are raised in them, and again dissipated instan-

taneously. And as they learnt before by degrees to laugh at
sudden unexpected noises, or motions, where there was no fear,
or no distinguishable one, so it is after some time in respect of
words. Children, and young persons, are diverted by every little
jingle, pun, contrast, or coincidence, which is level to their
capacities, even though the harshness and inconsistency, with
which it first strikes the fancy, be so minute as scarce to be perceived. And this is the origin of that laughter, which is excited
by wit, humour, buffoonry, &c.

But this species of laughter abates also by degrees, as the other
before-considered did, and, in general, for the same causes; so
that adults, and especially those that are judges of politeness and
propriety, laugh only at such strokes of wit and humour, as
surprise by some more than ordinary degree of contrast or coincidence; and have at the same time a due connexion with
pleasure and pain, and their several associations of fitness, decency, inconsistency, absurdity, honour, shame, virtue, and vice;
so as neither to be too glaring on the one hand, nor too faint on
the other. In the first case, the representation raises dislike and
abhorrence; in the last, it becomes insipid.

From hence may be seen, that in different persons the occasions
of laughter must be as different as their opinions and dispositions; that low similitudes, allusions, contrasts, and coincidences,
applied to grave and serious subjects, must occasion the most
profuse laughter in persons of light minds; and, conversely,
increase this levity of mind, and weaken the regard due to things
sacred; that the vices of gluttony, lewdness, vain-glory, self-
conceit, and covetousness, with the concomitant pleasures and
pains, hopes, fears, dangers, &c. when represented by indirect
circumstances, and the representation heightened by contrasts
and coincidences, must be the most frequent subject of mirth,
wit, and humour, in this mixed degenerate state, where they
are censured upon the whole; and yet not looked upon with a
due degree of severity, distance, and abhorrence; that company, feasting, and wine, by putting the body into a pleasure-
able state, must dispose to laughter upon small occasions; and

that persons who give themselves much to mirth, wit, and humour, must thereby greatly disqualify their understandings for the search after truth; inasmuch as by the perpetual hunting after apparent and partial agreements and disagreements, as in words, and indirect accidental circumstances, whilst the true natures of the things themselves afford real agreements and disagreements, that are very different, or quite opposite, a man must by degrees pervert all his notions of things themselves, and become unable to see them as they really are, and as they appear to considerate sober-minded inquirers. He must lose all his associations of the visible ideas of things, their names, symbols, &c. with their useful practical relations and properties; and get, in their stead, accidental, indirect, and unnatural conjunctions of circumstances, that are really foreign to each other, or oppositions of those that are united; and, after some time, habit and custom will fix these upon him.

The most natural occasions of mirth and laughter in adults seem to be the little mistakes and follies of children, and the smaller inconsistencies and improprieties, which happen in conversation, and the daily occurrences of life; inasmuch as these pleasures are, in great measure, occasioned, or at least supported, by the general pleasurable state, which our love and affection to our friends in general, and to children in particular, put the body and mind into. For this kind of mirth is always checked where we have a dislike; also where the mistake or inconsistency rises beyond a certain limit; for then it produces concern, confusion, and uneasiness. And it is useful not only in respect of the good effects which it has upon the body, and the present amusement and relaxation that it affords to the mind; but also, because it puts us upon rectifying what is so amiss, or any other similar error, in one another, or in children; and has a tendency to remove many prejudices from custom and education. Thus we often laugh at children, rustics, and foreigners, when yet they act right, according to the truly-natural, simple, and uncorrupted dictates of reason and propriety, and are guilty of no other inconsistency, than what arises from the usurpations of custom over nature; and we often take notice of this, and correct ourselves, in consequence of being diverted by it.

[Propositions 95—98 treat the pleasures and pains of ambition, self-interest, sympathy, and theopathy.]

PROP. 99

To examine how far the pleasures and pains of the moral sense are agreeable to the foregoing theory....

All meditations upon God, who is the inexhaustible fountain, and infinite abyss, of all perfection, both natural and moral; also all the kinds of prayer, *i.e.* all the ways of expressing our love, hope, trust, resignation, gratitude, reverence, fear, desire, &c. towards Him; transfer, by association, all the perfection, greatness, and gloriousness of his natural attributes upon his moral ones, *i.e.* upon moral rectitude. We shall by this means learn to be merciful, holy, and perfect, because God is so; and to love mercy, holiness, and perfection, wherever we see them.

And thus we may perceive, that all the pleasures and pains of sensation, imagination, ambition, self-interest, sympathy, and theopathy, as far as they are consistent with one another, with the frame of our natures, and with the course of the world, beget in us a moral sense, and lead us to the love and approbation of virtue, and to the fear, hatred, and abhorrence of vice. This moral sense therefore carries its own authority with it, inasmuch as it is the sum total of all the rest, and the ultimate result from them; and employs the force and authority of the whole nature of man against any particular part of it, that rebels against the determinations and commands of the conscience or moral judgment.

It appears also, that the moral sense carries us perpetually to the pure love of God, as our highest and ultimate perfection, our end, centre, and only resting-place, to which yet we can never attain.

.   .   .   .   .

Conclusion to Part I

Besides the consequences flowing from the doctrine of association, which are delivered in the corollaries to the 14th Proposition, there is another, which is thought by many to have a pernicious tendency in respect of morality and religion; and which therefore it will be proper that I should consider particularly.

The consequence I mean is that of the mechanism or necessity of human actions, in opposition to what is generally termed free-will. . . .

By the mechanism of human actions I mean, that each action results from the previous circumstances of body and mind, in the same manner, and with the same certainty, as other effects do from their mechanical causes; so that a person cannot do indifferently either of the actions *A*, and its contrary *a*, while the previous circumstances are the same; but is under an absolute necessity of doing one of them, and that only. Agreeably to this I suppose, that by free-will is meant a power of doing either the action *A*, or its contrary *a;* while the previous circumstances remain the same.

If by free-will be meant a power of beginning motion, this will come to the same thing; since, according to the opinion of mechanism, as here explained, man has no such power; but every action, or bodily motion, arises from previous circumstances, or bodily motions, already existing in the brain, *i.e.* from vibrations, which are either the immediate effect of impressions then made, or the remote compound effect of former impressions, or both.

But if by free-will be meant any thing different from these two definitions of it, it may not perhaps be inconsistent with the mechanism of the mind here laid down. Thus, if free-will

be defined the power of doing what a person desires or wills to
do, of deliberating, suspending, choosing, &c. or of resisting
the motives of sensuality, ambition, resentment, &c. free-will,
under certain limitations, is not only consistent with the doctrine
of mechanism, but even flows from it; since it appears from the
foregoing theory, that voluntary and semivoluntary powers of
calling up ideas, of exciting and restraining affections, and of
performing and suspending actions, arise from the mechanism
of our natures. This may be called free-will in the popular and
practical sense, in contradistinction to that, which is opposed
to mechanism, and which may be called free-will in the
philosophical sense.

·   ·   ·   ·   ·

PART II

PROP. I

*Something must have existed from all eternity; or, there never
was a time when nothing existed.*

·   ·   ·   ·   ·

PROP. 2

*There cannot have been a mere succession of finite dependent
beings from all eternity; but there must exist, at least, one
infinite and independent being.*

·   ·   ·   ·   ·

PROP. 3

*The infinite independent being is endued with infinite power
and knowlege.*

·   ·   ·   ·   ·

PROP. 4

God is infinitely benevolent.

As all the natural attributes of God may be comprehended under power and knowlege, so benevolence seems to comprehend all the moral ones. This Proposition therefore, and the foregoing, contain the fundamentals of all that reason can discover to us concerning the divine nature and attributes.

Now, in inquiring into the evidences for the divine benevolence, I observe, first, that as we judge of the divine power and knowlege by their effects in the constitution of the visible world, so we must judge of the divine benevolence in the same way. Our arguments for it must be taken from the happiness, and tendencies thereto, that are observable in the sentient beings, which come under our notice.

Secondly, that the misery, to which we see sentient beings exposed, does not destroy the evidences for the divine benevolence, taken from happiness, unless we suppose the misery equal or superior to the happiness. A being who receives three degrees of happiness, and but one of misery, is indebted for two degrees of happiness to his Creator. Hence our inquiry into the divine benevolence is reduced to an inquiry into the balance of happiness, or misery, conferred, or to be conferred, upon the whole system of sentient beings, and upon each individual of this great system. If there be reason to believe, that the happiness which each individual has received, or will receive, be greater than his misery, God will be benevolent to each being, and infinitely so to the whole infinite system of sentient beings; if the balance be infinitely in favour of each individual, God will be infinitely benevolent to each, and infinito-infinitely to the whole system.

It is no objection to this reasoning, that we desire pure happiness, and prefer it to an equal balance of happiness mixed with misery; or that the consideration of misery, amidst the works of an infinitely benevolent being, gives us perplexity. For this disappointment of our desires, and this perplexity, can amount to no more than finite evils, to be deducted from the sum total of happiness; and our obligations to the Author of our beings must always be in proportion to this remaining sum. We may add, that as this disappointment and perplexity are sources of misery at present, they may, in their future consequences, be much ampler sources of happiness; and that this seems to be the natural result of supposing, that happiness prevails over misery. . . .

Let us now come to the evidences for the divine benevolence, and its infinity.

First, then, it appears probable, that there is an over-balance of happiness to the sentient beings of this visible world, considered both generally and particularly. For though disorder, pain, and death, do very much abound every-where in the world, yet beauty, order, pleasure, life, and happiness, seem to superabound. This is indeed impossible to be ascertained by any exact computation. However, it is the general opinion of mankind, which is some kind of proof of the thing itself. For since we are inclined to think, that happiness or misery prevails, according as we ourselves are happy or miserable (which both experience, and the foregoing doctrine of association, shew), the general prevalence of the opinion of happiness is an argument of the general prevalence of the thing itself. Add to this, that the recollection of places, persons, &c. which we have formerly known, is in general pleasant to us. Now recollection is only the compound vestige of all the pleasures and pains, which have been associated with the object under consideration. It seems therefore, that the balance must have been in favour of pleasure. And yet it may be, that small or moderate actual pains are in recollection turned into pleasures. But then this will become an argument, in another way, for the prevalence of the pleasures, and particularly of those of recollection, *i.e.* mental ones. It appears also, that the growth and health of the body infer the general prevalence of happiness, whilst they continue. Afterwards, the mental happiness may overbalance the bodily misery.

Secondly, if we should lay down, that there is just as much misery as happiness in the world (more can scarce be supposed by any one), it will follow, that if the laws of benevolence were to take place in a greater degree than they do at present, misery would perpetually decrease, and happiness increase, till, at last, by the unlimited growth of benevolence, the state of mankind, in this world, would approach to a paradisiacal one. Now, this shews that our miseries are, in a great measure, owing to our want of benevolence, *i.e.* to our moral imperfections, and to that which, according to our present language, we do and must call *ourselves*. It is probable therefore, that, upon a more accurate examination and knowlege of this subject, we should find, that our miseries arose not only in great measure, but intirely, from this source, from the imperfection of our benevolence, whilst all that is good comes immediately from God, who must therefore be deemed perfectly benevolent. And since the course of the world, and the frame of our natures, are so ordered, and so adapted to each other, as to enforce benevolence upon us, this is a farther argument of the kind intentions of an over-ruling Providence. It follows hence, that malevolence, and consequently misery, must ever decrease. . . .

If we suppose a system of beings to be placed in such a situation, as that they may occasion either much happiness, or much misery, to each other, it will follow, that the scale will turn more and more perpetually in favour of the production of happiness: for the happiness which *A* receives from *B*, will lead him by association to love *B*, and to wish and endeavour *B*'s happiness, in return: *B* will therefore have a motive, arising from his desire of his own happiness, to continue his good offices to *A*: whereas the misery that *A* receives from *B*, will lead him to hate *B*, and to deter him from farther injuries. This must necessarily be the case, if we only admit, that every intelligent being is actuated by the view of private happiness, and that his memory and trains of ideas are of the same kind with ours. Now, the first supposition cannot be doubted, and to exclude the last would be to forbid all reasoning upon other intelligent beings: not to mention, that these two suppositions cannot, perhaps, be separated, since the desire of happiness seems in us to be the mere result of association, as above explained; and association itself the general law, according to which the intellectual world is framed and conducted. Now this different tendency of benevolence and malevolence, *viz.* of the first to augment itself without limits, of the latter to destroy itself ultimately, appears to be a very strong argument for the infinite benevolence of God. . . .

Some light may, perhaps, be cast upon this most difficult subject of the origin of evil, if we lay down the several notions of infinite goodness, which offer themselves to the mind, and compare them with one another, and with the appearances of things. Let us suppose then, that we may call that infinite benevolence, which makes either,

1. Each individual infinitely happy always. Or,

2. Each individual always finitely happy, without any mixture of misery, and infinitely so in its progress through infinite time. Or,

3. Each individual infinitely happy, upon the balance, in its progress through infinite time, but with a mixture of misery. Or,

4. Each individual finitely happy in the course of its existence, whatever that be, but with a mixture of misery as before; and the universe infinitely happy upon the balance. Or,

5. Some individuals happy and some miserable upon the balance, finitely or infinitely, and yet so that there shall be an infinite overplus of happiness in the universe.

All possible notions of infinite benevolence may, I think, be reduced to some one of these five; and there are some persons who think, that the infinity of the divine benevolence may be vindicated upon the last and lowest of these suppositions. Let us consider each particularly.

The first, *viz.* that each individual should be always happy infinitely, is not only contrary to the fact at first view, but also seems impossible, as being inconsistent with the finite nature of the creatures. . . .

The second supposition is that which is most natural as a mere supposition. We think that pure benevolence can give nothing but pure happiness, and infinite benevolence must give infinite happiness. But it is evidently contrary to the fact, to what we see and feel, and therefore we are forced, though with great unwillingness, to give up this notion also. . . .

The third supposition is possible in itself; but then it can neither be supported, nor contradicted, by the facts. If there appear an unlimited tendency towards the prevalence of happiness over misery, this may be some presumption for it. But all our judgments, and even conjectures, are confined within a short distance from the present moment. A divine revelation might give us an assurance of it. And it seems, that this supposition is, upon an impartial view, equally eligible and satisfactory with the foregoing. We estimate every quantity by the balance, by what remains after a subtraction of its opposite; and if this be an allowed authentic method, in the several kinds of happiness, why not in happiness considered in the abstract? But we must not conclude, that this is the genuine notion of the divine benevolence. There may perhaps be some presumptions for it, both from reason and Scripture; but I think none, in the present infancy of knowlege, sufficient to ground an opinion upon. However, there seem to be no possible presumptions against it; and this may encourage us to search both the book of God's word, and that of his works, for matter of comfort to ourselves, and arguments whereby to represent his moral character in the most amiable light.

The fourth supposition is one to which many thinking, serious, benevolent, and pious persons are now much inclined. All the arguments here used for the divine benevolence, and its infinity, seem to infer it, or, if they favour any of the other suppositions, to favour the third, which may be said to include this fourth. There are also many declarations in the Scriptures concerning the goodness, bounty, and mercy of God to all his creatures, which can scarce be interpreted in a lower sense.

As to the fifth supposition, therefore, it follows, that it is opposed by the preceding arguments, *i.e.* by the marks and footsteps of God's goodness in the creation, and by the declarations of the Scriptures to the same purpose. However, there are a few passages of Scripture, from whence some very learned and devout men still continue to draw this fifth supposition; they do also endeavour to make this supposition consistent with the divine benevolence, by making a farther supposition, *viz.* that of philosophical liberty, as it is called in these Observations, or the power of doing different things, the previous circumstances remaining the same. . . .

These observations seem naturally to occur, upon considering these five suppositions, and comparing them with one another, and with the word and works of God. But there is also another way of considering the third supposition, which, as it is a presumption for it, though not an evidence, agreeably to what was intimated above, I shall here offer to the reader.

First then, association has an evident tendency to convert a state of superior happiness, mixed with inferior misery, into one of pure happiness, into a paradisiacal one, as has been shewn in the first part of these Observations, Prop. 14. Cor. 9. Or, in other words, association tends to convert the state of the third supposition into that of the second.

Secondly, when any small pain is introductory to a great pleasure, it is very common for us, without any express reflection on the power of association, to consider this pain as coalescing with the subsequent pleasure, into a pure pleasure, equal to the difference between them; and, in some cases, the small pain itself puts on the nature of a pleasure, of which we see many instances in the daily occurrences of life, where labour, wants, pains, become actually pleasant to us, by a lustre borrowed from the pleasures to be obtained by them. And this happens most particularly, when we recollect the events of our past lives, or view those of others. It is to be observed also, that this power of uniting different and opposite sensations into one increases as we advance in life, and in our intellectual capacities; and that, strictly speaking, no sensation can be a monad, inasmuch as the most simple are infinitely divisible in respect of time, and extent of impression. Those, therefore, which are esteemed the purest pleasures, may contain some parts which afford pain; and, conversely, were our capacities sufficiently enlarged, any sensations connected to each other in the way of cause and effect, would be esteemed one sensation, and be denominated a pure pleasure, if pleasure prevailed upon the whole.

Thirdly, as the enlargement of our capacities enables us thus to take off the edge of our pains, by uniting them with the subsequent superior pleasures, so it confers upon us more and more the power of enjoying our future pleasures by anticipation, by extending the limits of the present time, *i.e.* of that time in which we have an interest. For the present time, in a metaphysical sense, is an indivisible moment; but the present time, in a practical sense, is a finite quantity of various magnitudes, according to our capacities, and, beginning from an indivisible moment in all, seems to grow on indefinitely in beings who are ever progressive in their passage through an eternal life.

Suppose now a being of great benevolence, and enlarged intellectual capacities, to look down upon mankind passing through a mixture of pleasures and pains, in which, however, there is a balance of pleasure, to a greater balance of pleasure perpetually, and, at last, to a state of pure and exalted pleasure made so by association: it is evident, that his benevolence to man will be the source of pure pleasure to him from his power of uniting the opposite sensations, and of great present pleasure from his power of anticipation. And the more we suppose the benevolence and capacities of this being enlarged, the greater and more pure will his sympathetic pleasure be, which arises from the contemplation of man. It follows therefore, that, in the eye of an infinite mind, creatures conducted, as we think, according to the third of the foregoing suppositions, are conducted according to the second, and these according to the first; or, in other words, that the first, second, and third, of the foregoing suppositions, are all one and the same in the eye of God. For all time, whether past, present, or future, is present time in the

eye of God, and all ideas coalesce into one to him; and this
one is infinite happiness, without any mixture of misery, *viz.* by
the infinite prepollence of happiness above misery, so as to
annihilate it; and this merely by considering time as it ought
to be considered in strictness, *i.e.* as a relative thing, belonging to
beings of finite capacities, and varying with them, but which is
infinitely absorbed in the pure eternity of God. Now the appearance of things to the eye of an infinite being must be called their
real appearance in all propriety. And tho' it be impossible for
us to arrive at this true way of conceiving things perfectly, or
directly, yet we shall approach nearer and nearer to it, as our
intellectual capacities, benevolence, devotion, and the purity
of our happiness, depending thereon, advance: and we seem
able, at present, to express the real appearance, in the same way
as mathematicians do ultimate ratios, to which quantities ever
tend, and never arrive, and in a language which bears a sufficient analogy to other expressions that are admitted. So that now
(if we allow the third supposition) we may in some sort venture
to maintain that, which at first sight seemed not only contrary to
obvious experience, but even impossible, *viz.* that all individuals
are actually and always infinitely happy. And thus all difficulties
relating to the divine attributes will be taken away; God will be
infinitely powerful, knowing, and good, in the most absolute
sense, if we consider things as they appear to him. . . .

[Propositions 5–45 continue the description "Of the Being and
Attributes of God, and of Natural Religion" and "The Truth
of the Christian Religion"; Propositions 46–76 proceed with
"The Rule of Life," or practical applications of the doctrines
previously advanced, and "The Rule of Faith."]

PROP. 55

*The pleasures of imagination ought not to be made a primary
pursuit.*

For, first, it does not appear, that those who devote themselves to the study of the polite arts, or of science, or to any other pleasure of mere imagination, as their chief end and pursuit, attain to a greater degree of happiness than the rest of the world. . . . Secondly, it is evident, that the pleasures of imagination were not intended for our primary pursuit, because they are, in general, the first of our intellectual pleasures, which are generated from the sensible ones by association, come to their height early in life, and decline in old age. . . . It deserves particular notice here, that the language used in respect of the ideas, pleasures, and pains of imagination, is applicable to those of the moral sense with a peculiar fitness and significancy; as, *vice versa*, the proper language of the moral sense does, in many cases, add great beauty to poetry, oratory, &c. when used catachrestically. And we may observe in general, that as the pleasures of imagination are manifestly intended to generate and augment the higher orders, particularly those of sympathy, theopathy, and the moral sense; so these last may be made to improve and perfect those, as I shall now endeavour to shew under the Proposition that follows.

PROP. 56

The pursuit of the pleasures of imagination ought to be regulated by the precepts of benevolence, piety, and the moral sense.

For, first, those parts of the arts and sciences which bring glory to God, and advantage to mankind, which inspire devotion, and instruct us how to be useful to others, abound with more and greater beauties, than such as are profane, mischievous, unprofitable, or minute. . . . It may be remarked, that the pleasures of imagination point to devotion in a particular manner by their unlimited nature.

For all beauty, both natural and artificial, begins to fade and
languish after a short acquaintance with it: novelty is a never-
failing requisite: we look down, with indifference and contempt, upon what we comprehend easily; and are ever aiming at,
and pursuing, such objects as are but just within the compass of
our present faculties. What is it now, that we ought to learn
from this dissatisfaction to look behind us, and tendency to press
forward; from this endless grasping after infinity? Is it not, that
the infinite Author of all things has so formed our faculties, that
nothing less than himself can be an adequate object for them?
That it is in vain to hope for full and lasting satisfaction from
any thing finite, however great and glorious, since it will itself
teach us to conceive and desire something still more so? That,
as nothing can give us more than a transitory delight, if its relation to God be excluded; so every thing, when considered as
the production of his infinite wisdom and goodness, will gratify
our utmost expectations, since we may, in this view, see that
every thing has infinite uses and excellencies? There is not an
atom perhaps in the whole universe, which does not abound
with millions of worlds; and, conversly, this great system of
the sun, planets, and fixed stars, may be no more than a single
constituent particle of some body of an immense relative magnitude, &c. In like manner, there is not a moment of time so small,
but it may include millions of ages in the estimation of some
beings; and, conversly, the largest cycle which human art is
able to invent, may be no more than the twinkling of an eye in
that of others, &c. The infinite divisibility and extent of space
and time admit of such infinities upon infinities, ascending and
descending, as make the imagination giddy, when it attempts
to survey them. But, however this be, we may be sure, that the
true system of things is infinitely more transcendent in greatness and goodness, than any description or conception of ours
can make it; and that the voice of nature is an universal chorus
of joy and transport, in which the least and vilest, according to
common estimation, bear a proper part, as well as those whose
present superiority over them appears indefinitely great, and may

bear an equal one in the true and ultimate ratio of things. And thus the consideration of God gives a relish and lustre to speculations, which are otherwise dry and unsatisfactory, or which perhaps would confound and terrify. Thus we may learn to rejoice in every thing we see, in the blessings past, present, and future; which we receive either in our own persons, or in those of others; to become partakers of the divine nature, loving and lovely, holy and happy.

· · · · ·

PROP. 72

To deduce practical rules concerning the theopathetic affections, faith, fear, gratitude, hope, trust, resignation, and love. . . .

SCHOLIUM

If we consider the love of the world, the fear of God, and the love of God, in the first ratio which they bear to each other, it will appear, that the love of the world is infinitely greater than the fear of God, and the fear infinitely greater than the love; so that the fear of God is a middle proportional between the love of the world and the love of God, in the first or nascent ratio of these affections. In like manner, if we take their last ratio, or that in which the love of the world, and the fear of God, vanish into the love of God, the love of the world will be infinitely less than the fear of God, and the fear infinitely less than the love; so that the fear of God will still be a middle proportional between the love of the world and the love of God. Let us suppose the fear of God to be a middle proportional between the love of the world and the love of God in all the intermediate states of these affections, from their first rise in infancy, till their ultimate absorption and evanescence in the love of God; and see how this supposition will tally with experience, and how each affection varies in respect of the other two. Call therefore the love of the world W, the fear of God F, and the love of God L. Since then $W : F :: F : L$, $W = \dfrac{F^2}{L}$. If now F be supposed to remain the same $W :: L$, *i.e.* every diminution of the love of the world will increase the love of God, and *vice versa;* so that, if the love of the world be nothing, the love of God will be infinite, also infinitely greater than the fear, *i.e.* we shall be infinitely happy. If, on the contrary, the love of the world be greater than the love of God, the fear will also be greater than it, and our religion be chiefly anxiety and superstition. If, farther, F, supposed still to remain the same, be greater than W, it is our truest interest to diminish W as much as we can, because then the gain in L is far greater than the loss in W. If L remain the same, then $W = F^2$; *i.e.* every increase of W will increase F also, *i.e.* every increase of the love of the world will increase the fear of God, which therefore, since the love is not increased by supposition, must incline to a superstitious dread: as, on the contrary, if W vanishes, F must vanish also; *i.e.* the love of the world and fear being both annihilated, we shall receive pure happiness, of a finite degree, from the love of God. If W remain the same, then $F^2 :: L$; *i.e.* every accession made to the fear of God will be the cause of a greater accession to the love, and every accession to the love the cause of only a less accession to the fear; *i.e.* we shall be gainers upon the whole by all motives either to the fear or love of God, losers by all contrary motives. For if F be supposed even infinite, L will be infinito-infinite, *i.e.* will absorb it infinitely; and, if F be infinitesimal, L will be infinito-infinitesimal; *i.e.* we shall become mere selfish worldlings; which is the case with those practical atheists, who succeed in their endeavours to put God, and a future state, out of their thoughts, that they may give themselves up to this world. W now occupies the place of L, and extinguishes both F and it; *i.e.* self and the world are their God. Upon the whole, it follows from this speculation concerning the quantities W, F, and L, that W ought to be diminished, and F and L to be increased, as much as possible, that so W may be indefinitely less than F, and F indefinitely less than L; *i.e.* we ourselves indefinitely happy in the love of God, by the previous annihilation of self and the world. And it may not perhaps be quite unuseful to have represented this most important of all conclusions, with the steps that lead to it, in this new and compendious light.

· · · · ·

PROP. 77

It is probable, that most or all men receive more happiness than misery in their passage thro' the present life.

· · · · ·

PROP. 78

The balance cannot be much in favour even of the most happy, during the present life.

· · · · ·

PROP. 79

Virtue has always the fairest prospect, even in this life; and vice is always exposed to the greatest hazards.

· · · · ·

PROP. 80

It does not seem at all probable, that happiness is exactly proportioned to virtue in the present life.

· · · · ·

PROP. 81

It is probable, that all the present civil governments will be over-turned.

. . . . .

PROP. 82

It is probable, that the present forms of church-government will be dissolved.

. . . . .

PROP. 83

It is probable, that the Jews will be restored to Palæstine.

. . . . .

PROP. 84

The Christian religion will be preached to, and received by, all nations.

. . . . .

PROP. 85

It is not probable, that there will be any pure or complete happi-ness, before the destruction of this world by fire.

. . . . .

PROP. 86

It is probable from the mere light of nature, that there will be a future state.

. . . . .

PROP. 87

The Christian revelation gives us an absolute assurance of a future state.

. . . . .

PROP. 88

The rewards and punishments of a future life will far exceed the happiness and misery of this, both in degree and duration.

. . . . .

PROP. 89

It is probable, that the future happiness of the good will be of a spiritual nature; but the future misery of the wicked may be both corporeal and mental.

. . . . .

PROP. 90

It seems probable, that the soul will remain in a state of inactivity, though perhaps not of insensibility, from death to the Resurrection.

. . . . .

PROP. 91

It follows from the foregoing theory of our intellectual pleasures and pains, that the bulk of mankind are not qualified for pure unmixed happiness.

. . . . .

PROP. 92

It follows from the declarations of the Scriptures, that the bulk of mankind are not qualified for the mansions of the blessed.

. . . . .

PROP. 93

To apply the foregoing doctrine, as well as we can, to the real circumstances of mankind.

. . . . .

PROP. 94

It is probable from reason, that all mankind will be made happy ultimately.

. . . . .

PROP. 95

It is probable from the Scriptures, that all mankind will be made ultimately happy.

. . . . .

Conclusion to Part II

I have now gone through with my Observations on the Frame, Duty, and Expectations of Man, finishing them with the doctrine of ultimate, unlimited happiness to all. This doctrine, if it be true, ought at once to dispel all gloominess, anxiety, and sorrow, from our hearts; and raise them to the highest pitch of love, adoration, and gratitude towards God, our most bountiful Creator, and merciful Father, and the inexhaustible source of all happiness and perfection. Here self-interest, benevolence, and piety, all concur to move and exalt our affections. How happy in himself, how benevolent to others, and how thankful to God, ought that man to be, who believes both himself and others born to an infinite expectation! Since God has bid us rejoice, what can make us sorrowful? Since he has created us for happiness, what misery can we fear? If we be really intended for ultimate unlimited happiness, it is no matter to a truly resigned person, when, or where, or how. Nay, could any of us fully conceive, and be duly influenced by, this glorious expectation, this infinite balance in our favour, it would be sufficient to deprive all present evils of their sting and bitterness. It would be a sufficient answer to the πόθεν τὸ κακὸν, to all our difficulties and anxieties from the folly, vice, and misery, which we experience in ourselves, and see in others, to say, that they will all end in unbounded knowlege, virtue, and happiness; and that the progress of every individual in his passage through an eternal life is from imperfect to perfect, particular to general, less to greater, finite to infinite, and from the creature to the Creator.

But, alas! this is chiefly speculation, and must be to the bulk of mankind. Whilst we continue entangled in the fetters of sin, we cannot enjoy the glorious liberty and privileges of the children of God. We cannot exalt ourselves to Heaven, and make a right estimate of things, from the true point of view, till we get clear of the attraction, and magic influences, of the earth. Whence it follows, that this doctrine, however great and glor-

ious in itself, in the eye of a being sufficiently advanced in purity
and comprehension, must be to us like the book given to St. John,
bitter in the belly, though *sweet in the mouth.* . . .

There is also another consideration, which though of less moment than the foregoing, is yet abundantly sufficient to move the
compassion of the good, and alarm the fears of the wicked; I
mean the temporal evils and woes, which will probably fall upon
the nominally Christian states of these Western parts, the
Christian Babylon, before the great revolution predicted in the
Scriptures, before the kingdoms of this world become the kingdoms of our Lord, and of his Christ. These evils will be brought
upon us by our excess of wickedness, just as the deluge was upon
the old world, and the destruction of Sodom upon its lewd inhabitants, through theirs; they may also be somewhat delayed,
or alleviated, by reformations public or private, even partial and
temporary ones. I will therefore make a few short remarks concerning such things, as seem more particularly to call for the
attention of the present Christian world; at least of those good
Philadelphians, who are desirous to keep themselves and others
from that hour of temptation, which is coming upon us all. My
remarks must be supposed to relate chiefly to this kingdom; to
be suggested by what occurs in it; and to be calculated, as far
as my poor, but sincere and earnest endeavours can have any
weight, to stem for a while that torrent of vice and impiety,
which seem ready to swallow us up, and, if possible, to protract
the life of the body politic. But I presume, that the resemblance
between all the states of Christendom is so great in all the points
here considered, that the practical consequences are the same
upon the whole.

There are six things, which seem more especially to threaten
ruin and dissolution to the present states of Christendom.

First, the great growth of atheism and infidelity, particularly
amongst the governing part of these states.

Secondly, the open and abandoned lewdness, to which great
numbers of both sexes, especially in the high ranks of life, have
given themselves up.

Thirdly, the sordid and avowed self-interest, which is almost the sole motive of action in those who are concerned in the administration of public affairs.

Fourthly, the licentiousness and contempt of every kind of authority, divine and human, which is so notorious in inferiors of all ranks.

Fifthly, the great wordly-mindedness of the clergy, and their gross neglects in the discharge of their proper functions.

Sixthly, the carelessness and infatuation of parents and magistrates with respect to the education of youth, and the consequent early corruption of the rising generation.

[Hartley discusses these various evils for several pages.]

It would be great rashness to fix a time for the breaking of the storm that hangs over our heads, as it is blindness and infatuation not to see it; not to be aware, that it may break. And yet this infatuation has always attended all falling states. The kingdoms of Judah and Israel, which are the types of all the rest, were thus infatuated. It may be, that the prophecies concerning Edom, Moab, Ammon, Tyre, Egypt, &c. will become applicable to particular kingdoms before their fall, and warn the good to flee out of them. And Christendom, in general, seems ready to assume to itself the place and lot of the Jews, after they had rejected their Messiah the Saviour of the world. Let no one deceive himself or others. The present circumstances of the world are extraordinary and critical, beyond what has ever yet happened. If we refuse to let Christ reign over us, as our Redeemer and Saviour, we must be slain before his face, as enemies, at his second coming.

ADAM SMITH

(1723-90)

The author of *The Wealth of Nations* was born in Kirk-aldy, Scotland; attended the University of Glasgow, where he heard lectures by Francis Hutcheson; and also studied at Oxford. He lectured on rhetoric and belles lettres in Edinburgh under the patronage of Lord Kames and there became a good friend of David Hume. From 1751 to 1763 he was Professor of Logic at the University of Glasgow. After several years of travel and retirement in his native town, during which he wrote *The Wealth of Nations* (1776), he settled in Edinburgh for the last dozen years of his life.

The combination of practical morality and common-sense psychology in *The Theory of Moral Sentiments* (1759) is typical of the Scottish intellectual circles in which Smith moved. His method of approaching a moral problem by analysis of individual responses both evidences and helped confirm the new psychological orientation which the romantics inherited. His idea of sympathetic imagination, represented in the selection below, seems particularly to anticipate Hazlitt and Keats. In the background of the work is the running battle, still an important issue for the romantics, between those who, following Mandeville, maintained that virtuous actions arise from selfish motives, and those like Shaftesbury who defended individual benevolence.

The Theory of Moral Sentiments is one of three works abridged by Herbert W. Schneider in *Adam Smith's Moral and Political Philosophy* (New York: Hafner, 1948). His *Lectures on Rhetoric and Belles Lettres . . . Reported by a Student in 1762-63* is edited by

John M. Lothian (London: Nelson & Sons, 1963). The *Inquiry into the Nature and Causes of the Wealth of Nations* is available in many modern editions.

The text that follows is based on the fifth edition (London, 1781).

The Theory of Moral Sentiments

How selfish soever man may be supposed, there are evidently some principles in his nature, which interest him in the fortune of others, and render their happiness necessary to him, though he derives nothing from it except the pleasure of seeing it. Of this kind is pity or compassion, the emotion which we feel for the misery of others, when we either see it, or are made to conceive it in a very lively manner. That we often derive sorrow from the sorrow of others, is a matter of fact too obvious to require any instances to prove it; for this sentiment, like all the other original passions of human nature, is by no means confined to the virtuous and humane, though they perhaps may feel it with the most exquisite sensibility. The greatest ruffian, the most hardened violator of the laws of society, is not altogether without it.

As we have no immediate experience of what other men feel, we can form no idea of the manner in which they are affected, but by conceiving what we ourselves should feel in the like situation. Though our brother is upon the rack, as long as we ourselves are at our ease, our senses will never inform us of what he suffers. They never did and never can carry us beyond our own person, and it is by the imagination only that we can form any conception of what are his sensations. Neither can that faculty help us to this any other way, than by representing to us what would be our own, if we were in his case. It is the impressions of our own senses only, not those of his, which our imaginations copy. By the imagination we place ourselves in his situation, we conceive ourselves enduring all the same torments, we enter as it were into his body and become in some measure him, and thence form some idea of his sensations, and even feel something which, though weaker in degree, is not altogether unlike them. His agonies, when they are thus brought home to ourselves, when we have thus adopted and made them our own, begin at last to affect us, and we then tremble and shudder at the thought of what he feels. For as to be in pain or distress of any kind excites the most excessive sorrow, so to conceive or to imagine that we are in it, excites some degree of the same emotion, in proportion to the vivacity or dulness of the conception.

That this is the source of our fellow-feeling for the misery of others, that it is by changing places in fancy with the sufferer, that we come either to conceive or be affected by what he feels, may be demonstrated by many obvious observations, if it should not be thought sufficiently evident of itself. When we see a stroke aimed and just ready to fall upon the leg or arm of another person, we naturally shrink and draw back our own leg or our own arm; and when it does fall, we feel it in some measure, and are hurt by it as well as the sufferer. The mob, when they are gazing at a dancer on the slack rope, naturally writhe and twist and balance their own bodies, as they see him do, and as they feel that they themselves must do if in his situation. Persons of delicate fibres, and a weak constitution of body, complain that in looking on the sores and ulcers which are exposed by beggars in the streets, they are apt to feel an itching or uneasy sensation in the correspondent part of their own bodies. The horror which they conceive at the misery of those wretches affects that particular part in themselves more than any other; because that horror arises from conceiving what they themselves would suffer, if they really were the wretches whom they are looking upon, and if that particular part in themselves was actually affected in the same miserable manner. The very force of this conception is sufficient, in their feeble frames, to produce that itching or uneasy sensation complained of. Men of the most robust make, observe that in looking upon sore eyes they often feel a very sensible soreness in their own, which proceeds from the same reason; that organ being in the strongest man more delicate than any other part of the body is in the weakest.

Neither is it those circumstances only, which create pain or sorrow, that call forth our fellow-feeling. Whatever is the passion which arises from any object in the person principally concerned, an analogous emotion springs up, at the thought of his situation, in the breast of every attentive spectator. Our joy for the deliverance of those heroes of tragedy or romance who interest us, is as sincere as our grief for their distress, and our fellow-feeling with their misery is not more real than that with their happiness. We enter into their gratitude towards those faithful friends who did not desert them in their difficulties; and we heartily go along with their resentment against those perfidious traitors who injured, abandoned, or deceived them. In every passion of which the mind of man is susceptible, the emotions of the by-stander always correspond to what, by bringing the case home to himself, he imagines, should be the sentiments of the sufferer.

· · · · ·

CHAP. III

When the original passions of the person principally concerned are in perfect concord with the sympathetic emotions of the spectator, they necessarily appear to this last just and proper, and suitable to their objects; and, on the contrary, when, upon bringing the case home to himself, he finds that they do not coincide with what he feels, they necessarily appear to him unjust and improper, and unsuitable to the causes which excite them. To approve of the passions of another, therefore, as suitable to their objects, is the same thing as to observe that we entirely sympathize with them; and not to approve of them as such, is the same thing as to observe that we do not entirely sympathize with them. The man who resents the injuries that have been done to me, and observes that I resent them precisely as he does, necessarily approves of my resentment. The man whose sympathy keeps time to my grief, cannot but admit the reasonableness of my sorrow. He who admires the same poem, or the same picture, and admires them exactly as I do, must surely allow the justness of my admiration. He who laughs at the same joke, and laughs along with me, cannot well deny the propriety of my laughter. On the contrary, the person who, upon these different occasions, either feels no such emotion as that which I feel, or feels none that bears any proportion to mine, cannot avoid disapproving my sentiments on account of their dissonance with his own. If my animosity goes beyond what the indignation of my friend can correspond to; if my grief exceeds what his most tender compassion can go along with; if my admiration is either too high or too low to tally with his own; if I laugh loud and heartily when he only smiles, or, on the contrary, only smile when he laughs loud and heartily; in all these cases, as soon as he comes from considering the object, to observe how I am affected by it, according as there is more or less disproportion between his sentiments and mine, I must incur a greater or less degree of his disapprobation: and upon all occasions his own sentiments are the standards and measures by which he judges of mine. . . .

Philosophers have, of late years, considered chiefly the tendency of affections, and have given little attention to the relation which they stand in to the cause which excites them. In common life, however, when we judge of any person's conduct, and of the sentiments which directed it, we constantly consider them under both these aspects. When we blame in another man the excesses of love, of grief, of resentment, we not only consider the ruinous effects which they tend to produce, but the little occasion which was given for them. The merit of his favourite, we say, is not so great, his misfortune is not so dreadful, his provocation is not so extraordinary, as to justify so violent a passion. We should have indulged, we say, perhaps, have approved of the violence of his emotion, had the cause been in any respect proportioned to it.

When we judge in this manner of any affection, as proportioned or disproportioned to the cause which excites it, it is scarce possible that we should make use of any other rule or canon but the correspondent affection in ourselves. If, upon bringing the case home to our own breast, we find that the sentiments which it gives occasion to, coincide and tally with our own, we necessarily approve of them as proportioned and suitable to their objects; if otherwise, we necessarily disapprove of them, as extravagant and out of proportion.

Every faculty in one man is the measure by which he judges of the like faculty in another. I judge of your sight by my sight, of your ear by my ear, of your reason by my reason, of your resentment by my resentment, of your love by my love. I neither have, nor can have, any other way of judging about them.

· · · · ·

Part III

CHAP. II

· · · · ·

As to the eye of the body, objects appear great or small, not so much according to their real dimensions, as according to the nearness or distance of their situation; so do they likewise to

what may be called the natural eye of the mind: and we remedy
the defects of both these organs pretty much in the same
manner. . . .

To the selfish and original passions of human nature, the
loss or gain of a very small interest of our own, appears to be
of vastly more importance, excites a much more passionate joy
or sorrow, a much more ardent desire or aversion, than the
greatest concern of another with whom we have no particular
connexion. His interests, as long as they are surveyed from this
station, can never be put into the balance with our own, can never
restrain us from doing whatever may tend to promote our own,
how ruinous soever to him. Before we can make any proper
comparison of those opposite interests, we must change our
position. We must view them, neither from our own place,
nor yet from his, neither with our own eyes nor yet with his,
but from the place, and with the eyes of a third person, who has
no particular connexion with either, and who judges with im-
partiality between us. Here too, habit and experience have
taught us to do this so easily and so readily, that we are scarce
sensible that we do it; and it requires, in this case too, some degree of reflection, and even of philosophy, to convince us, how
little interest we should take in the greatest concerns of our
neighbour, how little we should be affected by whatever relates
to him, if the sense of propriety and justice did not correct the
otherwise natural inequality of our sentiments.

Let us suppose that the great empire of China, with all its
myriads of inhabitants, was suddenly swallowed up by an earth-
quake, and let us consider how a man of humanity in Europe,
who had no sort of connexion with that part of the world,
would be affected upon receiving intelligence of this dreadful
calamity. He would, I imagine, first of all, express very strongly
his sorrow for the misfortune of that unhappy people, he would
make many melancholy reflections upon the precariousness of
human life, and the vanity of all the labours of man, which
could thus be annihilated in a moment. He would too, perhaps,
if he was a man of speculation, enter into many reasonings con-

cerning the effects which this disaster might produce upon the commerce of Europe, and the trade and business of the world in general. And when all this fine philosophy was over, when all these humane sentiments had been once fairly expressed, he would pursue his business or his pleasure, take his repose or his diversion, with the same ease and tranquillity, as if no such accident had happened. The most frivolous disaster which could befal himself would occasion a more real disturbance. If he was to lose his little-finger to-morrow, he would not sleep to-night; but provided he never saw them, he will snore with the most profound security over the ruin of a hundred millions of his brethren, and the destruction of that immense multitude seems plainly an object less interesting to him, than this paultry misfortune of his own. To prevent, therefore, this paultry misfortune to himself, would a man of humanity be willing to sacrifice the lives of a hundred millions of his brethren, provided he had never seen them? Human nature startles with horror at the thought, and the world, in its greatest depravity and corruption, never produced such a villain as could be capable of entertaining it. But what makes this difference? When our passive feelings are almost always so sordid and so selfish, how comes it that our active principles should often be so generous and so noble? When we are always so much more deeply affected by whatever concerns ourselves, than by whatever concerns other men; what is it which prompts the generous, upon all occasions, and the mean upon many, to sacrifice their own interests to the greater interests of others? It is not the soft power of humanity, it is not that feeble spark of benevolence which Nature has lighted up in the human heart, that is thus capable of counteracting the strongest impulses of self-love. It is a stronger power, a more forcible motive, which exerts itself upon such occasions. It is reason, principle, conscience, the inhabitant of the breast, the man within, the great judge and arbiter of our conduct. It is he, who, whenever we are about to act so as to affect the happiness of others, calls to us with a voice capable of astonishing the most presumptuous of our passions, that we are but one of the multitude, in no respect better than any other in it; and that when we prefer ourselves so shamefully and so blindly to others, we become the proper objects of resentment, abhorrence, and execration. It is from him only that we learn the real littleness of ourselves, and of whatever relates to ourselves, and the natural misrepresentations of self-love can be corrected only by the eye of this impartial spectator. It is he who shows us the propriety of generosity and the deformity of injustice; the propriety of resigning the greatest interests of our own, for the yet greater interests of others, and the deformity of doing the smallest injury to another, in order to obtain the greatest benefit to ourselves. It is not the love of our neighbour, it is not the love of mankind, which upon many occasions prompts us to the practice of those divine virtues. It is a stronger love, a more powerful affection, which generally takes place upon such occasions, the love of what is honourable and noble, of the grandeur, and dignity, and superiority of our own characters.

WILLIAM DUFF

(1732–1815)

This Scottish minister wrote, in addition to the book represented here, *Critical Observations on the Writing of the Most Celebrated Original Geniuses in Poetry* (1770); *The History of Rhedi, the Hermit of Mount Ararat, an Oriental Tale* (1773); *Sermons* (1786); *Letters on the Intellectual and Moral Character of Women* (1807); and *The Last Address of a Clergyman in the Decline of Life* (1814). The work for which he is now remembered, the *Essay on Original Genius* (1767), was never either novel or profound enough to be a great influence on anyone; but it deserves a small niche in literary history for bringing together in a few pages many eighteenth-century ideas on its subject. Duff's argument in the section below, "that original Poetic Genius will in general be displayed in its utmost vigour in the early and uncultivated periods of Society, which are peculiarly favourable to it," is substantially the same as Hazlitt's in several essays where he maintains that "the arts are not progressive." And Duff's more general belief that the poetic imagination is spontaneous and little improved by artificial cultivation is echoed at times not only by Hazlitt but by Keats, Blake, Shelley, and their literary descendants.

In the course of the book Duff discusses genius as it appears in science, philosophy, and the arts; but he is particularly interested in poetic genius and "original genius," which he describes as "that native and radical power which the mind possesses, of discovering something new and uncommon in every subject on which it employs its faculties." Duff also analyzes genius into its "principal ingredients" of imagination, judgment, and taste. By far the most important of these is imagination, "that faculty whereby the mind not only reflects on its own operations, but which assembles the various ideas conveyed to the understanding by the canal of sensation, and treasured up in the repository of the memory, compounding or disjoining them at pleasure; and which, by its plastic power of inventing new associations of ideas, and of combining them with infinite variety, is enabled to present a creation of its own, and to exhibit scenes and objects which never existed in nature."

A facsimile of *An Essay on Original Genius* is edited, with an introduction, by John L. Mahoney (Gainesville, Fla.: Scholars' Facsimiles & Reprints, 1964). This text follows the second edition (London, 1767), with a few modernizations of italics and small capitals.

An Essay on Original Genius

Book II

Section V

To assert that this divine art [poetry], to an excellence in
which the highest efforts of human Genius are requisite, should
attain its utmost perfection in the infancy of society, when mankind are only emerging from a state of ignorance and barbarity,
will appear a paradox to some, though it is an unquestionable
truth; and a closer attention will convince us, that it is agreeable
to reason, as well as confirmed by experience.

While Arts and Sciences are in their first rude and imperfect
state, there is great scope afforded for the exertions of Genius.
Much is to be observed; much is to be discovered and invented.
Imagination however in general exerts itself with more success
in the Arts than in the Sciences; in the former of which its success is more rapid than in the latter. Active as this faculty is in its
operations, its discoveries in science are for the most part attained by slow and gradual steps. They are the effect of long
and severe investigation; and receive their highest improvement
in the most civilized state of society. On the other hand the
efforts of Imagination, in Poetry at least, are impetuous, and

attain their utmost perfection at once, even in the rudest form of social life. . . .

It is very remarkable . . . that in the earliest and most un-cultivated periods of society, Poetry is by one great effort of nature, in one age, and by one individual, brought to the highest perfection to which human Genius is capable of advancing it; not only when the other Arts and Sciences are in a languishing state, but when they do not so much as exist. Thus Homer wrote his *Iliad* and *Odyssey*, when there was not a single picture to be seen in Greece; and Ossian composed *Fingal* and *Temora*, when none of the Arts, whether liberal or mechanical, were known in his country. . . .

The first reason we shall assign of original poetic genius being most remarkably displayed in an early and uncultivated period of society, arises from the antiquity of the period itself, and from the appearance of novelty in the objects which Genius contem-plates. A Poet of real Genius, who lives in a distant uncultivated age, possesses great and peculiar advantages for original com-position, by the mere antiquity of the period in which he lives. He is perhaps the first Poet who hath arisen in this infant state of society; by which means he enjoys the undivided empire of Imagination without a rival. The mines of Fancy not having been opened before his time, are left to be digged by him; and the treasures they contain become his own, by a right derived from the first discovery. The whole system of nature, and the whole region of fiction, yet unexplored by others, is subjected to his survey, from which he culls those rich spoils, which adorn his compositions, and render them original. . . . We may farther observe, that the objects with which he is surrounded, have an appearance of novelty, which, in a more cultivated period, they in a great measure lose; but which, in that we are speaking of, excites an attention, curiosity and surprise, highly favourable to the exertion of Genius. . . .

The next reason we shall give, why original Poetic Genius appears in its utmost perfection in the first periods of social life, is the simplicity and uniformity of manners peculiar to such periods.

Manners have a much greater effect on the exertions of Poetic Genius, than is commonly imagined. The simple manners which prevail among most nations in the infancy of society, are peculiarly favourable to such exertions. In this primitive state of nature, when mankind begin to unite in society, the manners, sentiments, and passions are (if we may use the expression) perfectly original. They are the dictates of nature, unmixed and undisguised: they are therefore more easily comprehended and described. The Poet in describing his own feelings, describes also the feelings of others; for in such a state of society, these are similar and uniform in all. Their tastes, dispositions, and manners are thrown into the same mould, and generally formed upon one and the same model. Artless and tender loves, generous friendships, and warlike exploits, compose the history of this uncultivated period; and the Poet who relates these, feeling the inspiration of his subject, is himself animated with all the ardor of the Lover, the Friend, and the Hero. Hence as his sensations are warm and vivid, his sentiments will become passionate or sublime, as the occasion may require; his descriptions energetic; his stile bold, elevated, and metaphorical; and the whole, being the effusion of a glowing fancy and an impassioned heart, will be perfectly natural and original. . . .

A third cause of this quality's being remarkably exerted in an early period of society, is the leisure and tranquillity of uncultivated life, together with the innocent pleasures which generally attend it.

Genius naturally shoots forth in the simplicity and tranquillity of uncultivated life. The undisturbed peace, and the innocent rural pleasures of this primeval state, are, if we may so express it, congenial to its nature. A Poet of true Genius delights to contemplate and describe those primitive scenes, which recal to our remembrance the fabulous era of the golden age. Happily exempted from that tormenting ambition, and those vexatious desires, which trouble the current of modern life, he wanders with a serene, contented heart, through walks and groves consecrated to the Muses; or, indulging a sublime, pensive, and sweetly-soothing melancholy, strays with a slow and

solemn step, through the unfrequented desert, along the naked
beach, or the bleak and barren heath. In such a situation, every
theme is a source of inspiration, whether he describes the beauties of nature, which he surveys with transport; or the peaceful
innocence of those happy times, which are so wonderfully
soothing and pleasing to the imagination. His descriptions therefore will be perfectly vivid and original, because they are the
transcript of his own feelings. . . .

The last cause we shall assign why original Poetic Genius appears in its utmost perfection in the uncultivated ages of society,
is, its exemption from the rules and restraints of Criticism, and
its want of that knowledge which is acquired from books. . . .

Let us inquire into the effects of these, upon the mind of a
Poet possessed of a high degree of original Genius. By an
acquaintance with that Literature which is derived from books,
it will be granted, he may attain the knowledge of a great
variety of events, and see human nature in a great variety of
forms. By collecting the observations and experience of past
ages, by superadding his own, and by reasoning justly from
acknowledged principles, he may, no doubt, acquire more accurate and extensive ideas of the works of Nature and Art, and
may likewise be thereby qualified to inrich the Sciences with
new discoveries, as well as most of the Arts with new inventions
and improvements. In his own art only he can never become an
original Author by such means; nor, strictly speaking, so much
as acquire the materials, by the use of which he may justly attain
this character: for the ideas derived from books, that is, from
the ideas of others, can by no process of poetical chymistry confer perfect Originality. Those ideas which are the intire creation of the mind, or are the result of the Poet's own observations,
and immediately drawn from nature, are the only original ones
in the proper sense. A Poet who adopts images, who culls out
incidents he has met with in the writings of other Authors, and
who imitates characters which have been portrayed by other
Poets, or perhaps by Historians, cannot surely with any propriety be considered as an Original, though he may at the same

time discover considerable powers of Imagination in adapting those images and incidents, as well as transforming and molding these characters to the general design of his poem. In order to become a Poet perfectly original (of whom only it must be remembered we are here treating) he must, if he should attempt Epic Poetry, invent images, incidents and characters: tradition may indeed supply him with the groundwork of the poem, as it did Homer, but the superstructure must be altogether his own. In executing such a work, what aid can a truly original Poet receive from books? If he borrows aid from the performances of others, he is no longer a complete Original. To maintain this character throughout, he must rely on his own fund: his own plastic imagination must supply him with every thing. . . .

We may add, that another effect of learning is, to encumber and overload the mind of an original Poetic Genius. Indeed it has this effect upon the mind of every man who has not properly arranged its scattered materials, and who by thought and reflection has not "digested into sense the motley meal" [Young's *Night Thoughts*]. But however properly arranged those materials may be, and however thoroughly digested this intellectual food, an original Genius will sometimes find an inconveniency resulting from it; for as no man can attend to and comprehend many different things at once, his mental faculties will in some cases be necessarily oppressed and overcharged with the immensity of his own conceptions, when weighed down by the additional load of learning. The truth is, a Poet of original Genius has very little occasion for the weak aid of Literature: he is self-taught. He comes into the world as it were completely accomplished. Nature supplies the materials of his compositions; his senses are the under-workmen, while Imagination, like a masterly Architect, superintends and directs the whole. Or, to speak more properly, Imagination both supplies the materials, and executes the work, since it calls into being "things that are not," and creates and peoples worlds of its own. It may be easily conceived therefore, that an original Poetic Genius, possessing such innate treasure (if we may be allowed an unphilosophical expression) has no use for that which is derived from books, since he may be encumbered, but cannot be inriched by it; for though the chief merit of ordinary Writers may consist in arranging and presenting us with the thoughts of others, that of an original Writer will always consist in presenting us with such thoughts as are his own.

We observed likewise, that an exemption from the rules and restraints of Criticism, contributed greatly to the more remarkable display of original Poetic Genius in the first ages of society. Every species of original Genius delights to range at liberty, and especially original Poetic Genius, which abhors the fetters of Criticism, claims the privilege of the freeborn sons of Nature, and never relinquishes it without the utmost regret. This noble talent knows no law, and acknowledges none in the uncultivated ages of the world, excepting its own spontaneous impulse, which it obeys without control, and without any dread of the censure of Critics. . . .

Upon the whole, from the reasons above assigned, it seems evident, that the early uncultivated ages of society are most favourable to the display of original Genius in Poetry; whence it is natural to expect, that in such ages the greatest Originals in this art will always arise. Unhappily for us, this point does not admit of proof from an induction of many particulars; for very few original Poems of those nations among whom they might have been expected, have descended through the vicissitudes and revolutions of so many ages to our times. Most of the monuments of Genius, as well as the works of Art, have perished in the general wreck of empire; and we can only conjecture the merit of such as are lost from that of the small number of those which remain. While the Works of Homer and Ossian however are in our hands, these, without any other examples, will be sufficient to establish the truth . . . of our assertion, That in the early periods of society, original Poetic Genius will in general be exerted to its utmost vigour.

ABRAHAM TUCKER

(1705-74)

The most exciting adventures of this amiable country gentleman seem to have occurred in his armchair pursuit of the Light of Nature; he ran down a metaphysical point with the gusto of a Squire Western after a fox. According to his grandson, who later edited *The Light of Nature Pursued*, he spent most of his time quietly living on his estate, which he managed conscientiously, collecting information on rural economy from neighbors and "authors, both ancient and modern." He always refused to enter politics: his one attendance at a county meeting, though he was only an observer, resulted in his being lampooned in a ballad—which amused him so much that he set it to music. After the death of his wife, he collected all their letters and transcribed them in a manuscript entitled "The Picture of Artless Love," which he often read over to his two daughters.

Tucker published the first two parts of *The Light of Nature Pursued* in 1768, under the name of Edward Search. Earlier he had published a short excerpt on free will, using the same pseudonym; and he answered attacks on this in a pamphlet signed Cuthbert Comment. In 1778, after his death, his daughter Judith published the remainder of *The Light of Nature Pursued*, and in 1805 his grandson, H. P. St. John Mildmay, brought out a second edition with a biographical sketch. Hazlitt published an abridgment in 1807, encouraged by Coleridge, who promised an introduction, never written.

Tucker's discussion of the creative and "esemplastic" powers of the imagination is closer to the theories of Coleridge, Wordsworth, and Hazlitt than anything previously written in England. But his real attraction for the romantics, as, indeed, for the modern reader, must have been his combination of ingenuity, naïveté, and lively fancy. He can split hairs in distinguishing the powers of the mind, yet become so carried away with his description of the "vehicular people" (see below) that he describes them as confidently as he would a next-door neighbor. Hazlitt in his preface particularly praises Tucker's delightful illustrations for their unexpectedness, aptness, and accuracy of observation. Tucker, for all his protestations of being a plodding, microscopic reasoner, is a romancer among metaphysicians. In the long chapter, "The Vision," which follows that on "The Mundane Soul" included below, he slips from his philosopher's boots entirely, and in an extended flight of fancy imagines himself in the vehicular state: floating in an amoeba-like bag, pelted by corpuscles of light, he meets the vehicular John Locke, who adopts him, teaches him vehicular ways, and introduces him to various other vehicular personages, including his late wife. At one point Tucker's bag is punctured, and his soul merges for a moment with the world soul.

   The Light of Nature Pursued consists of three divisions: the first is "Human Nature," made up largely of an analysis of the faculties and activities of the mind, plus chapters on related topics such as "Use," "Honour," "Ultimate Good," and a series of virtues; the second is "Theology," which considers man's spiritual nature, including his fate after death; and the third is "Lights of Nature and Gospel Blended," which accommodates Tucker's ideas more or less with Christian orthodoxy, in such chapters as "Miracles," "Grace," "Trinity," "Redemption," "Divine Economy," "Fondness for Pleasures," and "Education." The text below is from the five-volume, 1768 edition.

The Light of Nature Pursued

HUMAN NATURE

CHAP. I

FACULTIES OF THE MIND

Whoever considers the frame and constitution of Man must observe that he consists of two parts, Mind and Body. And this division holds equally good whatever opinion we may entertain concerning the nature of the mind; for be it an immaterial substance, be it a harmony, or be it a certain configuration of corporeal particles, at all events it does not extend to the whole of the human composition. There are several things within us which cannot belong to the mind under any notion we may conceive of it; such as the bones, the muscles, the sinews, the blood, the humours, and even the limbs and organs of sensation, because by losing some of these we lose nothing of our mind: when an arm is cut off or an eye beat out, tho' the man become less perfect the mind remains entire as before; the harmony is not dissolved, the mental compound disunited or the spiritual substance destroyed. . . .

2. Now in pursuit of this enquiry we shall find it requisite to distinguish between the faculties of the mind and the faculties of the man, of whom the mind is only a part. For in all compounds there are some properties belonging to the parts separately, and others resulting from the composition or joint action of the united parts. . . .

We hear of many faculties ascribed to man, such as walking, handling or speaking, hearing, seeing or feeling, which manifestly do not belong to the mind, since it can exercise none of them without aid of the body: we can neither walk without legs, handle without arms, nor speak without a tongue; neither hear without ears, see without eyes, nor touch without fingers. But tho' the mind has some share in the performance of all these actions, yet the faculties it exerts are not so various as the operations it produces: for it is by one and the same faculty of the mind that we walk, handle or speak, and by one and the same faculty that we hear see or touch; which faculty produces different effects according to the different bodily organs whereto it is applied.

Nevertheless there is this difference observable with respect to the mind itself, that upon some occasions, as in walking, handling, speaking, it affects and acts upon the body; on others, as hearing, seeing, feeling, it is itself affected and acted upon by the body. Hence we reasonably gather that the mind possesses two faculties; one by which we perform whatever we do, and another by which we discern whatever presents itself to our apprehension. The former has usually been stiled the Will, and the latter the Understanding.

3. Faculty is the same as Power, or rather a particular sort of power; being generally appropriated to those powers only which belong to animals. . . .

Of the two faculties of the mind before spoken of one is active and the other passive: for on every exertion of our Will the mind causes some motion, change of situation, or alteration of the subject it acts upon; and in every exercise of our understanding the mind passes either from a state of insensibility to a

state of discernment, or from one kind of discernment to another, as from sights to sounds or tastes or reflections, according to the variety of objects that act upon it.

4. We readily enough conceive ourselves active in the exertions of our Will, but by the common turn of our language we
seem to claim an activity in the exercises of our understanding
too; for we generally express them by active verbs, such as to
discern, to see, to observe, and apply the passives of those very
verbs to the objects when we say they are discerned, seen, observed; all which carry an import of something done by ourselves and something suffered by the objects from us. Yet a
very little consideration may show us that in all sensations at
least the objects are agents and ourselves the patients. For what
is sight but an impression of things visible upon our eyes and by
them conveyed to the mind? what is sound but the percussion
of air upon our ears and thence transmitted thro' the like conveyance? In all these cases the sensations are caused by bodies
without us, and are such as the respective bodies are fitted to
produce: the mind can neither excite nor avoid nor change them
in any manner; it can neither see blue in a rose nor hear the
sound of a trumpet from a drum, but remains purely passive
to take whatever happens to it from external objects. Nor is the
case different in hunger and thirst, the pleasant feel of health
or uneasiness of distempers, tho' proceeding from internal
causes: for nobody can doubt of these sensations being raised
by the humours or some parts of our body, which tho' within
the man yet lie without the mind, and therefore with respect to
that are truly external agents.

8. Let us now consider voluntary reflection such as recollect-
ing, studying, meditating, reasoning, deliberating and the like,
wherein the mind from time to time calls up the thoughts it
wants and is if ever both agent and patient in the same act. Yet
even here, if we examine the matter closely, we shall find that
the mind does not call up all our thoughts directly by its own
immediate command, but seizes on some clue whereby it draws
in all the rest. In meditation, tho' we choose our subject we do

not choose the reflections from time to time occurring thereupon. In reasoning we seek after some conclusion which we
cannot obtain without help of the premises: or hit upon some
discovery, a stranger to our thoughts before, and therefore not
under our obedience. Deliberation and investigation are like
the hunting of a hound, he moves and sniffs about by his own
activity, but the scent he finds is not laid nor the trail he follows
drawn by himself. The mind only begins a train of thinking or
keeps it in one particular track, but the thoughts introduce one
another successively. . . . Whoever will carefully observe what
he does when he sets himself down to study may perceive that
he produces none of the thoughts passing in his mind, not even
that which he uses as the clue to bring in all the others: he first
withdraws his attention from sensible objects, nor does he then
instantly enter upon his work; some little time must be given
for reflection to begin its play, which presently suggests the
purpose of his enquiries to his remembrance and some methods
of attaining it; that which appears most likely to succeed he
fixes his contemplation upon and follows whithersoever that
shall lead, or checks his thoughts from time to time when he
perceives them going astray, or stops their course if he finds it
ineffectual, and watches for its falling into some new train: for
imagination will be always at work, and if restrained from
roving in all that variety of sallies it would make of its own
accord, it will strike into any passages remaining open. Therefore we may compare our student to a man who has a river running through his grounds which divides into a multitude of
channels: if he damms up all the rest, the stream will flow in
the one he leaves open; if he finds it breaking out into side
branches he can keep it within bounds by stopping up the out-
lets; if he perceives the course it takes ineffectual for his purpose he can throw a mound across and let it overflow at any
gap he judges convenient. The water runs by its own strength
without any impulse from the man, and whatever he does to it,
will find a vent some where or other: he may turn, alter or direct
its motion, but neither gave nor can take it away. So it is with our

thoughts which are perpetually working so long as we wake, and sometimes longer, beyond our power to restrain: we may controul them, divert them into different courses, conduct them this way or that as we deem requisite, but can never totally prevent them from moving. Which shows they have a motion of their own independent of the mind and which they do not derive from its action nor will lay aside upon its command.

10. . . . Idea is the same as image, and the term imagination implies a receptacle of images: but image being appropriated by common use to visible objects could not well be extended to other things without confusion; wherefore learned men have imported the Greek word idea signifying image or appearance, to which being their own peculiar property they might affix as large a signification as they pleased. . . .

When a peacock spreads his tail in our sight we have a full view of the creature with all his gaudy plumage before us: the bird remains at some distance, but the light reflected from him paints an image upon our eyes, and the optic nerves transmit it to the sensory. This image when arrived at the ends of the nerves becomes an idea and gives us our discernment of the animal; and after the bird is gone out of view we can recall the idea of him to perform the same office as before, tho' in a duller and fainter manner. So when the nightingale warbles, the sound reaches our ears and passing thro' the auditory nerves exhibits an idea affecting us with the discernment of her music: and after she has given over singing, the same idea may recur to our remembrance or be raised again by us at pleasure. In like manner our other senses convey ideas of their respective kinds, which recur again to our view long after the objects first exciting them have been removed.

These ideas having entered the mind intermingle, unite, separate, throw themselves into various combinations and postures, and thereby generate new ideas of reflection strictly so called, such as those of comparing, dividing, distinguishing, of abstraction, relation, with many others: all which remain with us as stock for our further use upon future occasions.

11. . . . When we look upon a peacock what is that image conveyed to us considered in the several stages thro' which it passes? Not any thing brought away by the light from the bird and thrown in upon us thro' our organs, but a certain disposition of the rays striking upon our eyes, a certain configuration of parts arising in our retina, or a certain motion excited thereby in our optic nerves: which disposition configuration and motion are not substances but accidents in ancient dialect, or modifications according to modern philosophers. But accident or modification cannot exist by itself, it must have some substance to inhere in or belong to, which substance is indeed the agent upon all occasions. Nevertheless we commonly ascribe the action to the modification because what kind it shall be of depends entirely upon that: for the same rays, the same retina, the same nerves differently modified by the impulse of external objects might have served to convey the image of an owl or a bear or any other animal to our discernment. Therefore that last substance, whatever it be, which immediately gives us the sensation is the agent acting upon our mind in all cases of vision: and in like manner that something so or so modified which presents to our discernment is the agent in all cases of mental reflection, which modification we call our idea: but because we know nothing more of the substance than the operation it performs, therefore if we would speak to be understood we can say no otherwise than that the idea is the thing we discern.

What those substances are whereof our ideas are the modification, whether parts of the mind as the members are of our body, or contained in it like wafers in a box, or enveloped by it like fish in water, as many expressions current in use might lead us to imagine, whether of a spiritual corporeal or middle nature between both, I need not now ascertain. . . . All I mean at present to lay down is this. That in every exercise of the understanding that which discerns is numerically and substantially distinct from that which is discerned: and that an act of understanding is not so much our own proper act as the act of something else operating upon us.

·   ·   ·   ·   ·

CHAP. III

CAUSES OF ACTION

. . . . .

2. Dr. Hartley gives us a very different account of sensation and muscular motion from all we ever learned before from our masters and tutors. We used to hear that the muscles and organs were so many bundles of nerves and fibres, which were little hollow pipes containing a very fine liquor called animal spirits; that these spirits were the carriers serving us in our traffic upon all occasions, perpetually hurrying to and fro, some carrying sensation from external objects to the mind and others bringing back motion from thence to the limbs. But he tells us the nerves are solid capilaments having neither hollowness nor liquor within them but surrounded on all sides with Ether, which is a subtile fluid extremely moveable and elastic, intimately pervading all bodies whatever, even the most compact and solid. That the nerves lie constantly upon the stretch like the strings of a harpsichord and like them quiver and vibrate upon the slightest touch received at either end, which vibrating causes similar vibrations in the circum-ambient Ether. That those vibrations of ether, which he calls sensory vibratiuncles, excite perceptions in the mind and at the same time agitate the ether standing round the muscular fibres, which agitation termed by him motory vibratiuncles, causes those fibres to vibrate and propagate their motion along one another quite to the fingers ends. That the sensory vibratiuncles, like waves raised in a pond upon throwing in a stone, extend to distant parts out of view, and being reverberated by the banks recoil again at other times, or mixing together form new vibratiuncles thereby furnishing us with ideas of reflection.

Thus the mind remains totally inactive, reduced to one faculty alone, for the Will, which he terms expressly a certain state of the vibratiuncles, belongs to the ether not to her: she sits a spectator only and not an agent of all we perform, she may indeed discern what is doing but has no share in what is done: like the fly upon the chariot wheel she fancies herself raising a cloud of dust but contributes nothing towards encreasing it: she may lay mighty schemes and rejoice in the execution but in reality does nothing herself, she can neither move the limbs nor call ideas to her reflection, the whole being brought to pass by the action of vibratiuncles upon one another. The mind in this case resembles a man who thrusts his hand among the works of a clock, he may feel the movements and by long practice may acquire a skill in distinguishing the hours and knowing when the clock will strike; if he perceives the hour of dinner approach, this may set his mouth a watering and raise an appetite of hunger, which he thinks influences his Will to strike and thereby give notice to the cook that it is time to take up dinner.

3. On the other hand the late bishop of Clogher [*sic* for Cloyne, i.e., Berkeley] goes into a contrary extreme, for he allows us neither ether nor nerves nor organs nor limbs nor external substances nor space nor distance. He does not deny we have perceptions of all these matters, but says we have no communion with the things themselves nor can penetrate into them, and therefore can know nothing of their existence, our knowledge consisting wholly of perceptions existent only in the mind: and since we find some perceptions totally dissimilar from any thing in the objects exciting them, as colour, sound, pain and pleasure, how can we assure ourselves the rest are not so likewise, such as magnitude, solidity, figure, situation and motion? Therefore for aught we can tell our perceptions may arise from other guised objects than these whereto we attribute them, or perhaps may all flow continually from one and the same source: and because they possibly may, he concludes, by an inference common among persons of lively imagination, that they certainly do. Thus the life of man turns out a meer vision and delusion. We dream of taking long journies, traversing countries, encompassing the globe, but really never stir a foot from

home: we please ourselves with the thought of traversing among an infinite variety of objects, whereas in good truth we sit in perpetual solitude having nothing but ourselves to converse with. . . .

But here occurs an objection from the regularity of perceptions arising upon the application of proper objects to excite them which seldom frustrate our expectation. When my fingers are cold, upon holding them to the fire I shall find them grow warm: if then I have neither fingers nor fire how comes it that I feel a real warmth from an imaginary fire? If I have neither mouth nor meat how comes it that I taste the savour of visionary roast beef? Oh! says the right reverend, our perceptions are thrown upon us by an invisible intelligent Agent, who supplies them in such regular order that they may seem to come in a chain of causes and effects. If you have a perception of cold in your fingers and of a fire in the room, this is followed by a perception of approaching them to the fire, which again is followed by a perception of warmth. And this succession of perceptions often extends to different persons in order to keep up our intercourse with one another. . . .

4. Thus these two gentlemen represent the mind as an idle insignificant thing never acting at all but always gaping and staring at what passes. Both equally divest her of all employment whatsoever tho' in different ways: one by finding other hands to compleat all her business for her and so leaving her no work to do: and the other by sweeping away her whole stock of materials and so leaving her nothing to work upon.

But tho' they seem to stand directly in my way I have so little the spirit of opposition that I shall not endeavour to push them if I can any how slip by them. Wherefore to avoid dispute I shall not put myself upon the country leaving the matter in issue to a fair trial by my neighbours upon a full and fair examination of such evidence as their own experience shall offer. And as I find the opinions above cited have not made many converts among mankind I need not be in much pain for the verdict.

In the mean while I shall venture to proceed upon these

Postulata: That the bodies we daily see and handle actually exist in as great variety of magnitudes forms and situations as we commonly suppose, and our operations upon them are of our own performance: that Westminster hall is bigger than a nutshell and the Moon somewhat higher than the weather-cock: that the cloaths I wear are not the same thing with the glass window I look at; that I hold a real pen and have a real paper before me, that my hand would not write unless I moved it, that the thoughts I write down are the products of my own labour and study; and that the ideas floating in my brain would produce neither meditation nor outward action if I forbore to exert myself. . . .

6. But notwithstanding that we have assumed the mind an efficient cause we must acknowledge she has not strength enough to do our business alone without some foreign help. . . . The old notion of the mind's existing like the estate of a coparcener in law jargon per my and per tout, or being all in every part throughout the whole human frame has been long since exploded: we now rest convinced that the mind does not act herself upon the limbs but draws them to and fro by tendons, muscles, nerves and fibres, which latter our anatomists have traced to the brain where they find them grow smaller and smaller till at last they quite lose them thro' their extreme minuteness: and tho' we cannot thoroughly agree where she resides yet wherever her place of residence be she keeps constantly there in kingly state, never making wanton excursions to the toes or fingers but exercising her executive power upon them by the ministry of those imperceptible fibres.

Now there needs not much argument to show that if you are to act upon bodies at a distance by some string or other medium you cannot exert more strength upon them than your medium will bear: consequently the mind be she as mighty as a giant can impart no more of her might to the limbs than her fibres are capable of conveying: what could Goliah or Sampson do if you allowed them only a single cobweb to work with? . . .

8. Wherefore it seems more than probable the mind has always

some good friend at hand ready to assist her weakness, and the main of that strength she exerts upon the limbs comes from some other quarter than her own store-house. Whether this help flows from the animal spirits ether or that unknown pressure causing gravitation and cohesion or what else you please 'tis no matter: but that there is another force within us besides our own capable of acting upon the muscles we may be convinced by convulsive motions wherein the mind has no concern nor volition any share, yet they sometimes imitate and generally exceed the vigour of our voluntary actions. Perhaps there lies a mighty weight of some subtile fluid thereon from our animal circulation and bearing constantly against the orifices of our nerves, but prevented from entring by certain little sliding valves kindly provided by nature for our use: the mind then has nothing more to do than draw aside the valves and in rushes the torrent. The mind in this case works like the miller of an over-shot mill, he has shoots lying over every one of his wheels stopped by flash-boards at their upper ends, against which the water lies bearing always ready to drive the wheels whenever it can find a passage: so the miller by drawing a little board which any child might pull up with a finger, turns the stream upon this wheel or that as he pleases and twirls round a massive stone which he could not stir with both his arms. . . .

As we ascribe the grinding of our corn to an act of the miller because he sets the mill at work when and in what manner he pleases; we may with equal justice ascribe our actions to the performance of the mind because it depends entirely upon her of what kind they shall be. If we consider them as acts of the mind they extend no further than to drawing back the valves whereof she remains the sole efficient cause: if as acts of the man we may still deem her an efficient cause, because the other powers co-operating stand always ready in waiting for her direction, and whatever happens afterwards follows necessarily in the nerves muscles or limbs in consequence of the motion by her first begun.

·   ·   ·   ·   ·

CHAP. IX

COMBINATION OF IDEAS

From the ideas thus received by sensation and reflection there grows a new stock framed up of these as of so many materials by their uniting together in various assemblages and connections. This their junction I choose to call by the name of Combination, as being more comprehensive than Composition, the term usually employed. For our ideas combine together in two several manners: one by composition, when they so mix and as I may say melt together as to form one single complex idea, generally denoted by one name, as a man, a table, a dozen; the other by association, when they appear in couples strongly adhering to each other but not blended into the same mass, as darkness and apparitions, the burst of a cannon or push of a drawn sword and the dread of mischief accompanying them. For when we think of a man we conceive him to be one thing, and his body, limbs, rationality, with other ingredients of his essence as parts of the same whole: but when we reflect on a naked sword we do not consider that and the terror occasioned thereby as parts of any compound, altho' the one constantly attends the other beyond all possibility of separating them in the mind of a fearfull person.

2. To begin with composition, wherein I shall not attempt to reckon up how many sorts of complex ideas we have, that having been done already by Mr. Locke much better than I can pretend to, but shall examine how composition itself is effected, which it did not fall in his way directly to consider. . . .

3. Composition I apprehend is preceeded by a selection of some ideas from the rest exhibited at the same time to our view, as a necessary preparative thereto. For as a lady who would make a curious piece of shell-work must first pick out the proper shells from the drawers wherein they lie before she can dispose them into figures: so there can be no compound formed in the imagination until the particular ideas whereof it is to con-

sist be disengaged from all others presented in company with them. This separation is partly made by the objects themselves striking more strongly upon the senses and appearing eminently above their fellows; but I conceive the mind has a principal share in the business by turning her notice upon some particular objects preferably to others standing together before her.

Nature at first presents her objects in a chaos or confused multitude wherein there is nothing distinct, nothing connected. When the new born babe comes into the world, the sight of things in the chamber, the gabblings and handlings of the gossips and perhaps some smells and tastes, rush in at all the five avenues of sensation and accost the mind in one act of perception. The nurse's arms appear no more belonging to her body than the wainscot seen on each side of them: and the midwife's voice has no more relation to the person than to the bedpost. But as objects do not strike with equal force, the more glaring and striking give a stronger impulse to the organs, which continue the motion imparted therefrom after that of the feebler impulses have entirely ceased: and thus the former become selected in the reflection out of the rest entring in company with them. And as our organs acquire a disposition of falling more readily into modifications they have been thrown into before, hence frequency of appearance produces the same effect with vigour of impression, and sensations continually repeated become distinguished from others received more rarely.

4. Both those causes, strength of impression and frequency of appearance, are greatly assisted by the operation of the mind: for some objects affecting us agreably and others appearing indifferent, she fixes her notice upon the former for sake of the satisfaction received therefrom, which gives them an advantage above their fellows. Every one remarks how constantly the eyes of a young child follow the candle about the room whithersoever you carry it: and when we come to man's estate we often pursue particular objects through all the motions and turnings they make before us. We have not indeed quite the same command over our ears and other senses, yet among variety of

sounds, smells, tastes or touches accosting us at the same time we can pick out some in disregard to the rest; and we can do the like with respect to different senses. A man who reads in a room where there is company talking may mind his book without taking notice of anything they say, or may listen to their discourse without minding a word of what he reads. . . .

5. But objects that shine eminently above their fellows or on which the notice fixes are not always single objects; for two or more may appear equally conspicuous, or may give a pleasure jointly which each of them separately could not have afforded: this happening often cements them together and makes them coalesce into one assemblage. Another cause of coalescence arises from objects constantly presenting themselves together: most of the bodies we are conversant amongst being compound bodies, the parts of them preserve their contiguity to one another while they move from place to place altho' they change their situation with respect to other bodies surrounding them; hence the ideas of those parts uniting together form an assemblage. When nurse walks about the room she carries her arms along with her, but not the wainscot seen on each side of them: when she goes out every part of her disappears, and when she returns the whole of her figure presents again to the eye, and by frequent use becomes apprehended by the child in one complex idea. Nor can it be doubted what efficacy the consorting of objects has towards compounding them, when we reflect that we scarce know our own acquaintance in an unusual dress and how surprizing alteration a different coloured wig makes in a man's person: so that the cloaths we have been accustomed to see worn seem to enter into our complex idea of the wearer. So likewise ideas that use or conveniency has led us to consider frequently together become a compound, as a yoak of oxen, a flock of sheep, a city, a country. . . .

13. I shall have the less to say upon Association because of the near affiinity it bears to Composition, depending upon the same causes and subject to the same variations: and perhaps composition is nothing more than an association of the several ideas

entring into a complex. What shall be the one or the other seems to depend generally upon the use of language: for if things arising to the thought constantly in company have a name given them we deem them compounded, if none we can only call them associated. Names being a receptacle in great measure necessary for gathering our ideas and holding them together in a complex: like those cushions your gossips stick with pins in hearts, lozenges and various forms against a lying in; the cushion is no part of the figure, yet if that should chance to fall into the fire and be consumed, the pins must all tumble down in disorder and the figures composed of them vanish. It is not always easy to determine when ideas combined together belong to the class of compounds or associates: perhaps the connection between the looks and sentiments of persons, which I have mentioned under composition, others might call association: nor is it very material to ascertain the limits between the two classes exactly. But since there are combinations which cannot with any propriety be stiled complex ideas, I thought proper to take some notice of them apart.

· · · · ·

CHAP. XII

IMAGINATION AND UNDERSTANDING

We have observed at our entrance upon these enquiries that a compound may have properties resulting from the composition which do not belong to the parts singly whereof it consists. Therefore though the mind, taken in the strict and philosophical sence, possesses only two faculties, the active and the perceptive, this does not hinder but that the mind in the vulgar and grosser acceptation may possess a greater variety of faculties, such as discerning, remembring, thinking, studying, contemplating and a multitude of others; which are but different modes or species of perception, varying according to the state of the

ideas there are to be perceived, and are all reducible under two
general classes, Imagination and Understanding; neither of them
born with us, but acquired by use and practice, and the latter
growing out of the former. We come into the world a meer
blank, void of all inscription whatsoever. Sensation first begins
the writing and our internal sense or reflection encreases the
stock, which runs into various assortments and produces other
ideas different from the root whereout they spring; whence we
quickly become provided with store of assemblages, associations, trains and judgements.

These stores together with the repository containing them we
may stile the Imagination, the very word implying so much; for
being derived from image, which is the same as idea, it imports
the receptacle of ideas. And whatever number of them is excited
by external objects or presented by the mechanical workings
of our animal spirits or other causes I call an Act of imagination
or Scene exhibited thereby. I know that imagination is applied
in common discourse to ideas purely imaginary having no existence in truth and nature, such as a Cyclops, a Chimera, the
enchanted island of Circe, or whimsical adventures of Panta-
gruel. But we find rhetoricians and critics extending the term
to pictures of real originals drawn in the mind by descriptions
of scenes actually existing or occurrencies actually happening.
Mr. Addison in his essay on the pleasures of imagination treats
of those conveyed by the works of art and nature. Therefore I
shall not offend against propriety by taking the word in the
largest sence, as comprehending every representation to the
mind, whether of things real or fantastical, either brought into
view by some sensation or starting up of their own accord.

Among these ideas some being more engaging than the rest
attract the notice particularly to ourselves: the mental eye
singles them out from the whole scene exhibited before it, sees
them in a stronger light, holds them longer in view, and thereby
gives occasion to their introducing more of their own associates
than they could have done in the rapidity of their natural
course. This operation of the notice being frequently repeated

at length becomes itself an object of our observation, and thus we discover a power we have of heightning the colour of our ideas, of changing or directing their course by the application of our notice: and the exercise of this power I take to be what is commonly meant by an Act of the Understanding.

2. Thus there are three ways in which ideas are made to affect us: by mechanical causes, when either sensible objects excite them or the working of our animal spirits throws them up; by the notice being drawn to fix upon some appearing eminently inviting above their fellows; and by exerting this power of the notice purposely in order to discern them more fully or bring in others that do not occur of themselves. The two first belong to imagination and the last to understanding.

To render my notion of this division the clearer I shall endeavour to illustrate it by an example. Suppose a servant wench in London, after being fatigued with several hours hard labour, can get up stairs to repose herself a while in indolence. She squats down upon a chair, shuts her eyes, and falls into a state between sleeping and waking; but her fancy roves upon the work she has been doing, the utensils employed therein, and the chit chat of her fellow servants. If the cat mews at the door this changes the scene to puss's exploits in catching mice or her fondling tricks while she lay purring in somebody's lap; until some other sensation or turn of fancy leads on a new train of ideas. Hitherto all proceeds mechanically: volition remains wholly inactive, there being nothing alluring enough to raise a desire of retaining it in view, but the images pass lightly and nimbly along according to the impulse received from the causes exciting them, without leaving any trace of themselves behind. Presently there arises a great noise and hubbub in the street. This rouzes up the girl and carries her in all haste to the window. She sees a crowd of people and in the midst of them Mylord Mayor going by in procession. She minds nothing of the houses before her nor the mob jostling one another below, for the prancing horses with their gorgeous trappings engage her whole attention, until drawn from them by the great coach all glorious

with sculpture gold and paintings, which she follows with her
eye as far as it can be discerned distinctly. Then the sheriffs
and whatever else appear remarkable in the train have their share
in her notice: which impresses the objects whereon it fixes so
strongly that the traces of them remain in her reflection after
the objects themselves have been removed, and perhaps raise a
curiosity of knowing what could be the occasion of this parade.
Thus far imagination only is employed: but curiosity puts her
upon searching for the means of gratifying it, which not occurring readily she must use her understanding to discover and
pursue them. So she examines the sheet almanac pasted up behind the door to see what holiday it might be, but finding none
she casts about in her thoughts for some other way of account-
ing for the coach of state being brought out; when at last it may
be she recollects that somebody had told her there was to be an
address presented to day to his Majesty.

3. Although in the second article of the division abovemen-
tioned our active power be employed as well as in the third, yet
it is manifest we proceed in a different manner. In the former
we act inadvertently, heedlessly and without thinking, drawn
only to pursue certain objects that happen to strike upon our
fancy: in the other we act knowingly and designedly with a
view to introduce some other idea not already within our prospect, and with a consciousness and reflection upon what we
are a doing. For there is a reflex act whereby the mind turns inward upon herself to observe what ideas arise in her view or
what effect her activity has upon them or the bodily members,
distinct from that whereby she produces those effects. The one
is commonly called reflecting and the other acting, and both
may be performed at the same time, or the latter singly without
the former. The beginning of our lives I apprehend passes wholly
without this reflection, which we acquire in time and by degrees.
When we have discovered our power of directing the notice and
attained some expertness in the management of that power, we
may be said to have arrived at the use of our understanding.

The degrees of exertion in both faculties are very various,

from the intensest study down to that common reflection we make in the ordinary transactions of life; and from that steddy attention to very engaging scenes to the transient notice we take of objects moderately alluring when they pass swiftly in succession before us. All strong efforts of the understanding are laborious and fatiguing, visibly wasting the spirits and affecting the head and stomach if continued long, nor have the most abstracted reasonings less of that effect than others: which seems an undeniable evidence that when the mind is thought to be most retired and to converse solely with herself, she nevertheless uses some instrument or organ and employs the bodily forces in carrying on her work.

It is common to stile those actions mechanical that are performed without thought or forecast, especially if we cannot discover any inducement that led us into them, for we ascribe them to the force of habit or impulse of passion or fancy: but howmuchsoever habit or fancy may have thrown up the ideas, the motions ensuing thereupon could not have been produced without the agency of the mind. This was proper to be remarked, because if we take the microscope and examine the minute constituent parts of action, we shall find that far the greater number of them, although certainly performed by our active power, are yet directed by sudden transient ideas starting up from time to time spontaneously. But those ideas skim so lightly as to leave no print of their foot in the memory, therefore if we look for them the moment after we cannot find them and so persuade ourselves there were none. When a man walks he moves his legs himself, yet they seem to move habitually and involuntarily without any care of his to make them step right and left alternately or to ascertain the length of their paces: nor is it an easy matter for him with his utmost attention to discern the ideas that occasion this regularity of their motions.

4. To this inadvertent action of the mind we owe that dexterity in the use of our powers which is supposed to be an immediate gift of nature: for we are not born with the faculty of walking or handling or speaking. When little children go

to put their coral into their mouths they do not know how to get it thither, but hit it against their chin or rub it about their cheek: when you would set them to walk they jump with both legs at once or lift up their foot as if they were to step over a stile: and the first sounds they make are none other than those of grunting and crying. But the ideas formed daily in their imagination lead them on step by step to the management of their limbs and first rudiments of speech, before they are capable of anything that can be called learning or application. And afterwards we catch many little habits by accident or imitation, or fall into ways of acting by the force of example, or grow more perfect in our manner of proceeding meerly by dint of practice. Nor does imagination stand idle even in those seasons wherein we most employ our understanding, but makes many bye motions of her own or acts an under part assisting to execute the plan laid by her partner.

For understanding endeavours to extend her prospect as far and wide as she can stretch: she aims at distant ends, considers remote consequences, joins the past and future with the present, and contemplates imperfect ideas in order to strike out from thence something that may be a surer ground of our proceeding. Therefore she can direct only our larger actions, drawing the outlines of them or giving the main turns to our courses of behaviour, but leaves the intermediate spaces to be filled up by habit or the transient ideas starting up in train to our notice. She moves too slowly to give constant employment to our active power, which while she is deliberating must take its directions elsewhere.

5. Thus it appears that imagination actuates most of our motions and serves us perpetually in all the purposes of life, which understanding recommends, but the habitual and spontaneous rising of ideas prompts and directs us to compleat. . . .

6. Hence we may judge of how great importance it is to have a well regulated and well exercised imagination, which if we could possess compleatly it would answer all our occasions better with more ease and dispatch than we could compass them

in any other way. But as nature has not given us this faculty in perfection nor will it grow up to full stature of its own accord, she has endued us with the privilege of understanding to form and improve it. Therefore it is our business to range our ideas into such assortments and trains as are best adapted to our purposes; to bring them under command so as that they may be ready for any services to be required of them; and continually to keep a watchfull eye over them while at work to prevent their deviating into wrong channels.

Nor would understanding herself find so constant employment as she does were it not for some principles and views laid up in store which start up occasionally to set her at work. For who would consider or study or contrive unless to attain some purpose suggested to his reflection? Thus understanding often begins and terminates in imagination, which nevertheless does not derogate from its excellency, because very few of our most necessary and usefull purposes could ever be attained without it. And indeed understanding may justly claim the merit of those very exploits performed by habit or expertness, when it was owing to her care and diligence that they were acquired, or to her command and contrivance that they had their proper cues given and proper tasks assigned them.

7. For the most part both faculties go hand in hand co-operating in the same work, one sketching out the design and the other executing the performance: but sometimes we find them acting at once in different employments. When two persons engage earnestly together in discourse as they walk, their thoughts are wholly intent upon the subject of their conversation: but the transient notices of their senses and their habitual dexterity in the management of their limbs guide them in the mean while through all the turnings of their path. And thus they may go currently on while the path lies smooth and open: but should anything unusual happen in the way, and attention be so fully taken up as not to spare a glance away from the object that holds it, they may chance to run against a post or stumble over a stone. Your profound thinkers are sometimes absent in company and

commit strange mistakes for want of attending to the objects around them; or perhaps set out for one place and strike into the way leading to another. Which shows that the slightest and most common matters cannot be carried on safely without some degree of thought and observation: not that habit and imagination cannot find employment for our active powers of themselves, but it is a great chance they wander from the plan assigned them unless kept in order by frequent directions from understanding.

Thus the mind may be said to have two eyes, in their situation rather resembling those of a hare or a bird than a human creature, as being placed on opposite sides and pointed towards different sets of objects. Or may be more aptly compared to a man looking at a common field through a telescope with one eye, still holding the other open: with the naked eye he sees the several lands, their length and shape and the crops growing on each; with the glass he sees only one little spot, but in that he distinguishes the ears of corn, discerns butterflies fluttering about and swallows shooting athwart him. Sometimes both eyes turn upon the same prospect, one tracing the larger and tother the minuter parts: at other times they take different courses, one pursuing a train of little objects that have no relation to the scenes contemplated by the other.

8. Whatever knowledge we receive from sensation, or fall upon by experience, or grow into by habit and custom, may be counted the produce of imagination: and to this we may refer the evidence of the senses, the notices of appetite, our common notions and conceptions of things, and all that rises up spontaneously in our memory. Whatever has been infused into us by carefull instruction, or worked out by thought and industry, or gained by attentive observation, may be stiled the attainments of understanding: among which may be reckoned what skill we have in any art or science, or in language, or in conducting the common affairs of life, or what we bring to our remembrance by recollection. Our tastes, sentiments, opinions and

moral senses I apprehend belong partly to one class and partly to the other: their seat lies in the imagination, but they are introduced there sometimes by an industrious use of the understanding, and sometimes by the mechanical influence of example and custom.

· · · · ·

VOLUME II

THEOLOGY

CHAP. XXI

VEHICULAR STATE

When death puts an end to the animal circulation we see the body remains a meer lump of sluggish matter showing no signs either of perception or activity, from whence we naturally conclude that the spirit is departed from her: but whether or no it carries any thing away with it we are wholly uncertain, we see nothing fly off upon the last groan, but our senses are not acute enough to assure us that nothing does fly off. Therefore by virtue of the privilege constantly claimed in making an hypothesis I may fairly assume, what nobody can disprove, that the spirit upon quitting her present mansion does not go out naked nor entirely disengaged from matter, but carries away with her an integument from among those wherewith she was before invested. And I am far from being singular in this notion, for many wiser men have assigned a fine vehicle for the habitation of the spirit after its being divested of flesh and blood; and the ancients generally painted the soul or Psyche with butterflies wings, to represent that she came out with a new body as a butterfly does from the Chrysalis: nor do I want the best established authority in my support, for the apostle Paul compares the body to a seed which rots and perishes in the ground, nevertheless a germ survives producing another plant bearing some resemblance to that which generated the seed.

2. But we must suppose this vehicle extremely small so that the nicest eye may not discern it when going, nor the finest scales discover an abatement of weight in what remains after it is gone: yet it must contain an organization capable of exhibiting a greater variety of ideas than we now experience. No doubt it will appear strange and extravagant to the generality to imagine that so many organs of sensation and reflection and instruments of action as a man possesses in his present condition can ever be contained in a body so small as to be undiscoverable by the finest balance or the most piercing eye; for so must every thing appear that differs widely, whether in size or composition, from the objects we have been constantly conversant with. The young fellow who has never been in a nursery since he has left his own, the first time he sees a new born babe he is apt to wonder at its littleness: and if he dips into a treatise on the formation of a fœtus, can scarce believe the lineaments of a human body could be comprized within so narrow a compass as he sees there described. Thus every further reduction of size gives a fresh shock to his imagination until familiarized thereto by frequent contemplation; for things are no longer strange than while new to the thought. . . . What clogs our comprehension in . . . minute divisions is that we commonly think of making them by dividing the whole without dividing the parts, which must certainly spoil the composition. If St. Paul's church were cut in halves, each half would not be a church; if into quarters or lesser proportions they would still be more remote from the plan of the architect; but were all the stones, the timbers, the ornaments proportionably lessened, the whole form, disposition and symmetry might still remain the same though reduced to the bigness of a nut-shell. This indeed is what the clumsy hand of man could never do, but nature is a finer artificer than man, and I doubt not might succeed if she would undertake it. So if she were to waste away one half of a

man from the head downward without destroying his vital and animal functions, yet he would have but one arm and one leg and must lose many of his powers: but if she lessened all his component parts, his bones, his muscles, his fibres, the globules of his blood and other juices in equal degree, he might still continue a man, how small soever reduced, with the same variety of powers and faculties as before. He could not indeed exercise them upon the same objects he used, but she wants not means of furnishing him with other materials useless and unknown to him before but suitable to the condition she has thrown him into. And it may be presumed he would be better able to manage them, his strength not decreasing in proportion to his size, because small bodies are more compact and solid than the larger made up of them, for composition always adds to the quantity of pore in the compound. A bushel of pease has less specific gravity than the single pease it contains, because there will be hollow spaces between each pea and its neighbours besides the pores within their substances: and if a multitude of bushels be packed up in a room there will be vacancies between them besides those among their contents. Therefore the finer parts a body contains, the fewer atoms they must severally consist of (for these cannot be divided), the less of pore there will be among them, and consequently its nerves and sinews will be so much tougher and stronger.

3. And as the limbs and instruments of action in such a little body will be stronger with respect to the materials they have to deal with, so likewise must they be more agile and pliant: for this we find to be the case between animals of similar make, whose motions are commonly more unwieldy in proportion to their largeness. A little horse shifts his legs quicker than a tall one; the vulture and the eagle cannot flutter their wings so fast as the sparrow; nor did you ever see a hornet crawl so nimbly along the table as a fly; and little men are generally the quickest in their motions. Imagine a race of giants as big as Hampstead hill placed on an earth which with all its animals, fruits, corn, trees and vegetables should be proportionably vast: they might

then have the same accommodations as we have but could not find the same uses and convenience in them by reason of the tediousness of their motions. Consider how long they must be at dinner; if they sat down at eight in the morning they would scarce finish their repast by night, having a mile to carry every morsel from their plate to their mouths; when they went to bed it must take an hour to get up stairs, and after having unbuttoned their coat they must give their arm a swing of two or three miles round to pull down the sleeve behind; when they talked together it would require four or five seconds for their voices to reach one another's ears; and as it may be supposed their mental organs are conformable in size to their bodily, if you asked what's o'clock it might be necessary to consider half an hour before they could think of the proper answer. In short they must needs be a slow, solemn and heavy generation, without any spark of wit or liveliness belonging to them. If one of us were migrated into their enormous hulks, should we not, think ye, wish ardently to get back again into our less than six-foot bodies? and by parity of reason it may be presumed that when delivered from our present cumbersome bodies, if we remember anything of our situation therein, we shall be as much rejoiced to find ourselves in a body proportionably less and proportionably more alert and vigorous, wherein we may dispatch as much business in a minute as we can now in an hour, and perhaps be able to read through Guicciardine in the time we are now poring over all the nothings in a four-columned newspaper. . . .

4. I have hitherto spoken of the vehicles as little diminutive men with arms, legs and so forth such as we have; but I do not think so narrowly of nature as to pronounce with Epicurus that she cannot form a reasonable creature unless in a human shape. It seems to me more agreable to reason, at least more soothing to the imagination and better suited to our expectations of exchanging this present mansion for a more commodious, to suppose them not made in the shape nor provided with the limbs of any animal whatever, but consisting all of muscle and fibre,

tough and strong but extremely flexible and obedient to the Will, susceptible of any shape and in every part capable of being cast into any member of any animal, of being made soft as a feather or hard as a bone. We have some few imperfect samples of this changeableness in our own composition: our tongue lies round and yielding in our mouths, yet we can thrust it out to a considerable length, make it push with some force or support a small weight hung upon it by a string. . . . We can open our hands into five movable fingers for any nice or nimble work, or we can close them into a kind of hammer for striking, or bend them in rigid hooks for pulling. We have but one windpipe to sing, to talk, to whine, to rant, to scold with, nevertheless we can cast this single instrument into as many various forms as there are voices and tones of voice we utter: whereas were it necessary to have a different pipe for every articulate sound our throats must have been made bigger than a chamber organ. Thus we see how great advantage and convenience must accrue upon the members being convertible to many uses: and at the same time this may lessen our amazement at the multitude of powers we suppose comprized within so narrow a compass, for there may be more powers of action without requiring more works than we have in our present machinery; especially if the works be simpler, not consisting of a multitude of parts whose operation must be propagated from one to another and all concur to perform every single action, whereby the variety of our motions must needs be greatly contracted. You may have a bell-handle hanging by your chimney side with which by means of strings and pulleys you may ring a bell at tother end of the house: but you can only jerk it towards you, and cannot give it so many shakes up and down, to and fro, quick and gentle, as if you held the bell itself in your hand. In like manner we act upon external bodies with gross members lying at an immense distance from the seat of our activity, requiring a long contrivance of strings and pulleys to give us any command of them; we move our limbs by our bones, the bones by tendons, the tendons by muscles, the muscles by nerves, and the nerves perhaps by a series of imperceptible fibres which no anatomy can investigate: whereas were the externals needfull for our uses so sized as that we could apply our first fibres immediately to them, we might manage them a hundred times more handily, expeditiously and cleverly.

5. And the same advantage accruing from the great flexibility of fibres to cast themselves into the form of any limb occasionally as shall be wanted may be extended likewise to the organs of sensation, which are only so many textures of network variously woven from similar threads. The retina of the eye, whereon all our visible objects are painted, takes its name from a net; the auditory nerves are represented to us by anatomists as expanded in a reticular form at the bottom of the ear; the like is told us of the olfactory nerves spread over the lamellæ composing the ossa spongiosa of the nose; of the gustatory papillæ of the tongue, and tactile papillæ of the fingers and all the rest of our body. Now if we had the power of changing the position of our threads, what should hinder but that we might cast them into any texture fitted to receive the vibrations exciting any sensation we pleased; so as to see or hear or smell or taste or feel with the same organ according to the qualities of external objects striking upon it? . . .

6. Such little bodies likewise must be directly under the action of the mind in more of their parts without needing the complicated machinery of strings or engines to propagate it to them: for the minds immediate activity reaches no further than the sphere of her presence, which can never be enlarged, therefore the smaller body she inhabits the greater proportion of it will fall within her presence and subject to her command. . . .

10. Perhaps it may give disturbance to some folks to think of being reduced to such contemptible animals tenderer than a worm and weaker than a flea: but let them consider that the strongest creatures upon earth are not the most favoured by nature, the mighty elephant, the vigorous horse and the unwearied ox are governed by man, and among our own species the most robust and athletic are generally of the lowest rank.

... We in our present state have large works to do in providing for our sustenance, our cloathing, our habitation and accommodations of life, powerfull enemies to cope with and great beasts to employ in our services, all which we could not manage without a consistency of flesh and bones and some competency of bodily strength: but the vehicular people have no such bulky wares to move about. . . .

11. For their bodies contain nothing superfluous nor that number of vessels concerned in our animal circulation, but consist chiefly of sensory and motory fibres; so that every part lies within the observation and under command of the mind. If anything insinuate into their composition which might create diseases they can remove it as easily as we can wash the dirt off from our hands: their faculties are more piercing, their understandings better furnished with materials and less liable to be overclouded than ours: and they can throw their vehicle occasionally into such form as to receive what kind of sensation they choose from external objects, so as to make it all eye or all ear or some other sense we know nothing of, or a mixture of several. Nor need we fear lest a multiplicity of ideas should perplex and confound them, for perceptions take up no room in the mind nor does she ever find herself unable to receive as many as her organs can excite. Confusion springs from the darkness and imperfection of our ideas, not from an incapacity in the mind to perceive such as are presented clear and distinct. And as they are fitted for discerning minuter objects than we can distinguish, they will have an opportunity of observing the motions of those subtil fluids whereon gravitation, cohesion, magnetism, electricity, heat, explosion, vegetation, muscular motion and sensation depend, which will furnish them with sciences to us unknown. We find that light discovers to us the form and situation of bodies at an immense distance, and when we reflect how extremely movable and elastic the ether is known to be, we may conclude that no single particle of gross matter can stir without affecting its vibrations to a prodigious distance: this then may answer their purposes better than light does ours,

and inform them accurately of the positions, the distances, the magnitudes, the motions of all the visible universe. By which means they will have a full display of nature before them from the most magnificent of her works to the most curious and minute: nor can they fail of rising from thence to a compleater knowledge of the author of nature, his greatness, his wisdom, his goodness, than we can attain. And perhaps they may fathom that to us inscrutable mystery, the origin of evil, so as to reconcile it perfectly with their ideas of unlimited power and infinite goodness.

12. Nor can we deny them the means of discourse and correspondence with one another: ours we know is carried on by arbitrary signs either of sounds or letters, and any other marks that might be exhibited with equal facility, variety and distinctness would do as well: therefore we cannot but suppose that such agile creatures, all nerve and sensory, may form characters upon their vehicle, or throw off little particles of the fluids surrounding them, or find twenty other ways of communicating their thoughts. Nor can we deny them methods of transporting themselves from place to place, not in the manner we walk by pushing our feet against the stable ground, but rather like the steerage of a ship whose sails are set before or sidelong to the wind, receiving the direct or oblique impulse of the little streams passing continually on all sides of them, with such dextrous management as not to be thrown aside from their intended course. It would be in vain to conjecture what are their common employments and amusements, but enough has been suggested to show they do not want for either, and perhaps we may find more subjects to occupy their time than these: but amid the variety of objects and ideas continually presenting it cannot be doubted there will be some of the agreable and disagreable kind which will demand their care to procure the one and avoid the other or to assist one another upon occasion, from whence will arise desires and aims, prudential maxims and rules of conduct, the one perpetually instigating their activity, the other directing their measures. And if the idea of evil be requisite to action, they

will not want samples of actual suffering in some of their compatriots who will come infirm and maimed into their world by reason of hurts received in ours. . . .

14. . . . [The] vehicle or inner sensory constituting us rational creatures we received before our birth: it continues with us during our lives, enabling us to perceive and understand the notices brought from external objects by our bodily organs, the traces lying in our memory and all those stores of knowledge contained in the repository of our ideas: it remains entire after dissolution of the body, and though it can neither think nor reason after losing all its former ideas and materials to work upon, yet retains its rationality and cogitative faculty ready to be exercised upon whatever objects a fresh set of senses shall throw in or new experience supply. Nor let it be objected that I make the memory one of those parts that shall be left behind, so that the naked soul, how quick soever its perceptions may be, will have no retention. . . . Without troubling ourselves to conjecture the particular manner we may depend upon that wisdom by which all the laws of nature are established to provide means of exercising so necessary a faculty without which there can be neither understanding nor reason, neither prudence nor judgement. Thus we may conclude that the soul will be born into another life as much a blank paper as ever she came into this, having all the characters formerly written upon her totally expunged but capable of receiving any new ones that shall be written from thence forward. . . .

15. But this vehicle lying so long enclosed in the human body cannot fail of receiving some little changes in its texture from the continual play of our sensitive organs and action of our animal circulation thereupon: for every sensation and every suggestion from our memory or reflection passes through that in its way to the mind and though each singly may affect it no longer than for the moment of its passage, yet by being frequently repeated they will work a durable effect. . . . And as we have each of us particular courses of thinking wherein we are led to travel more frequently than in any others by our sev-

eral habits, our passions, our desires, our education, our situation
in life and the objects most familiar to our senses, the ideas passing almost continually in the same track will work the tender
sensory thinner in some places and leave it thicker in others,
separate the fibres or drive them closer together, stretch or contract them, and cause various alterations in their condition and
texture. So that every man goes out of the world with a differently modelled vehicle according as he has been a soldier or a
scholar, a merchant or a mechanic, a gentleman or a labourer,
according to the pursuits and expectations that have taken up
his thoughts, the successes and disappointments, the joys and
afflictions that have hung upon his mind, the occupations and
amusements that have filled up his time. . . .

17. Thus we work out our future fortunes by our present
behaviour and fit ourselves unknowingly for the several parts we
are to act upon the next stage by practising those assigned us
in this: so that we may look upon life as a necessary preparation
to qualify us for the employments of another state. . . .

18. And if the next life begins for the most part like the
present in tender infancy, this will require the cares of the old
inhabitants to overlook and cherish it: so that the business of
nurture, education and parental fondness will be no less considerable sources of employment and amusement among them than
among us. For there being neither marriage nor generation in
that country, they will provide themselves families by a kind of
adoption out of the new comers continually flocking in upon
them. Nor will they want means to direct them in their choice:
for though we have denied them all remembrance of what
passed during their abode here, there are other ways of discovering former relations and connections beside that of inspecting
the traces in our memory. If it were not so common among us we
should be astonished to think how a man, by looking upon a few
scratches upon paper, according to the shapes in which they
are drawn shall come to the knowledge of what his senses and
his experience could not have informed him. By this way my
friend at a hundred miles distance may know where I was yester-

day, what I was doing and what I thought of in my most retired meditations: and by this way we know what was done two thousand years ago in the days of Hannibal and Scipio. But though this be accomplished by the consent of mankind affixing certain ideas to certain characters, let us consider whether the like intelligible writing may not be exhibited by nature in the dependence of effects upon their causes: so that disembodied souls, having acuter faculties than ours, and improved them by long application and exercise, may acquire a dexterity at investigating causes from their effects, know precisely what has happened from what they see happening, discover their own pre-existence, trace out all that has befaln them in their former state, become acquainted with the history of mankind, learn by the manner and condition wherein the new comers arrive from what parts they must come and discern from a resemblance of features that the same causes must have operated upon them which have affected themselves. . . .

21. But tho' the rational soul or vehicle survive the body we cannot conclude from thence that it will live for ever. . . . Nor is it likely the soul should return again to her former confinement: for we see every thing that has life grows therein, animals as well as plants, and whatever lay enclosed in integuments, bursts forth too large to be contained in them any more: the little silk-worm just crawled from its egg or the moth from her chrysalis could not creep into them again, nor could any art replace the seeds of vegetables in their husks. But if the vehicle be not sustained by nutriment which might encrease its growth, nor swell instantly upon coming out of its case, nevertheless it may gradually expand by the continual action of the spirit within so as to be no more capable of lying within its former receptacle than a man is of re-entering his mother's womb. And this expansion cannot fail of introducing stages into the vehicular life similar to those of youth, maturity and age; the last not indeed attended with the pains and infirmities accompanying it here, but distending and separating the fibres of the vehicle until at last they open and let loose the enclosed spirit, which

will then fly off naked and alone. But tho the spirit, no longer
vitally united to any corporeal particles, either ethereal or
elementary, which used to serve for a conveyance of ideas and
instrument of volition, must lose its rationality, percipience and
active powers, it will retain its two primary faculties of perceptivity and activity: and whoever admits the doctrine of final
causes and nothing made in vain can hardly suppose they shall
lie overwhelmed in eternal sleep, or that means shall ever be
wanting of exercising them. . . .

CHAP. XXII

MUNDANE SOUL

•   •   •   •   •

2. The doctrine of a Soul of the World, otherwise called the
Mundane or Universal Soul, must be acknowledged of very
ancient date, as old at least as the Ionic philosophy; and seems
to have been generally embraced by the most eminent sages of
antiquity. They held it eternal, immutable, compleatly wise and
happy, extended throughout the universe, penetrating and in-
vigorating all things, the maker of the world and all creatures
therein, the fountain of sence, life and motion from whence the
souls of men and animals were discerped and, after dissolution
of their bodies, absorbed thereinto again; and they gave it the
appellation of God. . . .
    3. But I apprehend the mundane soul originally was not in-
tended to be understood of the Supreme Being, but a created
God dependent on him for its existence and faculties, produced
from everlasting by his almighty power and good pleasure: and
though it was supposed the maker, it was not supposed the
creator of all things, but to have formed the world out of pre-
existent materials according to a plan assigned it. . . .
    6. . . . The mundane soul is one no otherwise than as the sea is
one, by a similitude and contiguity of parts, being composed of

an innumerable host of distinct spirits as that is of aqueous particles: and as the rivers continually discharge into the sea, so the vehicular people upon the disruption of their vehicles discharge and incorporate into that ocean of spirits making the mundane soul. As for the discerption of souls from thence to inhabit human bodies I have no concern with that, the doctrine of preexistence being now universally exploded: for every good woman knows for certain that we were created some little time before our birth for this plain reason, because if we had existed a hundred years before, some or other of us to be sure must have remembered what passed with us in our former state. And since many learned divines admit an intermediate state between death and the final consummation of all things, I hope that what has been offered in the last chapter concerning the vehicular people will not be counted heterodox. Nor let it be objected that the mundane soul already full and not having a proportionable discharge cannot contain the fresh supplies continually poured in upon it: for some have supposed that the fallen angels have actually occasioned a considerable discharge therefrom. Or if this will not satisfy, let us consider that since creation is currently esteemed so common as to be practised every day in furnishing souls for children in the womb, we may as well suppose the same creative power constantly employed in producing new spaces, extending the bounds of the universe, and giving room for the mundane soul to expand according to the new members it continually receives.

7. We have found reason to conclude in the course of this work that all created spirit, as well as all matter, is homogeneous, and as bodies receive their difference and secondary qualities from the various forms and combinations whereinto the similar atoms composing them are thrown, so spirits derive their characters, their percipience, their rationality, their powers and faculties from the organizations whereto they are united or means of conveying perceptions supplied them: so that the spirit of an angel, a politician, a shoe cleaner, an ideot, a man and a child are intrinsically the same, differing only in their

being variously lodged and circumstanced. From hence it follows that the spirits composing the universal soul are all of
similar nature, having the same capacities, the same primary
properties of perceptivity and activity, and altogether such as
ourselves except these bonds of flesh wherein we lie imprisoned.
. . . As we live here separate and alone, each immured within his
several cell, we have nothing to discern besides the modifications
of the organs in our sensory, nor can we converse together unless
by the intervention of some bodily medium, as of sounds or
letters: but if we could have immediate intercourse with one
another, who can say how much more expeditely, easily and
clearly we might carry on our conversations? . . . Perhaps whatever either of us saw or heard or apprehended by any of our
senses or rose up in our imagination might instantly be discerned
by the other. . . . Suppose one of us intending to partake in the
diversions of Scarborough while the other stays in London: as
soon as he is gotten there we will suppose a string of spirits
reaching from him to me. . . . Having this channel of conveyance
ready at hand we should despise the tedious method of correspondence by the post, wherein we might sometimes be mis-
apprehended or imperfectly understood or at best could give
but a partial account of what had happened to us. . . . Imagine
further that we had a friend at Plymouth, another at Paris, another at Amsterdam, and that there were the like spiritual strings
of communication from every one to every one: we should
then all five have immediate knowledge of all that was worth
knowing in the five places by perceptions continually transmitted along those conveyances.

   8. . . . I must proceed to one assumption more, . . . and this is
that all space not occupied by matter is replete with spiritual
substance called the mundane soul, each part whereof, that is,
each component spirit lies contiguous to others: so that there
runs a continuity throughout the whole as there does throughout the waters of the ocean; for lines might be drawn from any
drop in the Atlantic sea to every spot in the European, African or
American shores surrounding it which should pass over rows of

drops contiguous to one another. This being premised it will follow that by the mutual communication of perceptions every one may have those arising in every other. . . .

9. If we suppose every component spirit to perceive all that every other does, it will appear impossible that so vast an infinitude of knowledge can be contained in any created mind; and we find a multitude of objects, although distinct in themselves, confounds us merely by their number: but this is owing to the scantiness of our organs, for according as they are more copious in one person than another we find the same number of ideas appear clear or confused. Cesar could dictate to three amanuenses at once, and call all the Roman citizens by their names; and if it would perplex any of us to attempt the like it is because we have not the same quickness of parts, that is, the same fineness of organization. . . . So that in our present condition 'tis our organs that set the limits to our understanding, nor do we know what our mental capacity is, our sources being too scanty ever to fill the vessel. We may possibly be capable of twenty senses, but being provided with inlets only for five, have no more conception of the others than a blind man has of light. Therefore we have no reason to confine the extent of the mundane understanding to the narrowness of our own, but rather to believe it much larger than any thing we have experienced or can imagine. . . . The parts of the universal soul will serve for organs to each other conveying perceptions instantaneously from the most distant regions of nature, distributing to every one whatever information it concerns him to receive: for we know of nothing so quick as thought, nor that it takes up any time in its progress. And their knowledge being derived from one common fund they will all have the same sentiments, the same motives and rules of conduct. . . .

17. This entire unanimity of sentiment and perfect harmony of action may well warrant us to look upon the whole as one thing, to which the material world will serve as a sensory exciting sensations and reflections and exhibiting ideas, and the spiritual part as a percipient to receive them and a vivifying principle

to invigorate and actuate the motions of the other; having in a manner one understanding, one design, and one volition, making all together one compound as the human soul and body make one man. So that with the Stoics we may call the universe an immense animal, or say with Pope, All are but parts of one stupendous Whole whose body nature is and God, not the Almighty but this created god we have been speaking of, the soul. This god or animal or glorified man containing all men (for it matters not what name we use so our ideas be clear) which is the world, will have a full discernment of all his parts with their combinations, proportions, symmeteries, situations and uses: nor will anything minute escape his notice, for being not confined like us to one little cell in the brain where we know nothing of the many secretions, circulations and other transactions passing in our frame, but his spirit insinuating and penetrating every where, not an atom can stir without his knowledge and observation. . . .

20. Having given the fullest explication I could of that exalted Being the universal soul, the head and principal of creatures, let us now consider how well he may deserve the glorious things said of him in former times. And first we need not scruple to admit him for maker of the world, that is, the agent employed in executing that stupendous work: for penetrating into every pore of material substance, being all intelligence and activity throughout, he might discern all the particles in Chaos, if ever there was one, know what they were severally fit for, assort them into elements and of them compose habitable earths. Upon the word given Let there be light, he might twist the sevenfold rays and dart them about in all directions, or upon a second word collect the main body of them into a Sun. He might give the heavy planets their tangential motion by one strong and exactly poised stroke. He might gather the waters from the dry land, having first scooped the capacious bed of ocean and raised the equatorial parts lest the diurnal rotation should cast up the sea above them. He might give the earth a twirl as easily as a child twirls round his whirlagig to produce the vicissitudes of day and night. He might thrust the poles askance twice ten de-

grees and more that summer and winter, seed time and harvest should never fail. He might draw out strings of viscous juices from the ground, and perforating them into tubes and interlacing them artfully together, compose therewith the tree yielding fruit after his kind and the herb after his kind whose seed is in itself. He might form the dust of the earth into animal organizations with proper members for walking or flying or creeping or swimming as soon as the breath of life should be breathed into them: and extracting the finer particles from the grosser might work them into mental organs and sensories fit for the reception of perceptive spirits who should be created for them to begin the race of men upon earth. And as he went on compleating his task the Lord Almighty looked forth from heaven and saw every handy work of his minister and behold it was very good. The six days formation being ended, though God rested from commanding his agent did not rest from acting: for his reason could now direct him how to proceed in sustaining the work he had been taught to make. He still continued to turn the grand wheel of repulsion, that first mover in the wondrous machine of visible nature, all whose movements follow one another uninterruptedly for ages according to stated laws and in regular courses without failure or disorder in any single wheel. Until the fulness of time being come or the signal given from the throne of Glory, the same agent, turning the wheel of repulsion the contrary way, will rend the mighty fabric asunder, throw the parts of compounds out of their order, dissipate them with a sudden explosion and reduce all into Chaos again. From whence upon a new plan assigned new systems may be formed, new earths stretched out, new vegetables and animals produced to cover and inhabit them. . . .

22. The powers and operations of the universal soul being settled we will proceed next to consider his state and condition within himself: and we may agree with the ancient sages in pronouncing him immortal, unchangeable, compleatly intelligent, wise and happy. For having nothing external he will be secure against dangers and accidents from without: being not vitally

united to systems of matter their dissolution can affect him no
otherwise than a change of objects or of one thing for another
taken into our hands does us: and consisting of similar parts
whose qualities do not depend upon their order or combinations, he will not suffer by their taking new positions, as we
should do upon the misplacing an eye or an ear or any little
fibre in our bodies; for every component spirit would be able to
perform the same office with that into whose place it
succeeded. . . .

23. With all these accomplishments and perfections we cannot doubt of his being unspeakably happy; and if any sparks of
evil should be sprinkled upon him by contemplation of the miserable wretches in the two embodied states, they would be so
overwhelmed with the joys flowing from elsewhere that he
would feel no more disturbance thereat than a man having just
received news of some great good fortune befaln him would feel
upon happening to break a china saucer. Nor need we apprehend his being satiated with the sameness of his prospect, having
no other objects beside his own immense body to entertain him,
with which being long since perfectly acquainted he can make
no new discoveries for his amusement. For though pleasure cannot subsist without novelty in ourselves because our bodily organs, losing their quickness upon repetition of the same objects,
will not continue the relish they gave at first; yet where the
spirits serve as organs to one another it is not certain the same
inconvenience must ensue. But supposing variety of objects and
employments necessary to happiness he will not want for plenty
of either: for his immense body, the universe, though but one
and he have nothing external to gaze at, consists of numberless
systems each containing a multitude of under parts whose incessant movements perpetually change the face of nature and
exhibit a diversity of scenes as well among the larger members
as in the minuter particles. Nor is it necessary that every component spirit should have the whole in contemplation at once;
for large as their capacity may be we have never represented it
as infinite; therefore their streams of communication may be

varied by the pouring sometimes one kind of perceptions upon each other and sometimes another. . . . Nor need we fear their want of employment to engage them, for considering the vast consumption of motion every where which requires their continual efforts to renew it, besides the mutual communication of perceptions and choice of those proper to be communicated, they will constantly have enough to do in giving impulse to the matter falling within their reach. For as they do not run along with the bodies they actuate but hand them on to one another, they will have different functions to execute: sometimes busied in pushing forward the corpuscles of light, spreading the tails of comets, or regulating the vibrations of ether according to their proximity or distance from masses of gross matter: sometimes in gravitating heavy weights to earths, or holding the parts of metals in cohesion, or giving fluidity to liquors, or agitating the particles of fire, or contracting and dilating the circulating vessels in plants and animals. . . .

25. This host of happy spirits called by one name, the universal soul, from their uniformity of action and sentiment, we suppose the receptacle for particular spirits as they can disengage themselves from their vital union with matter, and that upon disruption of a vehicle the perceptive inhabitant will be discharged therein and incorporated therewith: whereby the communication with spiritual substance being opened it will instantly partake of all the knowledge and designs of its neighbours and immediately take its share in their operations according to the station wherein it happens to fall. And tho' leaving the traces of its former memory behind, it will have the records of the universal sensory to inspect wherein is preserved the remembrance of events happening throughout nature more exactly and fully than can be comprized in any animal organization. Thus in this state there will be no infancy nor growth of faculties or advancement in learning, but the new comers upon their first arrival will stand upon the same footing with the old members as if they had resided among them from everlasting. As they act in concert carrying on one plan of operation the act

of all will seem the act of every one and each feel a kind of consciousness of what is performed by the whole company. For as among men concurring heartily in one undertaking all claim the credit to themselves, the majority at an election exult as much as if the choice had depended upon their single votes, and a tradesman at a coffee house triumphs in a victory and thinks himself entitled to say We have beat the enemy, because he pays some trifle towards the supplies, or is a member of the nation whose quarrel it is; so the members of this mighty agent, the universal soul, altho singly feeble, will partake in the joy of those stupendous works carried on by their united strength. For all contributing their activity to roll the celestial orbs in their appointed courses, to diffuse light throughout the vast expanse, to keep the elements in order, to distribute all things upon earth by number weight and measure, to produce and preserve the several species of plants and animals, to direct the affairs of men and turn the wheels of fortune, to fulfill invariably the Will of God and execute the mighty plan assigned them, the pleasure of the performance will redound entire to every one as if he had been the sole agent employed.

26. ... We may well admit this the happiest state created substance can be placed in, therefore we need seek no higher but may take this for our idea of the kingdom of heaven. ...

27. This spiritual community being heaven and all space not occupied by matter being replete with spiritual substance, it follows that heaven is not local but every where all around, above, below, on each side and within us, filling not only the starry regions but likewise the air, the earth and the seas, and permeating the pores of all compound bodies. Therefore that we are out of heaven is not owing to any distance we stand at from thence, but to our being pent up in walls of flesh which cut off our communication with the blessed spirits and shut us out from all participation in their lights and their joys. We are like persons inclosed each in a sentry box having all the chinks and crannies stopped that might let in the least light or sound, and in this condition set down among the splendid throng in a full

Ridotto: they would be alone in the midst of company as knowing nothing of the gaiety and diversions passing round them. If they had strings reaching to one another's boxes they might make signs by them, learn in time to understand one another's motions and carry on a sort of conversation together, but very imperfect in comparison of what they could do if let out and permitted to converse like other people. So we while imprisoned in these earthly tabernacles see little and know little of all that passes around us, and converse together imperfectly by the corporeal mediums of sights and sounds. Upon the dissolution of this gross body we may find an inner integument still clinging round us, but when the appointed time shall deliver us from this too we shall not have far to travel before we join our company: for wherever our vehicle leaves us there we shall find heaven, and take our place and occupation therein immediately without any of that surprize or aukwardness or agitation usually thrown upon our corporeal organs by scenes wholly new, but with the same readiness and familiarity as a man coming off a journey having his own house, his own family, his own furniture and conveniences about him; for we shall then understand and apprehend, not by our old ideas, but by those of the universal mind, and partake in the expertness and full digested remembrance belonging to that.

JACOB BRYANT

(1715–1804)

This learned antiquarian, considered by a contemporary "in point of classical erudition . . . perhaps, without an equal in the world," spent most of his life as secretary, librarian, and pensioner of the Duke of Marlborough and his family. He had two rooms set aside for him at Blenheim, and was frequently visited for his wise conversation by the King and Queen. His magnum opus, *A New System* (1774–1776), demonstrates, mainly by breath-taking etymologies, that Egyptian, Greek, and other mythologies are only distorted versions of events, particularly Noah's flood, more accurately described in the book of Genesis. His other works include *Observations on the Poems of Thomas Rowley* (1781), proving their authenticity; *A Treatise on the Authenticity of the Scriptures, and the Truth of the Christian Religion* (1792); and *A Dissertation Concerning the War of Troy, and the Expedition of the Grecians, as Described by Homer; Shewing That No Such Expedition Was Ever Taken, and That No Such City as Phrygia Ever Existed* (1796). Of these only his defense of the Scriptures won the general assent of his contemporaries. Although he is said to be the prototype of George Eliot's Mr. Casaubon, his actual character seems to have been exceptionally unassuming and sweet-natured. He never married, but lived to the age of 89, clear-minded and pursuing his studies to the last. An early biographer mentions that "he was particularly fond of dogs, and was known to have thirteen spaniels at one time." On his deathbed he is reported to have "declared to his nephew, and others in the room, that 'all he had written was with a view to the promulgation of truth; and, that all he had contended for, he himself believed.' "

Blake is clearly indebted to Bryant for some of his ideas about the dispersal of the human race over the earth; for a discussion of Bryant's influence on Blake, see S. Foster Damon, *A Blake Dictionary* (Providence: Brown Univ. Press, 1965). J. B. Beer in *Coleridge the Visionary* (New York: Macmillan, 1959), thinks that Coleridge also drew directly from Bryant's mythology. At any rate, many people of the time believed that, in Blake's words, "the antiquities of every Nation under Heaven . . . are the same thing[,] as Jacob Bryant, and all antiquaries have proved" (*A Descriptive Catalogue of Pictures* [1809], Number V). Such works as Bryant's *New System*, Mallet's *Northern Antiquities*, and Horne Tooke's *Pantheon* created an atmosphere congenial to the mythopoeic talents of Southey, Keats, and Shelley. Edward B. Hungerford describes in *Shores of Darkness* (New York: Columbia Univ. Press, 1941) the influence on Blake, Keats, Shelley, and Goethe of such eighteenth-century "mythogogs."

The text below is based on the third edition (1807). This selection gives some idea of the quality, but not of the vast quantity and diffuseness, of the details that Bryant amasses. Even here a number of illustrations have been left out, particularly passages in Greek. (Bryant translates most of his Greek citations, explaining in the Preface that he realizes his reader's probable ignorance, though he laments it and hopes that "better days may perhaps come; when the Greek language will be in greater repute.")

A New System; or, An Analysis of Antient Mythology

PREFACE

It is my purpose, in the ensuing work, to give an account of the first ages, and of the great events which happened in the infancy of the world. In consequence of this I shall lay before the reader what the Gentile writers have said upon this subject, collaterally with the accounts given by Moses, as long as I find him engaged in the general history of mankind. By these means I shall be able to bring surprising proofs of those great occurrences, which the sacred penman has recorded. And when his history becomes more limited, and is confined to a peculiar people, and a private dispensation, I shall proceed to shew what was subsequent to his account after the migration of families, and the dispersion from the plains of Shinar. When mankind were multiplied upon the earth, each great family had, by divine appointment, a particular place of destination, to which they retired. In this manner the first nations were constituted, and kingdoms founded. But great changes were soon effected, and colonies went abroad without any regard to their original place of allotment. New establishments were soon made, from whence ensued a mixture of people and languages. These are events of the highest consequence; of which we can receive no intelligence, but through the hands of the Gentile writers.

It has been observed, by many of the learned, that some particular family betook themselves very early to different parts of the world, in all which they introduced their rites and religion, together with the customs of their country. They represent them as very knowing and enterprising; and with good reason. They were the first who ventured upon the seas, and undertook long voyages. They shewed their superiority and address in the numberless expeditions which they made, and the difficulties which they surmounted. Many have thought that they were colonies from Egypt, or from Phenicia, having a regard only to the settlements which they made in the west. But I shall shew hereafter, that colonies of the same people are to be found in the most extreme parts of the east; where we may observe the same rites and ceremonies, and the same traditional histories, as are to be met with in their other settlements. The country called Phenicia could not have sufficed for the effecting all that is attributed to these mighty adventurers. It is necessary for me to acquaint the Reader, that the wonderful people to whom I allude were the descendants of Chus, and called Cuthites and Cuseans. They stood their ground at the general migration of families; but were at last scattered over the face of the earth. They were the first apostates from the truth, yet great in worldly wisdom. They introduced, wherever they came, many useful arts, and were looked up to as a superior order of beings: hence they were styled Heroes, Dæmons, Heliadæ, Macarians. They were joined in their expeditions by other nations, especially by the collateral branches of their family, the Mizraim, Caphtorim, and the sons of Canaan. These were all of the line of Ham, who was held by his posterity in the highest veneration. They called him Amon: and having in process of time raised him to a divinity, they worshipped him as the Sun; and from this worship they were styled Amonians. . . .

What I have to exhibit is in great measure new; and I shall be obliged to run counter to many received opinions, which length of time, and general assent, have in a manner rendered sacred. What is truly alarming, I shall be found to differ, not only from some few historians, as is the case in common controversy, but in some degree from all; and this in respect to many of the most essential points, upon which historical precision has been thought to depend. My meaning is, that I must set aside many supposed facts which have never been controverted; and dispute many events which have not only been admitted as true, but have been looked up to as certain æras from whence other events were to be determined. All our knowledge of Gentile history must either come through the hands of the Grecians, or of the Romans, who copied from them. I shall therefore give a full account of the Helladian Greeks, as well as of the Iönim, or Ionians, in Asia: also of the Dorians, Leleges, and Pelasgi. What may appear very presumptuous, I shall deduce from their own histories many truths, with which they were totally unacquainted, and give to them an original, which they certainly did not know. They have bequeathed to us noble materials, of which it is time to make a serious use. It was their misfortune not to know the value of the data which they transmitted, nor the purport of their own intelligence. . . .

As it will be my business to abridge history of every thing superfluous and foreign, I shall be obliged to set aside many antient law-givers, and princes, who were supposed to have formed republics, and to have founded kingdoms. I cannot acquiesce in the stale legends of Deucalion of Thessaly, of Inachus of Argos, and Ægialeus of Sicyon; nor in the long line of princes who are derived from them. The supposed heroes of the first ages, in every country are equally fabulous. . . . I make as little account of the histories of Saturn, Janus, Pelops, Atlas, Dardanus, Minos of Crete, and Zoroaster of Bactria. Yet something mysterious, and of moment, is concealed under these various characters: and the investigation of this latent truth will be the principal part of my inquiry. In respect to Greece, I can afford credence to very few events, which were antecedent to the Olympiads. I cannot give the least assent to the story of Phryxus, and the golden fleece. It seems to me plain beyond doubt, that there were no such persons as the Grecian Argonauts: and that the expedition of Jason to Colchis was a fable. After having cleared my way, I shall proceed to the sources, from whence the Grecians drew. I shall give an account of the Titans, and Titanic war, with the history of the Cuthites and antient Babylonians. This will be accompanied with the Gentile history of the Deluge, the migration of mankind from Shinar, and the dispersion from Babel. The whole will be crowned with an account of antient Egypt; wherein many circumstances of high consequence in chronology will be stated. In the execution of the whole there will be brought many surprising proofs in confirmation of the Mosaic account: and it will be found, from repeated evidence, that every thing, which the divine historian has transmitted, is most assuredly true. And though the nations, who preserved memorials of the Deluge, have not perhaps stated accurately the time of that event; yet it will be found the grand epocha, to which they referred; the highest point to which they could ascend. This was esteemed the renewal of the world; the new birth of mankind; and the ultimate of Gentile history. . . .

Before I can arrive at this essential part of my inquiries, I must give an account of the rites and customs of antient Hellas; and of those people which I term Amonians. This I must do in order to shew, from whence they came: and from what quarter their evidence is derived. A great deal will be said of their religion and rites: also of their towers, temples, and Puratheia, where their worship was performed. The mistakes likewise of the Greeks in respect to antient terms, which they strangely perverted, will be exhibited in many instances: and much true history will be ascertained from a detection of this peculiar misapplication. It is a circumstance of great consequence, to which little attention has been paid. Great light however will accrue from examining this abuse, and observing the particular mode of error: and the only way of obtaining an insight must be by an etymological process, and by recurring to the primitive language of the people, concerning whom we are treating. As the Amonians betook themselves to regions widely separated; we shall find in every place where they settled, the same worship and ceremonies, and the same history of their ancestors. There will also appear a great similitude in the names of their cities and temples: so that we may be assured, that the whole was the operation of one and the same people. The learned Bochart saw this; and taking for granted, that the people were Phenicians, he attempted to interpret these names by the Hebrew language; of which he supposed the Phenician to have been a dialect. His design was certainly very ingenious, and carried on with a wonderful display of learning. He failed however: and of the nature of his failure I shall be obliged to take notice. It appears to me, as far as my reading can afford me light, that most antient names, not only of places, but of persons, have a manifest analogy. There is likewise a great correspondence to be observed in terms of science; and in the titles, which were of old bestowed upon magistrates and rulers. The same observation may be extended even to plants, and minerals, as well as to animals; especially to those which were esteemed at all sacred. Their names seem to be composed of the same, or similar elements; and bear a manifest relation to the religion in use among the Amonians, and to the Deity which they adored. This deity was the Sun: and most of the antient names will be found to be an assemblage of titles, bestowed upon that luminary. Hence there will appear a manifest correspondence between them, which circumstance is quite foreign to the system of Bochart. His etymologies are destitute of this collateral evidence; and have not the least analogy to support them. . . .

My purpose has been throughout to give a new turn to antient history, and to place it upon a surer foundation. The mythology of Greece is a vast assemblage of obscure traditions, which have been transmitted from the earliest times. . . . A great part of this intelligence has been derived to us from the Poets; by which means it has been rendered still more extravagant, and strange. . . . We must, however, make this distinction, that in the alle-

gorical representations of Greece, there was always a covert
meaning, though it may have escaped our discernment. In short,
we must look upon antient mythology as being yet in a chaotic
state, where the mind of man has been wearied with roaming
over the crude consistence without ever finding out one spot
where it could repose in safety. . . . It is my hope, and my presumption, that such a place of appulse may be found, where we
may take our stand, and from whence we may have a full view
of the mighty expanse before us; from whence also we may
descry the original design, and order, of all those objects, which
by length of time, and their own remoteness, have been rendered so confused and uncertain.

· · · · ·

OF THE DELUGE

The history of the Deluge, as it is transmitted to us by Moses,
may appear short and concise; yet abounds with matter: and
affords us a thorough insight into the most material circumstances, with which that calamity was attended. There seems to
have been a great convulsion in nature, insomuch that all flesh
died, eight persons only being saved: and the means of their
deliverance were so wonderful, that very lasting impressions
must have been left upon their minds, after they had survived the
fearful event. The sacred writer has moreover given us the
reasons, why it pleased God to bring this flood upon the world,
to the destruction of the work of his hands.
[Bryant here quotes, with a few omissions, Genesis 6:11–
7:24.] We find from the above, that the Patriarch and his family
were inclosed in an ark, or covered float; wherein there was only
one window of a cubit in dimensions. This was of small proportion in respect to the bulk of the machine, which was above
five hundred feet in length. It was moreover closed up, and fas-
tened: so that the persons within were consigned to darkness;
having no light, but what must have been administered to them

from lamps and torches. They therefore could not have been eye-witnesses to the general calamity of mankind. They did not see the mighty eruption of waters, nor the turbulence of the seas: when *the fountains of the great deep were broken up.* Yet the crash of mountains, and the noise of the cataracts could not but have sounded in their ears: and possibly the cries of people may have reached them; when families and nations were overwhelming in the floods. The motion too of the ark must have been very violent at this tempestuous season: all which added to the gloom, and uncertainty, in which they were involved, could not but give them many fearful sensations; however they may have relied on Providence, and been upheld by the hand of heaven. We find that the machine, in which they were secured, is termed Thebah, an ark, or chest. It was of such a model and construction as plainly indicated, that it was never designed to be managed, or directed by the hands of men. And it seems to have been the purpose of Providence throughout to signify to those, who were saved, as well as to their latest posterity, that their preservation was not in any degree effected by human means.

[Bryant quotes, with a few omissions, Genesis 8: 1–20.] These are the principal circumstances in this wonderful occurrence; which I have produced in the words of the divine historian, that I might not do injury to his narration: and they are of such a nature, as, one might well imagine, would be long had in remembrance. We may reasonably suppose, that the particulars of this extraordinary event would be gratefully commemorated by the Patriarch himself; and transmitted to every branch of his family: that they were made the subject of domestic converse; where the history was often renewed, and ever attended with a reverential awe and horror: especially in those, who had been witnesses to the calamity, and had experienced the hand of Providence in their favour. In process of time, when there was a falling off from the truth, we might farther expect that a person of so high a character as Noah, so particularly distinguished by the Deity, could not fail of being reverenced by his posterity:

and, when idolatry prevailed, that he would be one of the first among the sons of men, to whom divine honours would be paid. Lastly, we might conclude that these memorials would be interwoven in the mythology of the Gentile world: and that there would be continually allusions to these antient occurrences in the rites and mysteries; as they were practised by the nations of the earth. In conformity to these suppositions I shall endeavour to shew, that these things did happen: That the history of the deluge was religiously preserved in the first ages: That every circumstance of it is to be met with among the historians and mythologists of different countries: and traces of it are to be particularly found in the sacred rites of Egypt, and of Greece.

It will appear from many circumstances in the more antient writers, that the great Patriarch was highly reverenced by his posterity. They looked up to him as a person peculiarly favoured by heaven; and honoured him with many titles; each of which had a reference to some particular part of his history. They styled him Prometheus, Deucalion, Atlas, Theuth, Zuth, Xuthus, Inachus, Osiris. When there began to be a tendency towards idolatry; and the adoration of the Sun was introduced by the posterity of Ham; the title of Helius among others was conferred upon him. They called him also Mην, and Μαν, which is the Moon; the secret meaning of which name I shall hereafter shew. When colonies went abroad, many took to themselves the title of Minyadæ and Minyæ from him; just as others were denominated Achæmenidæ, Auritæ, Heliadæ, from the Sun. People of the former name are to be found in Arabia, and in other parts of the world. The natives at Orchomenos were styled Minyæ; as were also some of the inhabitants of Thessaly. It was the antient name of the Arcadians, interpreted Σεληνιται, Lunares: but grew obsolete. Noah was the original Ζευς, Zeus, and Dios. He was the planter of the vine, and the inventor of fermented liquors: whence he was denominated Zeuth, which signifies ferment; rendered Ζευς, Zeus, by the Greeks. He was also Dionusos, interpreted by the Latines Bacchus, but very improperly. Bacchus was Chus, the grandson of Noah; as Ammon may be in general esteemed Ham, so much reverenced by the Egyptians.

As many of these terms were titles, they were not always uniformly adapted: nor were the antients consistent in their mythology. But nothing has produced greater confusion in these antient histories than that fatal turn in the Greeks of reducing every unknown term to some word, with which they were better acquainted. In short, they could not rest till they had formed every thing by their own idiom, and made every nation speak the language of Greece. Among the people of the east the true name of the Patriarch was preserved: they called him Noas, Naus, and sometimes contracted Nous: and many places of sanctity, and many rivers were denominated from him. Anaxagoras of Clazomenæ had been in Egypt; and had there obtained some knowledge of this personage. He spoke of him by the name of Noas or Nous; and both he and his disciples were sensible that it was a foreign appellation: yet he has well nigh ruined the whole of a very curious history, which he had been taught, by taking the terms in a wrong acceptation, and then making inferences in consequence of this abuse. [Bryant here quotes the Greek which he translates in the following italics.] *The disciples of Anaxagoras say, that Nous is, by interpretation, the Deity Dis, or Dios: and they call Athena, Art or Science— They likewise esteem Nous the same as Prometheus.* He then proceeds to inform us why they looked upon Nous to have been Prometheus: *because he was the renewer of mankind; and was said,* μεταπεπλασθαι, *to have fashioned them again,* after that they had been in a manner extinct. All this is to be inferred from the words above. But the author, while he is giving this curious account, starts aside, and, forgetting that he is confessedly treating of a foreign term, recurs to his own language, and from thence frames a solution of the story. He tells us that Nous, which he had been speaking of as a proper name, was, after all, a Grecian term, νους, the mind: that *the mind was Prometheia; and Prometheus was said to renew mankind from new forming their minds,*

and leading them by cultivation from ignorance to knowledge.—
Thus have the Greeks, by their affectation, continually ruined
history: and the reader may judge how difficult it is to see the
truth through the mist, with which it is environed. . . .

[Bryant cites several ancient writers who refer to Noah
under names related by tenuous etymology.] However the
story may have been varied, the principal outlines plainly point
out the person who is alluded to in these histories. Many personages having been formed out of one has been the cause of
great confusion, both in these instances, and in numberless
others. Indeed, the whole mythology of the antients has, by
these means, been sadly clouded. It is, I think, manifest, that
Annacus and Nannacus, and even Inacus, relate to Noachus, or
Noah. And not only these, but the histories of Deucalion and
Prometheus have a like reference to the Patriarch, in the six
hundredth year (and not the three hundredth), of whose life the
waters prevailed upon the earth. He was the father of mankind,
who were renewed in him. Hence he is represented by another
author under the character of Prometheus, as a great artist, by
whom men were formed anew, and were instructed in all that
was good. He makes Minerva co-operate with him in making
images of clay, according to the history before given: but he
additionally gives to her the province of inspiring them with a
living soul, instead of calling the winds together for that purpose. Hence the soul of man, according to Lucian, is an emanation of Divine Wisdom.

Noah was the original Cronus, and Zeus; though the latter
is a title conferred sometimes upon his son, Ham. . . . There is
a very particular expression recorded by Clemens of Alexandria,
and attributed to Pythagoras; who is said to have called the
sea Κρονου δακρυον, *the tear of Cronus:* and there was a farther
tradition concerning this person, καταπινειν τα τεκνα, *that he
drank, or swallowed up, all his children.* The tears of Isis are
represented as very mysterious. They are said to have flowed,
whenever the Nile began to rise, and to flood the country. The
overflowing of that river was the great source of affluence to the

people: and they looked upon it as their chief blessing; yet it was ever attended with mystical tears, and lamentations. This was particularly observable at Coptos, where the principal Deity was Isis. . . . —Proventum fructuum Ægyptii quærunt usque ad veros planctus: namque irrigatio Nili supradictorum fletibus imploratur. [The Egyptians go so far as actual lamentations to make their crops grow: for they pray for the overflowing of the Nile with tears.] This writer [Lutatius Placidus] imagines, that the tears, and lamentations of the people were to implore an inundation: and the tears of Isis, according to Pausanias, were supposed to make the river swell. But all this was certainly said, and done, in memorial of a former flood, of which they made the overflowing of the Nile a type.

As the Patiarch was by some represented as a king called Naachus and Nauachus; so by others he was styled Inachus, and supposed to have reigned at Argos. For colonies, wherever they came, in process of time superadded the traditions, which they brought, to the histories of the countries, where they settled. . . .

He seems in the East to have been called Noas, Noasis, Nusus, and Nus, and by the Greeks his name was compounded Dionusus. The Amonians, wherever they came, founded cities to his honour: hence places called Nusa will often occur. . . . There was also a place called Nusa upon mount Caucasus; and upon Helicon: also in the island Eubœa; where was a notion, that grapes would blossom, and come to perfection in one day. . . . As it was the turn of the Greeks to place every thing to the account of conquest; they made him a great conqueror, who went over the face of the whole earth, and taught mankind the plantation of the vine. . . .

Though the Patriarch is represented.under various titles, and even these not always uniformly appropriated; yet there will continually occur such peculiar circumstances of his history, as will plainly point out the person referred to. The person preserved is always mentioned as preserved in an ark. He is described as being in a state of darkness, which is represented

allegorically as a state of death. He then obtains a new life, which
is called a second birth; and is said to have his youth renewed.
He is on this account looked upon as the firstborn of mankind:
and both his antediluvian and postdiluvian states are commemorated, and sometimes the intermediate is spoken of. . . .

    Part of the ceremony in most of the antient mysteries con-
sisted in carrying about a kind of ship or boat; which custom,
upon due examination, will be found to relate to nothing else
but Noah, and the Deluge. The ship of Isis is well known; and
the celebrity among the Egyptians, whenever it was carried in
public. The name of this, and of all the navicular shrines was
Baris: which is very remarkable; for it was the very name of
the mountain, according to Nicolaus Damascenus, on which the
ark of Noah rested; the same as Ararat in Armenia. . . . We may
be assured then that the ship of Isis was a sacred emblem: in
honour of which there was among the Egyptians an annual
festival. . . . They oftentimes, says Porphyry, describe the sun
in the character of a man sailing on a float. And Plutarch observes
to the same purpose, that they did not represent the sun and
the moon in chariots; αλλα πλοιοις οχημασι χρωμενους περιπλειν, *but
wafted about upon floating machines.* In doing which they did
not refer to the luminaries; but to a personage represented under those titles. The Sun, or Orus, is likewise described by
Iamblichus as sitting upon the lotus, and sailing in a vessel.

    It is said of Sesostris, that he constructed a ship, which was two
hundred and eighty cubits in length. It was of cedar; plated
without with gold, and inlaid with silver: and it was, when
finished, dedicated to Osiris at Thebes. It is not credible, that
there should have been a ship of this size, especially in an inland
district, the most remote of any in Egypt. It was certainly a
temple, and a shrine. The former was framed upon this large
scale: and it was the latter, on which the gold and silver were so
lavishly expended. There is a remarkable circumstance relating
to the Argonautic expedition; that the dragon slain by Jason was
of the dimensions of a Trireme: by which must be meant, that it
was of the shape of a ship in general; for there were no Triremes
at the time alluded to. And I have moreover shewn, that all these

dragons, as they have been represented by the poets, were in reality temples, Dracontia; where, among other rites, the worship of the serpent was instituted. There is therefore reason to think, that this temple, as well as that of Sesostris, was fashioned in respect to its superficial contents after the model of a ship: and as to the latter, it was probably intended in its outlines to be the exact representation of the ark, in commemoration of which it was certainly built. . . .

The same memorial is to be observed in other countries, where an ark, or ship, was introduced in their mysteries, and often carried about upon their festivals. . . .

I have before taken notice, that this history was pretty recent when these works were executed in Egypt, and when these rites were first established: and there is reason to think, that in early times most shrines among the Mizraim were formed under the resemblance of a ship, in memory of this great event. Nay, farther, both ships and temples received their names from hence; being styled by the Greeks, who borrowed largely from Egypt, Ναυς and Ναος, and Mariners Ναυται, Nautæ, in reference to the Patriarch, who was variously styled Noas, Naus, and Noah.

However the Greeks may, in their mysteries, have sometimes introduced a ship as a symbol, yet, in their references to the Deluge itself, and to the persons preserved, they always speak of an ark, which they call Λαρναξ, Larnax, Κιβωτος, and the like. And though they were apt to mention the same person under various titles, and by these means different people seem to be made principals in the same history; yet they were so far uniform in their accounts of this particular event, that they made each of them to be preserved in an ark. Thus it is said of Deucalion, Perseus, and Dionusus, that they were exposed upon the waters in a machine of this fabric. Adonis was hid in an ark by Venus; and was supposed to have been in a state of death for a year. . . . Theocritus introduces a pastoral personage Comates, who was exposed in an ark for the same term, and wonderfully preserved. . . . Of Osiris being exposed in an ark, we have a very remarkable account in Plutarch; who mentions that it was on account of Typhon; and that it happened on the seventeenth of the month Athyr, when the Sun was in Scorpio. This, in my judgment, was the precise time when Noah entered the ark, and when the flood came; which, in the Egyptian mythology, was termed Typhon.

From what has preceded, the reader will perceive, that the history of the Deluge was no secret to the Gentile world. They held the memory of it very sacred; and many colonies, which went abroad, styled themselves Thebeans, in reference to the ark. . . .

Noah was represented, as we may infer from Berosus, under the semblance of a fish by the Babylonians: and those representations of fishes in the sphere, probably related to him and his sons. The reasons given for their being placed there were, that Venus, when she fled from Typhon, took the form of a fish; and that the fish, styled Notius, saved Isis in some great extremity: pro quo beneficio simulacrum Piscis et *ejus filiorum*, de quibus ante diximus, inter astra constituit: *for which reason Venus placed the fish Notius and his sons among the stars.* By this we may perceive, that Hyginus speaks of these asterisms as representations of persons: and he mentions from Eratosthenes, that the fish Notius was the father of mankind: ex eo pisce natos homines.

It is said of Noah, that after the deluge he built the first altar to God: which is a circumstance always taken notice of in the history given of him by Gentile writers. He is likewise mentioned as the first planter of the vine; and the inventor of wine itself, and of Zuth or ferment, by which similar liquors were manufactured. We may therefore suppose that both the altar, and the crater, or cup, related to these circumstances. As the Patriarch was esteemed the author of the first ship, which was navigated, he was in consequence of it made the god of seamen; and his temple was termed ἱερον Ποσειδωνος Κανωβου. He was esteemed the same as Serapis: and inscriptions have been found dedicated to him under the title of Θεος Σωτηρ. In this temple, or rather college, was a seminary for astronomy, and other marine sciences. Ptolemy, the great Geographer, to whom the world is so much indebted, was a member of this society, and studied here forty years. The name of the temple was properly Ca Noubi: the latter part, Noubi, is the oracle of Noah.

Niobe was the same name, and person; though by the Greeks mentioned as a woman. She is represented as one, who was given up to grief, having been witness to the death of all her children. Her tears flowed day and night; till she at last stiffened with woe; and was turned into a stone, which was to be seen on mount Sipylus in Magnesia. . . .

As the antients described the ark, the ναυς αμφιπρυμναῖς, like a lunette; it was in consequence of it called Mην, and Σεληνη, which signify *a Moon:* and a crescent became a common symbol on this occasion. The chief person likewise, the Patriarch, had the name of Meen, and Menes: and was worshipped all over the east as Deus Lunus. . . .

Among the various personages under which the Patriarch was represented, the principal seems to have been that of Dionusus. He was by the mythologists supposed to have had a second birth, and a renewal of life in the Theba or Ark. Hence he was termed Θηζασγενης; which the Greeks interpreted a Theban born, and made him a native of Bœotia: but he was originally only worshipped there; and his rites and mysteries came from Egypt. This injustice of the Greeks, in taking to themselves every Deity, and hero, was complained of by the Egyptians. . . .

The principal terms, by which the antients distinguished the Ark, were Theba, Baris, Arguz, Argus, Aren, Arene, Arne, Laris, Boutus, Bœotus, Cibotus. Out of these they formed different personages: and as there was apparently a correspondence in these terms, they in consequence of it invented different degrees of relation. Hence a large family has arisen from a few antiquated words, which related to the same history, and of which many were nearly synonymous. In the account given above, we may perceive that the ark, and the chief person of the ark, are often confounded; but by the light, which is here afforded, the truth, I think, may be easily discovered.

WILLIAM GODWIN

(1756–1836)

Godwin might as easily be considered one of the romantics as their forerunner, since he was a friend of Coleridge, Wordsworth, Lamb, Hazlitt, and Shelley, and developed romantic characteristics in some of his own later writings. But he is mainly remembered for the influence of *Political Justice*, and this book, first published in 1793, is a product of the earlier revolutionary generation of Holcroft, Paine, and Priestley.

Hazlitt describes in *The Spirit of the Age* the original reception of Godwin's book: "Tom Paine was considered for the time as a Tom Fool to him; Paley an old woman; Edmund Burke a flashy sophist. Truth, moral truth, it was supposed, had here taken up its abode; and these were the oracles of thought." *Political Justice* was Coleridge's and Southey's handbook in planning Pantisocracy. Hazlitt reports that Wordsworth told a young man, "Throw aside your books of chemistry, and read Godwin on Necessity"—an anecdote, in the opinion of F. E. L. Priestley, "too unexpected to be false"; many critics have seen the influence of Godwin in Wordsworth's *Salisbury Plain* and in his ideas on education, and also, by reaction, in *The Borderers*. Godwinian rationalism, perfectibilitarianism, and necessitarianism run through much of Shelley's poetry.

Godwin's father was a dissenting minister, and Godwin himself preached for a time; but, according to Leslie Stephen, about 1787 Thomas Holcroft led him into atheism, where he remained until Coleridge returned him to "a sufficiently vague theism" about 1800. In 1797 he married Mary Wollstonecraft, author of *Vindication of*

the Rights of Women, although neither in theory believed in matri-
mony. Mary died the same year from the birth of a daughter, who
was to become Mary Shelley. Godwin's later life is a miserable story
of declining reputation and financial struggle never quite relieved
by constant literary industry. He had to support not only his infant
daughter Mary, but Fanny Imlay, a previous child of Mary Wollstonecraft; and eventually a new wife, Mrs. Clermont, who already
had two children and bore him another. He and his new wife for
a while published children's books (including the Lambs' *Tales from
Shakespeare*). In 1811 Shelley wrote him and became a disciple and
benefactor for the rest of his life: pity strives with disgust at the
cold, reproachful tone of Godwin's many shameless demands on
Shelley for money. Henry Noel Brailsford describes Godwin's
relations with Shelley and other contemporaries in *Shelley, Godwin
and Their Circle* (London: Oxford Univ. Press, 1951).

A two-volume facsimile of the 1798 edition of *Political Justice*,
with a third volume of commentary and textual notes, is edited by
F. E. L. Priestley, Univ. of Toronto Department of English Studies
and Texts, No. 2 (Toronto: Univ. of Toronto Press, 1946). Recent
books on Godwin include: David Fleisher, *William Godwin* (London: Allen & Unwin, 1951); A. E. Rodway, ed., *Godwin and the
Age of Transition* (New York: Barnes & Noble, 1952); and David
H. Munro, *Godwin's Moral Philosophy* (London: Oxford Univ.
Press, 1953). This selection is based on the third edition (1798).

Enquiry Concerning Political Justice and Its Influence on Morals and Happiness

SUMMARY OF PRINCIPLES

Established and Reasoned Upon in the Following Work

. . . . .

I.

The true object of moral and political disquisition, is pleasure or happiness.

The primary, or earliest, class of human pleasures, is the pleasures of the external senses.

In addition to these, man is susceptible of certain secondary pleasures, as the pleasures of intellectual feeling, the pleasures of sympathy, and the pleasures of self-approbation.

The secondary pleasures are probably more exquisite than the primary:

Or, at least,

The most desirable state of man, is that, in which he has access to all these sources of pleasure, and is in possession of a happiness the most varied and uninterrupted.

This state is a state of high civilisation.

II.

The most desirable condition of the human species, is a state of society.

The injustice and violence of men in a state of society, produced the demand for government.

Government, as it was forced upon mankind by their vices, so has it commonly been the creature of their ignorance and mistake.

Government was intended to suppress injustice, but it offers new occasions and temptations for the commission of it.

By concentrating the force of the community, it gives occasion to wild projects of calamity, to oppression, despotism, war, and conquest.

By perpetuating and aggravating the inequality of property, it fosters many injurious passions, and excites men to the practice of robbery and fraud.

Government was intended to suppress injustice, but its effect has been to embody and perpetuate it.

III.

The immediate object of government, is security.

The means employed by government, is restriction, an abridgment of individual independence.

The pleasures of self approbation, together with the right cultivation of all our pleasures, require individual independence.

Without independence men cannot become either wise, or useful, or happy.

Consequently, the most desirable state of mankind, is that which maintains general security, with the smallest incroachment upon individual independence.

IV.

The true standard of the conduct of one man towards another, is justice.

Justice is a principle which proposes to itself the production of the greatest sum of pleasure or happiness.

Justice requires that I should put myself in the place of an impartial spectator of human concerns, and divest myself of retrospect to my own predilections.

Justice is a rule of the utmost universality, and prescribes a specific mode of proceeding, in all affairs by which the happiness of a human being may be affected.

V.

Duty is that mode of action, which constitutes the best application of the capacity of the individual, to the general advantage.

Right is the claim of the individual, to his share of the benefit arising from his neighbours' discharge of their several duties.

The claim of the individual, is either to the exertion or the forbearance of his neighbours.

The exertions of men in society should ordinarily be trusted to their discretion; their forbearance, in certain cases, is a point of more pressing necessity, and is the direct province of political superintendence, or government.

VI.

The voluntary actions of men are under the direction of their feelings.

Reason is not an independent principle, and has no tendency to excite us to action; in a practical view, it is merely a comparison and balancing of different feelings.

Reason, though it cannot excite us to action, is calculated to regulate our conduct, according to the comparative worth it ascribes to different excitements.

It is to the improvement of reason therefore, that we are to look for the improvement of our social condition.

VII.

Reason depends for its clearness and strength upon the cultivation of knowledge.

The extent of our progress in the cultivation of knowledge, is
  unlimited.
Hence it follows,
  1. That human inventions, and the modes of social existence, are
     susceptible of perpetual improvement.
  2. That institutions calculated to give perpetuity to any par-
     ticular mode of thinking, or condition of existence, are per-
     nicious.

VIII.

The pleasures of intellectual feeling, and the pleasures of self-
  approbation, together with the right cultivation of all our
  pleasures, are connected with soundness of understanding.
Soundness of understanding is inconsistent with prejudice:
  consequently, as few falshoods as possible, either speculative
  or practical, should be fostered among mankind.
Soundness of understanding is connected with freedom of enquiry: consequently, opinion should, as far as public security
  will admit, be exempted from restraint.
Soundness of understanding is connected with simplicity of
  manners, and leisure for intellectual cultivation: consequently,
  a distribution of property extremely unequal, is adverse to
  the most desirable state of man.

· · · · ·

Book I

CHAP. II

. . . It is an old observation, that the history of mankind is
little else than a record of crimes. Society comes recommended
to us by its tendency to supply our wants and promote our well
being. If we consider the human species, as they were found
previously to the existence of political society, it is difficult not
to be impressed with emotions of melancholy. But, though the
chief purpose of society is to defend us from want and incon-

venience, it effects this purpose in a very imperfect degree. We are still liable to casualties, disease, infirmity and death. Famine destroys its thousands, and pestilence its ten thousands. Anguish visits us under every variety of form, and day after day is spent in languor and dissatisfaction. Exquisite pleasure is a guest of very rare approach, and not less short continuance.

But, though the evils that arise to us from the structure of the material universe are neither trivial nor few, yet the history of political society sufficiently shows that man is of all other beings the most formidable enemy to man. Among the various schemes that he has formed to destroy and plague his kind, war is the most terrible. Satiated with petty mischief and the retail of in-sulated crimes, he rises in this instance to a project that lays nations waste, and thins the population of the world. Man directs the murderous engine against the life of his brother; he invents with indefatigable care refinements in destruction; he proceeds in the midst of gaiety and pomp to the execution of his horrid purpose; whole ranks of sensitive beings, endowed with the most admirable faculties, are mowed down in an instant; they perish by inches in the midst of agony and neglect, lacerated with every variety of method that can give torture to the frame.

This is indeed a tremendous scene! Are we permitted to console ourselves under the spectacle of its evils, by the rareness with which it occurs, and the forcible reasons that compel men to have recourse to this last appeal of human society? Let us consider it under each of these heads . . . .

[Godwin traces the bloody history of mankind from Sesostris, Semiramis, and "the earliest records of time" through Alexander, the Romans, the Goths, the Huns, and Charlemagne, to modern Europe, "the most civilised and favoured quarter of the world," with its constant wars of succession, religion, and territorial gain.]

And what are in most cases the pretences upon which war is undertaken? What rational man could possibly have given himself the least disturbance, for the sake of choosing whether Henry the sixth or Edward the fourth should have the style of

king of England? What Englishman could reasonably have
drawn his sword for the purpose of rendering his country an
inferior dependency of France, as it must necessarily have been
if the ambition of the Plantagenets had succeeded? What can
be more deplorable, than to see us first engage eight years in
war rather than suffer the haughty Maria Theresa to live with a
diminished sovereignty or in a private station; and then eight
years more to support the free-booter who had taken advantage
of her helpless condition? . . .

If we turn from the foreign transactions of states with each
other, to the principles of their domestic policy, we shall not
find much greater reason to be satisfied. A numerous class of
mankind are held down in a state of abject penury, and are continually prompted by disappointment and distress to commit
violence upon their more fortunate neighbours. The only mode
which is employed to repress this violence, and to maintain the
order and peace of society, is punishment. . . .

Add to this the species of government which prevails over
nine tenths of the globe, which is despotism: a government, as
Locke justly observes, altogether "vile and miserable," and
"more to be deprecated than anarchy itself."

Certainly every man who takes a dispassionate survey of this
picture, will feel himself inclined to pause respecting the necessity of the havoc which is thus made of his species, and to question whether the established methods for protecting mankind
against the caprices of each other are the best that can be de-
vised. . . .

CHAP. III

. . . Two of the greatest abuses relative to the interior policy
of nations, which at this time prevail in the world, consist in the
irregular transfer of property, either first by violence, or secondly by fraud. . . .

First then it is to be observed, that, in the most refined states
of Europe, the inequality of property has risen to an alarming

height. Vast numbers of their inhabitants are deprived of almost every accommodation that can render life tolerable or secure. Their utmost industry scarcely suffices for their support. The women and children lean with an insupportable weight upon the efforts of the man, so that a large family has in the lower orders of life become a proverbial expression for an uncommon degree of poverty and wretchedness. If sickness or some of those casualties which are perpetually incident to an active and laborious life, be added to these burthens, the distress is yet greater. . . .

A second source of those destructive passions by which the peace of society is interrupted, is to be found in the luxury, the pageantry and magnificence, with which enormous wealth is usually accompanied. Human beings are capable of encountering with chearfulness considerable hardships, when those hardships are impartially shared with the rest of the society, and they are not insulted with the spectacle of indolence and ease in others, no way deserving of greater advantages than themselves. But it is a bitter aggravation of their own calamity, to have the privileges of others forced on their observation, and, while they are perpetually and vainly endeavouring to secure for themselves and their families the poorest conveniences, to find others revelling in the fruits of their labours. . . .

A third disadvantage that is apt to connect poverty with discontent, consists in the insolence and usurpation of the rich. If the poor man would in other respects compose himself in philosophic indifference, and, conscious that he possesses every thing that is truly honourable to man as fully as his rich neighbour, would look upon the rest as beneath his envy, his neighbour will not permit him to do so. He seems as if he could never be satisfied with his possessions, unless he can make the spectacle of them grating to others; and that honest self-esteem, by which his inferior might otherwise attain to tranquillity, is rendered the instrument of galling him with oppression and injustice. . . .

Such are the causes, that, in different degrees under the different governments of the world, prompt mankind openly or secretly to encroach upon the property of each other. Let us consider how far they admit either of remedy or aggravation from political institution. . . .

First then, legislation is in almost every country grossly the favourer of the rich against the poor. . . .

Secondly, the administration of law is not less iniquitous than the spirit in which it is framed. . . .

Thirdly, the inequality of conditions usually maintained by political institution, is calculated greatly to enhance the imagined excellence of wealth. . . .

CHAP. IV

[Godwin argues that education should be based on clear logical and moral principles rather than obscurely conjectured innate ideas and irrational traditions.] The actions and dispositions of men are not the offspring of any original bias that they bring into the world in favour of one sentiment or character rather than another, but flow entirely from the operation of circumstances and events acting upon a faculty of receiving sensible impressions.

. . . It is sufficient to recollect the nature of moral causes to be satisfied that their efficiency is nearly unlimited. The essential differences that are to be found between individual and individual, originate in the opinions they form, and the circumstances by which they are controled. It is impossible to believe that the same moral train [applied in the education of different children] would not make nearly the same man. . . .

Speak the language of truth and reason to your child, and be under no apprehension for the result. Show him that what you recommend is valuable and desirable, and fear not but he will desire it. Convince his understanding, and you enlist all his powers animal and intellectual in your service. How long has the genius of education been disheartened and unnerved by the pretence that man is born all that it is possible for him to become? How long has the jargon imposed upon the world, which would persuade us that in instructing a man you do not add to, but unfold his stores? The miscarriages of education do not proceed from the boundedness of its powers, but from the mistakes with which it is accompanied. We often inspire disgust, where we mean to infuse desire. We are wrapped up in ourselves, and do not observe, as we ought, step by step the sensations that pass in the mind of our hearer. We mistake compulsion for persuasion, and delude ourselves into the belief that despotism is the road to the heart. . . .

Multitudes will never exert the energy necessary to extraordinary success, till they shall dismiss the prejudices that fetter them, get rid of the chilling system of occult and inexplicable causes, and consider the human mind as an intelligent agent, guided by motives and prospects presented to the understanding, and not by causes of which we have no proper cognisance and can form no calculation.

Apply these considerations to the subject of politics, and they will authorise us to infer, that the excellencies and defects of the human character, are not derived from causes beyond the reach of ingenuity to modify and correct. If we entertain false views and be involved in pernicious mistakes, this disadvantage is not the offspring of an irresistible destiny. We have been ignorant, we have been hasty, or we have been misled. Remove the causes of this ignorance or this miscalculation, and the effects will cease. . . .

Children are a sort of raw material put into our hands, a ductile and yielding substance, which, if we do not ultimately mould in conformity to our wishes, it is because we throw away the power committed to us, by the folly with which we are accustomed to exert it. But there is another error not less decisive. The object we choose is an improper one. Our labour is expended, not in teaching truth, but in teaching falshood. When that is the case, education is necessarily and happily maimed of half its powers. The success of an attempt to mislead can never be complete. We continually communicate in spite of ourselves the materials of just reasoning; reason is the genuine exercise, and truth the native element of an intellectual nature; it is no won-

der therefore, that, with a crude and abortive plan to govern
his efforts, the preceptor is perpetually baffled, and the pupil,
who has been thus stored with systematic delusions, and partial,
obscure, and disfigured truths, should come out any thing rather
than that which his instructor intended him. . . .

As long as parents and teachers in general shall fall under the
established rule, it is clear that politics and modes of government
will educate and infect us all. They poison our minds, before we
can resist, or so much as suspect their malignity. Like the barbarous directors of the Eastern seraglios, they deprive us of our
virility, and fit us for their despicable employment from the
cradle. So false is the opinion that has too generally prevailed,
that politics is an affair with which ordinary men have little
concern.

CHAP. V

[Godwin demonstrates that rational understanding is the most
powerful human motivation; with proper training, it will always
override momentary fear, passion, and sensuous desire.] Volition
and foresight, in their strict and accurate construction, are inseparable. All the most important occasions of our lives, are
capable of being subjected at pleasure to a decision, as nearly as
possible, perfectly voluntary. . . . When the understanding clearly perceives rectitude, propriety and eligibility to belong to a
certain conduct, and so long as it has that perception, that conduct will infallibly be adopted. A perception of truth will inevitably be produced by a clear evidence brought home to the
understanding, and the constancy of the perception will be
proportioned to the apprehended value of the thing perceived.
Reason therefore and conviction still appear to be the proper
instrument, and the sufficient instrument for regulating the
actions of mankind. . . .

The corollaries respecting political truth, deducible from
the simple proposition, which seems clearly established by the

reasonings of the present chapter, that the voluntary actions of
men are in all instances conformable to the deductions of their
understanding, are of the highest importance. Hence we may
infer what are the hopes and prospects of human improvement.
The doctrine which may be founded upon these principles, may
perhaps best be expressed in the five following propositions:
Sound reasoning and truth, when adequately communicated,
must always be victorious over error: Sound reasoning and truth
are capable of being so communicated: Truth is omnipotent:
The vices and moral weakness of man are not invincible: Man is
perfectible, or in other words susceptible of perpetual improvement. . . .

[On the second proposition, that sound reasoning and truth
are capable of being communicated:]
In order to its due application in this point of view, opportunity
for the communication must necessarily be supposed. The incapacity of human intellect at present, requires that this opportunity should be of long duration or repeated recurrence. We
do not always know how to communicate all the evidence we
are capable of communicating, in a single conversation, and
much less in a single instant. But, if the communicator be sufficiently master of his subject, and if the truth be altogether on
his side, he must ultimately succeed in his undertaking. We
suppose him to have sufficient urbanity to conciliate the good
will, and sufficient energy to engage the attention, of the party
concerned. In that case, there is no prejudice, no blind reverence
for established systems, no false fear of the inferences to be
drawn, that can resist him. He will encounter these one after
the other, and he will encounter them with success. Our prejudices, our undue reverence, and imaginary fears, flow out of
some views the mind has been induced to entertain; they are
founded in the belief of some propositions. But every one of
these propositions is capable of being refuted. The champion
we describe, proceeds from point to point; if in any his success
have been doubtful, that he will retrace and put out of the reach

of mistake; and it is evidently impossible that with such qualifi-
cations and such perseverance he should not ultimately accomplish his purpose. . . .

[On the last proposition, that man is perfectible:]
By perfectible, it is not meant that he is capable of being brought
to perfection. But the word seems sufficiently adapted to express
the faculty of being continually made better and receiving perpetual improvement; and in this sense it is here to be understood.
The term perfectible, thus explained, not only does not imply
the capacity of being brought to perfection, but stands in express opposition to it. If we could arrive at perfection, there
would be an end to our improvement. There is however one
thing of great importance that it does imply: every perfection or
excellence that human beings are competent to conceive, human
beings, unless in cases that are palpably and unequivocally excluded by the structure of their frame, are competent to attain.

This is an inference which immediately follows from the
omnipotence of truth. Every truth that is capable of being communicated, is capable of being brought home to the conviction
of the mind. Every principle which can be brought home to the
conviction of the mind, will infallibly produce a correspondent
effect upon the conduct. If there were not something in the
nature of man incompatible with absolute perfection, the doctrine of the omnipotence of truth would afford no small prob-
ability that he would one day reach it. Why is the perfection of
man impossible?

The idea of absolute perfection is scarcely within the grasp
of human understanding. If science were more familiarised to
speculations of this sort, we should perhaps discover that the
notion itself was pregnant with absurdity and contradiction.

It is not necessary in this argument to dwell upon the limited
nature of the human faculties. We can neither be present to all
places nor to all times. We cannot penetrate into the essences of
things, or rather we have no sound and satisfactory knowledge
of things external to ourselves, but merely of our own sensations.
We cannot discover the causes of things, or ascertain that in the

antecedent which connects it with the consequent, and discern nothing but their contiguity. With what pretence can a being thus shut in on all sides lay claim to absolute perfection?

But, not to insist upon these considerations, there is one principle in the human mind, which must for ever exclude us from arriving at a close of our acquisitions, and confine us to perpetual progress. The human mind, so far as we are acquainted with it, is nothing else but a faculty of perception. All our knowledge, all our ideas, every thing we possess as intelligent beings, comes from impression. All the minds that exist, set out from absolute ignorance. They received first one impression, and then a second. As the impressions became more numerous, and were stored by the help of memory, and combined by the faculty of association, so the experience increased, and with the experience the knowledge, the wisdom, every thing that distinguishes man from what we understand by a "clod of the valley." This seems to be a simple and incontrovertible history of intellectual being; and, if it be true, then as our accumulations have been incessant in the time that is gone, so, as long as we continue to perceive, to remember or reflect, they must perpetually increase.

● ● ● ● ●

Book II

CHAP. II

From what has been said it appears, that the subject of our present enquiry is strictly speaking a department of the science of morals. Morality is the source from which its fundamental axioms must be drawn, and they will be made somewhat clearer in the present instance, if we assume the term justice as a general appellation for all moral duty.

That this appellation is sufficiently expressive of the subject will appear, if we examine mercy, gratitude, temperance, or any of those duties which, in looser speaking, are contradistinguished from justice. Why should I pardon this criminal, remunerate this favour, or abstain from this indulgence? If it partake of the nature of morality, it must be either right or wrong, just or unjust. It must tend to the benefit of the individual, either without trenching upon, or with actual advantage to the mass of individuals. Either way it benefits the whole, because individuals are parts of the whole. Therefore to do it is just, and to forbear it is unjust.—By justice I understand that impartial treatment of every man in matters that relate to his happiness, which is measured solely by a consideration of the properties of the receiver, and the capacity of him that bestows. Its principle therefore is, according to a well known phrase, to be "no respecter of persons."

Considerable light will probably be thrown upon our investigation, if, quitting for the present the political view, we examine justice merely as it exists among individuals. Justice is a rule of conduct originating in the connection of one percipient being with another. A comprehensive maxim which has been laid down upon the subject is, "that we should love our neighbour as ourselves." But this maxim, though possessing considerable merit as a popular principle, is not modelled with the strictness of philosophical accuracy.

In a loose and general view I and my neighbour are both of us men; and of consequence entitled to equal attention. But, in reality, it is probable that one of us is a being of more worth and importance than the other. A man is of more worth than a beast; because, being possessed of higher faculties, he is capable of a more refined and genuine happiness. In the same manner the illustrious archbishop of Cambray was of more worth than his valet, and there are few of us that would hesitate to pronounce, if his palace were in flames, and the life of only one of them could be preserved, which of the two ought to be preferred.

But there is another ground of preference, beside the private consideration of one of them being further removed from the state of a mere animal. We are not connected with one or two percipient beings, but with a society, a nation, and in some sense with the whole family of mankind. Of consequence that life ought to be preferred which will be most conducive to the general good. In saving the life of Fenelon, suppose at the moment he conceived the project of his immortal Telemachus, I should have been promoting the benefit of thousands, who have been cured by the perusal of that work, of some error, vice and consequent unhappiness. Nay, my benefit would extend further than this; for every individual, thus cured, has become a better member of society, and has contributed in his turn to the happiness, information and improvement of others.

Suppose I had been myself the valet; I ought to have chosen to die, rather than Fenelon should have died. The life of Fenelon was really preferable to that of the valet. But understanding is the faculty that perceives the truth of this and similar propositions; and justice is the principle that regulates my conduct accordingly. It would have been just in the valet to have preferred the archbishop to himself. To have done otherwise would have been a breach of justice.

Suppose the valet had been my brother, my father or my benefactor. This would not alter the truth of the proposition. The life of Fenelon would still be more valuable than that of the valet; and justice, pure, unadulterated justice, would still have preferred that which was most valuable. Justice would have taught me to save the life of Fenelon at the expence of the other. What magic is there in the pronoun "my," that should justify us in overturning the decisions of impartial truth? My brother or my father may be a fool or a profligate, malicious, lying or dishonest. If they be, of what consequence is it that they are mine?

"But to my father I am indebted for existence; he supported me in the helplessness of infancy." When he first subjected himself to the necessity of these cares, he was probably influenced by no particular motives of benevolence to his future offspring. Every voluntary benefit however entitles the bestower to some kindness and retribution. Why? Because a voluntary benefit is an evidence of benevolent intention, that is, in a certain degree, of virtue. It is the disposition of the mind, not the external action separately taken, that entitles to respect. But the merit of this disposition is equal, whether the benefit were conferred upon me or upon another. I and another man cannot both be right in preferring our respective benefactors, for my benefactor cannot be at the same time both better and worse than his neighbour. My benefactor ought to be esteemed, not because he bestowed a benefit upon me, but because he bestowed it upon a human being. His desert will be in exact proportion to the degree, in which that human being was worthy of the distinction conferred.

Thus every view of the subject brings us back to the consideration of my neighbour's moral worth, and his importance to the general weal, as the only standard to determine the treatment to which he is entitled. Gratitude therefore, if by gratitude we understand a sentiment of preference which I entertain towards another, upon the ground of my having been the subject of his benefits, is no part either of justice or virtue. . . .

There seems to be more truth, in the argument, derived chiefly from the prevailing modes of social existence, in favour of my providing, in ordinary cases, for my wife and children, my brothers and relations, before I provide for strangers, than in those which have just been examined. As long as the providing for individuals is conducted with its present irregularity and caprice, it seems as if there must be a certain distribution of the class needing superintendence and supply, among the class affording it; that each man may have his claim and resource. . . .

It is therefore impossible for me to confer upon any man a favour; I can only do him right. Whatever deviates from the law of justice, though it should be in the too much done in favour of some individual or some part of the general whole, is so much substracted from the general stock, so much of absolute injustice.

The reasonings here alleged, are sufficient, clearly to establish the competence of justice as a principle of deduction in all cases of moral enquiry. They are themselves rather of the nature of illustration and example, and, if error be imputable to them in particulars, this will not invalidate the general conclusion, the propriety of applying moral justice as a criterion in the investigation of political truth.

Society is nothing more than an aggregation of individuals. Its claims and duties must be the aggregate of their claims and duties, the one no more precarious and arbitrary than the other. What has the society a right to require from me? The question is already answered: every thing that it is my duty to do. Any thing more? Certainly not. Can it change eternal truth, or subvert the nature of men and their actions? Can it make my duty consist in committing intemperance, in maltreating or assassinating my neighbour?—Again, what is it that the society is bound to do for its members? Every thing that is requisite for their welfare. But the nature of their welfare is defined by the nature of mind. That will most contribute to it, which expands the understanding, supplies incitements to virtue, fills us with a generous consciousness of our independence, and carefully removes whatever can impede our exertions.

· · · · ·

Book III

[Godwin examines various bases of governments—brute force, divine right, and the social contract—and rejects them all as not reflecting the principle of justice.]

CHAP. VII

. . . "Different forms of government, are best adapted to the condition of different nations." Yet there is one form, in itself considered, better than any other form. Every other mode of society, except that which conduces to the best and most pleasurable state of the human species, is at most only an object of toleration. It must of necessity be ill in various respects; it must entail mischiefs; it must foster unsocial and immoral prejudices.

Yet upon the whole, it may be, like some excrescences and defects in the human frame, it cannot immediately be removed without introducing something worse. In the machine of human society all the wheels must move together. He that should violently attempt to raise any one part into a condition more exalted than the rest, or force it to start away from its fellows, would be the enemy, and not the benefactor, of his contemporaries.

It follows however, from the principles already detailed, that the interests of the human species require a gradual, but uninterrupted change. He who should make these principles the regulators of his conduct, would not rashly insist upon the instant abolition of all existing abuses. But he would not nourish them with false praise. He would show no indulgence to their enormities. He would tell all the truth he could discover, in relation to the genuine interests of mankind. Truth, delivered in a spirit of universal kindness, with no narrow resentments or angry invective, can scarcely be dangerous, or fail, so far as relates to its own operation, to communicate a similar spirit to the hearer. Truth, however unreserved be the mode of its enunciation, will be sufficiently gradual in its progress. It will be fully comprehended, only by slow degrees, by its most assiduous votaries; and the degrees will be still more temperate, by which it will pervade so considerable a portion of the community, as to render them mature for a change of their common institutions.

Again: if conviction of the understanding be the compass which is to direct our proceedings in the general affairs, we shall have many reforms, but no revolutions. As it is only in a gradual manner that the public can be instructed, a violent explosion in the community, is by no means the most likely to happen, as the result of instruction. Revolutions are the produce of passion, not of sober and tranquil reason. There must be an obstinate resistance to improvement on the one side, to engender a furious determination of realising a system at a stroke on the other. The reformers must have suffered from incessant counteraction, till, inflamed by the treachery and art of their opponents, they are wrought up to the desperate state of imagining that all must be secured in the first favourable crisis, as the only alternative for its being ever secured. It would seem therefore, that the demand of the effectual ally of the public happiness, upon those who enjoy the privileges of the state, would be, "Do not give us too soon; do not give us too much; but act under the incessant influence of a disposition to give us something."

Government, under whatever point of view we examine this topic, is unfortunately pregnant with motives to censure and complaint. Incessant change, everlasting innovation, seem to be dictated by the true interests of mankind. But government is the perpetual enemy of change. What was admirably observed of a particular system of government, is in a great degree true of all: They "lay their hand on the spring there is in society, and put a stop to its motion." Their tendency is to perpetuate abuse. Whatever was once thought right and useful, they undertake to entail to the latest posterity. They reverse the genuine propensities of man, and, instead of suffering us to proceed, teach us to look backward for perfection. They prompt us to seek the public welfare, not in alteration and improvement, but in a timid reverence for the decisions of our ancestors, as if it were the nature of the human mind, always to degenerate, and never to advance.

Man is in a state of perpetual mutation. He must grow either better or worse, either correct his habits or confirm them. The government under which we are placed, must either increase our passions and prejudices by fanning the flame, or, by gradually discouraging, tend to extirpate them. In reality, it is impossible to conceive a government that shall have the latter tendency. By its very nature positive institution has a tendency to suspend the elasticity and progress of mind. Every scheme for embodying imperfection must be injurious. That which is to-day a considerable melioration, will at some future period, if preserved unaltered, appear a defect and disease in the body politic. It is earnestly to be desired, that each man should be wise enough to govern himself, without the intervention of any compulsory restraint; and, since government, even in its best state, is an evil, the object principally to be aimed at is, that we should have as little of it, as the general peace of human society will permit.

·   ·   ·   ·   ·

Book IV

CHAP. II

[Godwin strongly opposes revolutions because they are irrational and inevitably do more harm than good.]

. . . The only method according to which social improvements can be carried on, with sufficient prospect of an auspicious event, is, when the improvement of our institutions advances, in a just proportion to the illumination of the public understanding. There is a condition of political society best adapted to every different stage of individual improvement. The more nearly this condition is successively realised, the more advantageously will the general interest be consulted. There is a sort of provision in the nature of the human mind for this species of progress. Imperfect institutions, as has already been shown, cannot long support themselves, when they are generally disapproved of, and their effects truly understood. There is a period, at which they may be expected to decline and expire, almost without an effort. Reform, under this meaning of the term, can scarcely be considered as of the nature of action. Men feel their situation; and the restraints that shackled them before, vanish like a deception. When such a crisis has arrived, not a sword will need to be drawn, not a finger to be lifted up in purposes of violence. The adversaries will be too few and too feeble, to be able to entertain a serious thought of resistance against the universal sense of mankind.

·   ·   ·   ·   ·

CHAP. VIII

[In Chapter VII Godwin establishes to his satisfaction "that all the actions of men are necessary." His main proof is that human behavior, like material phenomena, follows predictable patterns, and that anyone maintaining a doctrine of free will would have to deny any such regularity. Furthermore, he argues, any decision of the "will" is merely the result of previous mental preferences, which in turn arise from antecedent states of mind, and so ad infinitum, with never a moment when a "free" choice can be said to have been made.]

. . . But the doctrine of necessity does not overturn the nature of things. Happiness and misery, wisdom and error will still be distinct from each other, and there will still be a correspondence between them. Wherever there is that which may be the means of pleasure or pain to a sensitive being, there is ground for preference and desire, or on the contrary for neglect and aversion. Benevolence and wisdom will be objects worthy to be desired, selfishness and error worthy to be disliked. If therefore by virtue we mean, that principle which asserts the preference of the former over the latter, its reality will remain undiminished by the doctrine of necessity. . . .

But, if the doctrine of necessity do not annihilate virtue, it tends to introduce a great change into our ideas respecting it. According to this doctrine it will be absurd for a man to say, "I will exert myself," "I will take care to remember," or even "I will do this." All these expressions imply as if man were, or could be, something else than what motives make him. Man is in reality a passive, and not an active being. In another sense however he is sufficiently capable of exertion. The operations of his mind may be laborious, like those of the wheel of a heavy machine in ascending a hill, may even tend to wear out the substance of the shell in which it acts, without in the smallest degree impeaching its passive character. If we were constantly aware of this, our minds would not glow less ardently with the love of truth, justice, happiness and mankind. We should have a firmness and simplicity in our conduct, not wasting itself in fruitless struggles and regrets, not hurried along with infantine impatience, but seeing actions with their consequences, and calmly and unreservedly given up to the influence of those comprehensive views which this doctrine inspires.

As to our conduct towards others, in instances where we were concerned to improve and meliorate their minds, we should address our representations and remonstrances to them with double confidence. The believer in free-will, can expostulate with, or correct, his pupil, with faint and uncertain hopes, conscious that the clearest exhibition of truth is impotent, when brought into contest with the unhearing and indisciplinable faculty of will; or in reality, if he were consistent, secure that it could produce no effect. The necessarian on the contrary employs real antecedents, and has a right to expect real effects. . . .

At first sight it may appear as if, the moment I was satisfied that exertion on my part was no better than a fiction, and that I was the passive instrument of causes exterior to myself, I should become indifferent to the objects which had hitherto interested me the most deeply, and lose all that inflexible perseverance, which seems inseparable from great undertakings. But this cannot be the true state of the case. The more I resign myself to the influence of truth, the clearer will be my perception of it. The less I am interrupted by questions of liberty and caprice, of attention and indolence, the more uniform will be my constancy. Nothing could be more unreasonable, than that the sentiment of necessity should produce in me a spirit of neutrality and indifference. The more certain is the conjunction between antecedents and consequents, the more chearfulness should I feel in yielding to painful and laborious employments.

It is common for men impressed with the opinion of free will, to entertain resentment, indignation, and anger, against those who fall into the commission of vice. How much of these feelings is just, and how much erroneous? The difference between virtue and vice, will equally remain upon the opposite hypothesis. Vice

therefore must be an object of rejection, and virtue of preference; the one must be approved, and the other disapproved.
But our disapprobation of vice, will be of the same nature, as
our disapprobation of an infectious distemper.

One of the reasons why we are accustomed to regard the
murderer with more acute feelings of displeasure, than the knife
he employs, is that we find a more dangerous property, and
greater cause for apprehension, in the one than in the other. The
knife is only accidentally an object of terror, but against the
murderer we can never be enough upon our guard. In the same
manner we regard the middle of a busy street with less com-
placency, as a place for walking, than the side; and the ridge
of a house with more aversion than either. Independently therefore of the idea of freedom, mankind in general will find in the
enormously vicious a sufficient motive of apprehension and displeasure. With the addition of that idea, it is no wonder that
they should be prompted to sentiments of the most intemperate
abhorrence.

These sentiments obviously lead, to the examination of the
prevailing conceptions on the subject of punishment. The doctrine of necessity, would teach us to class punishment in the
list of the means we possess of influencing the human mind,
and may induce us to enquire into its utility, as an instrument
for reforming error. The more the human mind can be shown
to be under the influence of motive, the more certain it is that
punishment will produce a great and unequivocal effect. But
the doctrine of necessity will teach us to look upon punishment
with no complacence, and at all times to prefer the most direct
means of encountering error, the development of truth. Whenever punishment is employed under this system, it will be employed, not for any intrinsic recommendation it possesses, but
only as it shall appear to conduce to general utility.

On the contrary it is usually imagined, that, independently
of the supposed utility of punishment, there is proper desert in
the criminal, a certain fitness in the nature of things that renders
pain the suitable concomitant of vice. It is therefore frequently

said, that it is not enough that a murderer should be transported to a desert island, where there should be no danger that his malignant propensities should ever again have opportunity to act; but that it is also right the indignation of mankind against him, should express itself, in the infliction of some actual ignominy and pain. On the contrary, under the system of necessity, the terms, guilt, crime, desert and accountableness, in the abstract and general sense in which they have sometimes been applied, have no place.

•   •   •   •   •

CHAP. XI

. . . The doctrine of necessity teaches us, that all things in the universe are connected together. Nothing could have happened otherwise than it has happened. Do we congratulate ourselves upon the rising genius of freedom? Do we view with pride the improvements of mankind, and contrast with wonder, man in the state in which he once was, naked, ignorant and brutal, with man as we now sometimes behold him, enriched with boundless stores of science, and penetrated with sentiments of the purest philanthropy? These things could not have existed in their present form, without having been prepared by all the preceding events. Every thing the most seemingly insignificant, the most loathsome, or the most retrograde, was indissolubly bound to all that we most admire in the prospect before us. We may perhaps go a step further than this. The human mind is a principle of the simplest nature, a mere faculty of sensation or perception. It must have begun from absolute ignorance; it must obtain its improvement by slow degrees; it must pass through various stages of folly and mistake. Such is, and could not but be, the history of mankind. . . .

[Godwin attacks the optimistic belief that "everything that is, is right."] It may be worthy of remark, that the support the system of optimism derives from the doctrine of necessity, is of a very equivocal nature. The doctrine of necessity teaches, that each event is the only thing, under the circumstances, that could happen; it would, of consequence, be as proper, upon this system, to say that every thing that happens, is the worst, as that it is the best, that could possibly happen. . . .

Though there is some pain, or absolute evil, which, relatively taken, must be admitted to be attended with an overbalance of good, yet it is a matter of great delicacy and difficulty, in most instances, to decide in favour of pain, which, whatever be its relative value, is certainly a negative quantity to be deducted in the sum total of happiness. . . .

Let us not amuse ourselves with a pompous and delusive survey of the whole, but let us examine parts severally and individually. All nature swarms with life. This may, in one view, afford an idea of an extensive theatre of pleasure. But unfortunately every animal preys upon his fellow. Every animal, however minute, has a curious and subtle structure, rendering him susceptible, as it should seem, of piercing anguish. We cannot move our foot, without becoming the means of destruction. The wounds inflicted are of a hundred kinds. These petty animals are capable of palpitating for days in the agonies of death. It may be said, with little licence of phraseology, that all nature suffers. There is no day nor hour, in which, in some regions of the many-peopled globe, thousands of men, and millions of animals, are not tortured, to the utmost extent that organised life will afford. . . . The evil does not consist merely in the pain endured. It is the injustice that inflicts it, that gives it its sharpest sting. . . . The whole history of the human species, taken in one point of view, appears a vast abortion. Man seems adapted for wisdom and fortitude and benevolence. But he has always, through a vast majority of countries, been the victim of ignorance and superstition. Contemplate the physiognomy of the species. Observe the traces of stupidity, of low cunning, of rooted insolence, of withered hope, and narrow selfishness, where the characters of wisdom, independence and disinterestedness, might have been inscribed. Recollect the horrors of war, that last invention of deliberate profligacy for the misery of man. Think of the variety of wounds, the multiplication of anguish, the desolation of countries, towns destroyed, harvests flaming, inhabitants perishing by thousands of hunger and cold.

A sound philosophy will teach us to contemplate this scene without madness. Instructed in its lessons, we shall remember that, though there is much of evil, there is also much of good in the world, much pleasure, as well as much pain. We shall not even pronounce that some small portion of this evil is not relatively not an evil. Above all, we shall be cheered with the thought of brighter prospects and happier times. But the optimist must be particularly rash, who takes upon him to affirm of all this mass of evil without exception, that it is relatively not evil, and that nothing could have happened otherwise than it has happened, without the total being worse than it is.

.   .   .   .   .

Book VIII

CHAP. VIII—APPENDIX

It is a curious subject, to enquire into the due medium between individuality and concert. On the one hand, it is to be observed that human beings are formed for society. Without society, we shall probably be deprived of the most eminent enjoyments of which our nature is susceptible. In society, no man, possessing the genuine marks of a man, can stand alone. Our opinions, our tempers and our habits are modified by those of each other. This is by no means the mere operation of arguments and persuasives; it occurs in that insensible and gradual way, which no resolution can enable us wholly to counteract. He that would attempt to counteract it by insulating himself, will fall into a worse error than that which he seeks to avoid. He will divest himself of the character of a man, and be incapable of judging of his fellow men, or of reasoning upon human affairs.

On the other hand, individuality is of the very essence of intellectual excellence. He that resigns himself wholly to sympathy and imitation, can possess little of mental strength or accuracy. The system of his life is a species of sensual dereliction. He is like a captive in the garden of Armida; he may revel in the midst of a thousand delights; but he is incapable of the enterprise of a hero, or the severity of a philosopher. He lives forgetting and forgot. He has deserted his station in human society. Mankind cannot be benefited by him. . . .

Every thing that is usually understood by the term cooperation, is, in some degree, an evil. A man in solitude, is obliged to sacrifice or postpone the execution of his best thoughts, in compliance with his necessities, or his frailties. How many admirable designs have perished in the conception, by means of this circumstance? It is still worse, when a man is also obliged to consult the convenience of others. If I be expected to eat or to work in conjunction with my neighbour, it must either be at a time most convenient to me, or to him, or to neither of us. We cannot be reduced to a clock-work uniformity.

Hence it follows that all supererogatory cooperation is carefully to be avoided, common labour and common meals. "But what shall we say to a cooperation, that seems dictated by the nature of the work to be performed?" It ought to be diminished. There is probably considerably more of injury in the concert of industry, than of sympathies. At present, it is unreasonable to doubt, that the consideration of the evil of cooperation, is, in certain urgent cases, to be postponed to that urgency. Whether, by the nature of things, cooperation of some sort will always be necessary, is a question we are scarcely competent to decide. At present, to pull down a tree, to cut a canal, to navigate a vessel, require the labour of many. Will they always require the labour of many? When we recollect the complicated machines of human contrivance, various sorts of mills, of weaving engines, steam engines, are we not astonished at the compendium of labour they produce? Who shall say where this species of improvement must stop? . . .

It may be a curious speculation to attend to the progressive steps, by which this feature of human society may be expected to decline. For example: shall we have concerts of music? The miserable state of mechanism of the majority of the performers, is so conspicuous, as to be, even at this day, a topic of mortification and ridicule. Will it not be practicable hereafter for one man to perform the whole? Shall we have theatrical exhibitions? This seems to include an absurd and vicious cooperation. It may be doubted, whether men will hereafter come forward in any mode, formally to repeat words and ideas that are not their own? It may be doubted, whether any musical performer will habitually execute the compositions of others? We yield supinely to the superior merit of our predecessors, because we are accustomed to indulge the inactivity of our faculties. . . .

Another article which belongs to the subject of cooperation, is cohabitation. The evils attendant on this practice, are obvious. In order to the human understanding's being successfully cultivated, it is necessary, that the intellectual operations of men should be independent of each other. . . .

The subject of cohabitation is particularly interesting, as it includes in it the subject of marriage. It will therefore be proper to pursue the enquiry in greater detail. The evil of marriage, as it is practised in European countries, extends further than we have yet described. The method is, for a thoughtless and romantic youth of each sex, to come together, to see each other, for a few times, and under circumstances full of delusion, and then to vow eternal attachment. What is the consequence of this? In almost every instance they find themselves deceived. They are reduced to make the best of an irretrievable mistake. They are led to conceive it their wisest policy, to shut their eyes upon realities, happy, if, by any perversion of intellect, they can persuade themselves that they were right in their first crude opinion of each other. Thus the institution of marriage is made a system of fraud; and men who carefully mislead their judgments in the daily affair of their life, must be expected to have a crippled judgment in every other concern.

Add to this, that marriage, as now understood, is a monopoly, and the worst of monopolies. So long as two human beings are forbidden, by positive institution, to follow the dictates of their own mind, prejudice will be alive and vigorous. So long as I seek, by despotic and artificial means, to maintain my possession of a woman, I am guilty of the most odious selfishness. Over this imaginary prize, men watch with perpetual jealousy; and one man finds his desire, and his capacity to circumvent, as much excited, as the other is excited, to traverse his projects, and frustrate his hopes. As long as this state of society continues, philanthropy will be crossed and checked in a thousand ways, and the still augmenting stream of abuse will continue to flow.

The abolition of the present system of marriage, appears to involve no evils. We are apt to represent that abolition to ourselves, as the harbinger of brutal lust and depravity. But it really happens, in this, as in other cases, that the positive laws which are made to restrain our vices, irritate and multiply them. Not to say, that the same sentiments of justice and happiness, which, in a state of equality, would destroy our relish for expensive gratifications, might be expected to decrease our inordinate appetites of every kind, and to lead us universally to prefer the pleasures of intellect to the pleasures of sense.

· · · · ·

CHAP. X

. . . To the general mass of the adherents of equality, it may be proper to address a few words. "If there be any force in the arguments of this work, we seem authorised to deduce thus much from them, that truth is irresistible. Let then this axiom be the rudder of our undertakings. Let us not precipitately endeavour to accomplish that to-day, which the dissemination of truth will make unavoidable to-morrow. Let us not over-anxiously watch for occasions and events: of particular events the ascendancy of truth is independent. Let us anxiously refrain

from violence: force is not conviction, and is extremely un-
worthy of the cause of justice. Let us admit into our bosoms
neither contempt, animosity, resentment nor revenge. The
cause of justice is the cause of humanity. Its advocates should
be penetrated with universal good-will. We should love this
cause; for it conduces to the general happiness of mankind. We
should love it; for there is not a man that lives, who, in the
natural and tranquil progress of things, will not be made happier
by its approach. The most powerful circumstance by which it
has been retarded, is the mistake of its adherents, the air of rug-
gedness, brutishness and inflexibility which they have given to
that which, in itself, is all benignity. Nothing less than this could
have prevented the great mass of enquirers from bestowing upon
it a patient examination. Be it the care of the now increasing
advocates of equality, to remove this obstacle to the success of
their cause. We have but two plain duties, which, if we set out
right, it is not easy to mistake. The first is an unwearied attention
to the great instrument of justice, reason. We should communicate our sentiments with the utmost frankness. We should
endeavour to press them upon the attention of others. In this we
should give way to no discouragement. We should sharpen our
intellectual weapons; add to the stock of our knowledge; be per-
vaded with a sense of the magnitude of our cause; and perpetually
add to that calm presence of mind and self-possession which
must enable us to do justice to our principles. Our second duty
is tranquillity."

One objection may perhaps be inferred from these considerations. "If the inevitable progress of improvement insensibly lead
towards equality, what need was there of proposing it as a
specific object to men's consideration?" The answer to this objection is easy. The improvement in question consists in a knowledge of truth. But our knowledge will be very imperfect, so
long as this great branch of universal justice fails to constitute
a part of it. All truth is useful; can this truth, which is perhaps
the most fundamental of all moral principles, be without its
benefit? Whatever be the object towards which mind irresistibly

advances, it is of no mean importance to us to have a distinct view of that object. Our advances will thus become accelerated. It is a well known principle of morality, "that he who proposes perfection to himself, though he will inevitably fall short of what he pursues, will make a more rapid progress, than he who is contented to aim only at what is imperfect." The benefits to be derived in the internal from a view of equality as one of the great objects to which we are tending, are exceedingly conspicious. Such a view will strongly conduce to make us disinterested now. It will teach us to look with contempt upon mercantile speculations, commercial prosperity, and the cares of gain. It will impress us with a just apprehension of what it is of which man is capable, and in which his perfection consists; and will fix our ambition and activity upon the worthiest objects. Intellect cannot arrive at any great and illustrious attainment, however much the nature of intellect may carry us towards it, without feeling some presages of its approach; and it is reasonable to believe that, the earlier these presages are introduced, and the more distinct they are made, the more auspicious will be the event.

A selected list of MIDLAND BOOKS

(continued on next page)

MIDLAND BOOKS